T0347555

# BUILDING SECURITY IN EUROPE'S NEW BORDERLANDS

*Forthcoming*

BUILDING SECURITY IN THE NEW STATES OF EURASIA
Subregional Cooperation in the Former Soviet Space
Edited by
Renata Dwan and Oleksandr Pavliuk

## A project of the EastWest Institute

The EastWest Institute is an independent, not-for-profit organization working to defuse tensions and conflicts that threaten geopolitical stability while promoting democracy, free enterprise, and prosperity in Central and Eastern Europe, Russia, and other states of Eurasia. The EastWest Institute operates through a network of affiliated centers, including New York, Prague, Moscow, Kyiv, Kosice, and Brussels, and was formerly known as the Institute for EastWest Studies.

For more information, please contact us at:

EastWest Institute
700 Broadway, Second Floor
New York, NY 10003
Tel (212) 824-4100, Fax (212) 824-4149
Website: http://www.iews.org
E-mail: iews@iews.org

# BUILDING SECURITY IN EUROPE'S NEW BORDERLANDS

SUBREGIONAL COOPERATION
IN THE WIDER EUROPE

EDITED BY
RENATA DWAN

EASTWEST INSTITUTE
New York Prague Moscow Kyiv Brussels Košice

Routledge
Taylor & Francis Group

LONDON AND NEW YORK

First published 1999 by M.E. Sharpe

Published 2015 by Routledge
2 Park Square, Milton Park, Abingdon, Oxon OX14 4RN
711 Third Avenue, New York, NY, 10017, USA

*Routledge is an imprint of the Taylor & Francis Group, an informa business*

**Library of Congress Cataloging-in-Publication Data**

Building Security in Europe's new borderlands : subregional
cooperation in the wider Europe / Edited by Renata Dwan
p.  cm.
Includes bibliographical references and index.
ISBN 0-7656-0531-7 (cloth : alk paper)
1. Europe, Eastern—Foreign relations.  2. Europe, Eastern—
Economic integration.  3. European cooperation.  I. Dwan, Renata.
JZ1570.B85  1999
327.1'7'094—dc21          99-38505
CIP

ISBN 13: 9780765605313 (hbk)

# Contents

# Preface

Since 1996 the EastWest Institute has been running a major research and policy-forming project on the nature and function of subregional cooperation in the new Europe. The project aims to explore existing and emerging cooperative processes among groups of states; examine the contribution subregional cooperation can make to security and stability in post-Cold War Europe; and assess the factors that influence this form of cooperation. Examination of the policies of international organizations towards subregional cooperation and, where appropriate, recommendations to them constitute an important element of the project. The project is generously supported by the Carnegie Corporation of New York.

The first year of the project addressed six existing subregional groups: the Barents Euro-Arctic Council, the Council of Baltic Sea States, the Visegrad Group, the Central European Free Trade Initiative, the Central European Initiative, and the Black Sea Economic Cooperation. Emerging patterns of subregional cooperation in the borderlands of Europe were the focus of the project's second year. This book reflects the conclusions of this phase. In the third and final year of the project, the prospects for subregional cooperation in and around the CIS space will be explored in greater depth. A further edited volume will accompany this final stage.

Over the course of the project, seminars and meetings have taken place throughout Europe, bringing together academics, national policymakers, representatives of non-governmental organizations, and officials from international organizations to collectively explore various aspects and examples of subregional cooperation. The project has had the good fortune to be guided by an international steering board, the members of which are drawn from senior national and international positions and serve in their personal capacity. This group meets twice annually to review the progress of the project. EWI has also benefited from communication and coordination with the Organization for Security and Cooperation in Europe (OSCE), particularly in the organization of OSCE-led conferences on subregional security and cooperation. EWI would like to express its thanks to all those who have participated in one way or another in the project. The generosity with which individuals and other organizations have shared their knowledge, experience, and opinions has been greatly appreciated.

Particular thanks are due to a number of people who have assisted in the production of this book, not least the contributing authors and the project's steering board. The author would like to express special gratitude to Oleksandr Pavliuk for his comments and support. Michael Goldman Donally translated Arif Yunusov's text from the Russian. Editing assistance was provided by Kenneth Kronenberg and EWI interns Megan Phillips and Ondrej Simek. EWI's Scott Rogers was responsible for preparing the final text for publication. The contents of the book, however, remain solely the responsibility of the editor and the authors. They should not be construed as reflecting the views of the EastWest Institute, the Carnegie Corporation of New York, or the Subregional Project Steering Board.

*Renata Dwan*

# List of Abbreviations and Acronyms

| | |
|---|---|
| BCSCSE | *Balkan Conference of Stability and Cooperation in Southeast Europe* |
| BEAC | *Barents Euro-Arctic Council* |
| BSEC | *Black Sea Economic Cooperation* |
| CAEC | *Central Asian Economic Community* |
| CBSS | *Council of Baltic Sea States* |
| CEFTA | *Central European Free Trade Agreement* |
| CEI | *Central European Initiative* |
| CFE | *Conventional Armed Forces in Europe Treaty* |
| CIS | *Commonwealth of Independent States* |
| EAPC | *Euro-Atlantic Partnership Council* |
| ECO | *Economic Cooperation Organization* |
| EU | *European Union* |
| NATO | *North Atlantic Treaty Organization* |
| NIS | *Newly Independent States* |
| OSCE | *Organization for Security and Cooperation in Europe* |
| PFP | *Partnership for Peace* |
| RI | *Royaumont Initiative* |
| SBDI | *South Balkan Development Initiative* |
| SECI | *Southeast European Cooperation Initiative* |
| WEU | *Western European Union* |

# Note on Terminology

The delineation of Europe and its constituent parts has been, historically, a contested subject. The Cold War gave special political and geographical resonance to the terms "West" and "East." In the post-Cold War environment it seems more useful to write geographical signifiers in lower case terms: eastern Europe, central Asia. This is the format used in this book.

# Contributors

**Renata Dwan** is Deputy Director of the EastWest Institute's European Security Programme and is based at the Institute's Budapest Center. She writes on European security issues and is currently finishing a book on the European Defence Community (EDC).

**Anders Bjurner** is Deputy State Secretary for Foreign Affairs with principal responsibility for common security policy issues in the Swedish Ministry for Foreign Affairs. He has previously been Chairman of the Committee for Senior Officials of the Organization for Security and Cooperation in Europe (OSCE), and Chairman of the OSCE Minsk Group on the Nagorno-Karabakh conflict. He has also served as Deputy Director General for Political Affairs and Special Assistant to the Minister for Foreign Affairs on the Middle East peace process. Other postings have included the United Nations and in Africa. He has been Chairman of the Steering Board of the EastWest Institute's subregional project since 1996.

**Sophia Clément** is a Research Fellow at the WEU Institute for Security Studies, Paris. She was previously attached to the Centre d'Etudes et de Recherche Internationales (CERI) in Paris. She writes widely on European security issues and South East Europe and is author of "Conflict Prevention in the Balkans: the case of Kosovo and the FYR of Macedonia," Chaillot Paper 30, WEU-ISS.

**Andrew Cottey** is a Lecturer in the Department of Peace Studies at the University of Bradford. He has previously worked for the EastWest Institute, Saferworld and the British American Security Information

Council and was a 1996-98 NATO Research Fellow. He is author of *East-Central Europe After the Cold War: Poland, the Czech Republic, Slovakia and Hungary in Search of Security.*

**Charles King** is Assistant Professor in the School of Foreign Service and the Department of Government at Georgetown University where he holds the university's Ion Ratiu Chair of Romanian Studies. He is co-editor of *Nations Abroad: Diaspora Politics and International Relations in the Former Soviet Union* and is currently completing a history of the Moldovans.

**S. Neil MacFarlane** is Lester B. Pearson Professor of International Relations and Director of the Centre for International Studies at the University of Oxford. His work focuses on relations among the newly independent states and the role of international organizations in that development on which he has published widely.

**Plamen Pantev** is Founder and Director of the Institute for Security and International Studies in Bulgaria. He is Associate Professor in International Relations and International Law at Sofia University "St. Kliment Ohridsky," and author of two books and numerous articles on international relations and security policy issues.

**Oleksandr Pavliuk** is Director of the Kyiv Center of the EastWest Institute and Associate Professor at the University of "Kyiv-Mohyla Academy." He has published articles on regional cooperation and Ukrainian foreign policy and is the author of *Ukraine's Struggle for Independence and United States Policy.*

**Arif Yunusov** is head of the Department of Conflictology Studies at the Institute of Peace and Democracy, Azerbaijan. He is the author of more than thirty works on conflicts in Azerbaijan and the Muslim world and has written many articles on the Karabakh conflict and issues current in the Caucasus.

# BUILDING SECURITY IN EUROPE'S NEW BORDERLANDS

# Introduction

*Renata Dwan*

## Terms and Definitions

An encyclopedic number of new terms and acronyms have appeared in international relations literature and discourse over the course of the past ten post-Cold War years. Their appearance has not been heralded by all. Many academics and policymakers skeptically regard such terms as convenient new labels for what are, essentially, long familiar concepts. Others query the extent to which the search for new ways of thinking about international relations really does produce fundamentally different understandings of how order among states is achieved and sustained. Ultimately, the benefit of new approaches to practical international politics is considered, at best, unproven. Subregionalism and subregional cooperation represent two of these contested terms. In the first place, what is a subregion? What exactly is defined by the term "subregional cooperation"? And what distinguishes it from any other form of cooperation between states?

The conceptual and definitional weakness of the term "subregional" stem, in part, from the fact that it has belatedly come into vogue as a way of describing processes currently taking place in the new Europe. Over the past ten years, diverse groupings of states have emerged in different parts of Europe, often involving states that were previously either not independent or constrained in their freedom to choose their foreign alignments. These include the Barents

1

Euro-Arctic Council (BEAC) and the Council of Baltic Sea States (CBSS) in the north; the Visegrad group, the Central European Free Trade Association (CEFTA), and the Central European Initiative (CEI) in central Europe; and the Black Sea Economic Cooperation Organization BSEC), the Balkan Conference on Stability and Cooperation (BCSC), and the South-Eastern European Cooperation Initiative (SECI) in the south. These groupings are diverse in size, function, and scope. Collectively, however, they reflect a new trend among states from the Barents to the Black Sea for which the label, "subregional cooperation" has offered a conveniently broad umbrella.[1]

Subregional cooperation can be described as a process of regularized, significant political and economic interaction among a group of states. This interaction can take place at the state, that is, the national government level, or between sub-state actors such as regional and local authorities, civil society representatives, private business groups, and individuals. Functioning subregional cooperation usually involves interaction at both levels among a wide variety of actors across a range of issues. The forms of interaction may differ markedly in magnitude, intensity, and character. Nevertheless, an important feature of subregional cooperative groupings to date in Europe has been their relatively uninstitutionalized structure. Subregional cooperation, therefore, is not integration: No supranational authority is created, no ceding of sovereignty is involved, and no body of common laws and obligations is established.

It might be tempting, then, to dismiss subregionalism as merely the traditional practice of alignment between a certain group of states. That would, however, ignore the geographical and functional emphases of the process. A "region" usually refers to some comprehensive area with a subregion denoting a smaller grouping embedded within it. A region is not merely a geographical entity. The notion implies a certain degree of interdependency between the constituent parts, usually a product of geographical proximity, which affects economic, political, social, cultural, and security relations between them. What happens to one state of the region affects other states more than events outside the region, and patterns of what Barry Buzan calls "amity and enmity arising from a variety of issues that could not be predicted from a simple consideration of the distribution of power" play a major role in determining the security and stability of the region.[2] In this context, Europe can be regarded as a region and the OSCE space area postulated as an emerging regional system.

The subregion, existing within the region, shares the attribute of interdependency among its constituent parts. In the smaller subregion, however, the extent of interaction between the states that comprise it becomes even more significant. Some might argue, for example, that a state could be part of a region, without having direct interaction or particularly intense relations with another state of that region. In the smaller subregion, however, direct interaction between constituent states is more likely and the quantity of this interaction—economic, political, or military—is likely to be significant relative to other states in the larger region.[3]

The higher level of intensity of interaction between the states of a subregion shapes, in turn, the functional orientation of subregional processes. Because subregional actors are more interdependent, they are likely to share similar problems and challenges. These challenges may often be of a specific geographical nature, such as an environmental problem that affects each of the states of the subregion, or a problem arising out of their proximity or interaction, such as border management, ethnic relations, or trade regulation. Subregional cooperation, therefore, is usually directed at the specific challenges that a group of states face in their immediate neighborhood. It emerges from a degree of convergence of interests among highly interdependent states.

To that extent, subregionalism (the phenomenon of subregional cooperation) involves recognition of common interest and a resolution to work together in its pursuit. The construction of a subregion is thus a conscious task on the part of the states involved. Two important consequences follow from this: First, subregions are not given geographical or political subsets of a region but conscious groupings that may develop or decline over time. Second, although the directness and intensity of interaction that promote higher interdependency among a particular group of states suggests geographical proximity, it does not make geography a prerequisite. Geographical location is an important component in the construction of a subregion but it is not the sole or even essential condition.

## Purpose and Structure of this Book

Interest has grown in subregional cooperation over the course of the past few years. This is partly due to the proliferation of new subregional initiatives as well as to the growing strength of existing subregional groupings in central and eastern Europe. The impact of subregional groupings, both in their immediate locale and on the broader international stage, is likely to be more marked as they become more active in policy and practice. Another factor shaping interest is the activities and policies of wider European and Euro-Atlantic organizations: As western European economic, political, and security systems enlarge eastward, the institutions of these systems have to respond to and negotiate patterns of interstate relations among prospective members. Finally, interest in subregional cooperation is increasing as post-Cold War thinking on what constitutes security and how it can best be achieved continues. There is growing recognition that subregional cooperation can have an important role to play in widening the sense of what is meant by security, in offering practical new strategies for its pursuit, and in bringing non-traditional actors into the process of security-building.

This book has grown out of consideration of these three factors. It represents the continuation of a study begun as an examination of six subregional groupings: Barents Euro-Arctic Council, Council of Baltic Sea States, Visegrad Group, Central European Free Trade Association, Central European Initiative, and Black Sea Economic Cooperation. The volume produced by this study looked at the origins, structure and functioning of these groupings and explored the ways in which subregional cooperation processes contribute to security and integration in post-Cold War Europe.[4] This exercise demonstrated, first, that the phenomenon of subregional cooperation in the new Europe was far more prevalent in northern and central Europe than in other parts of the continent, i.e., areas that had not undergone the conflicts that have plagued other parts of Europe in recent years. Second, it also revealed the significant interrelationship between subregional cooperative processes and wider European integration movements, namely NATO and the EU. Pursuit of membership in the latter is, in general, a strong motivation (and explicit condition) for increased efforts at good-neighborliness and cooperation in much of central and eastern Europe. At the same time, desire for EU and NATO integration can also make applicant states hesitant to enter subregional arrangements for fear of giving the impression that they would be satisfied with alternative cooperative processes other than full NATO and EU membership. EU and NATO integration processes contain and shape subregional cooperation in Europe.

The conclusions reached by this study, therefore, provoked further questions: Is subregional cooperation possible in areas of current, recent, or unresolved conflict? Can subregional cooperation make a contribution to security in such areas? Where, in other words, does subregional cooperation fit within existing structures and hierarchies of security in the wider Europe? Anders Bjurner touches upon some of these questions in the opening chapter. He notes the interdependency of subregional cooperation with other security processes and underscores the limitations of subregional cooperation in meeting the security needs of states. These are important points to bear in mind in approaching the question of what subregional cooperation can do in "security-deficit" areas.

Another set of questions reflected the dominance of EU and NATO integration for the subregional groupings surveyed. How contingent is subregional cooperation on wider regional cooperative processes? What are the prospects for subregional cooperation between states on the European continent that are neither current EU or NATO members nor likely to join in the foreseeable future? What policies might larger international organizations develop toward subregional initiatives in order to promote and realize the positive results of increased cooperation among groups of states? It is this last question that Andrew Cottey tackles in the final chapter of the book. He examines EU and NATO policies toward subregional cooperation around its future borders and also assesses the policies of other principal European institutions, the Organization for Security and Cooperation in Europe (OSCE) and the Council of Europe (CoE), as well as the United Nations (UN).

This book, then, is concerned with the parts of wider Europe that remain outside of the dominant integration trends of the region. Those areas are the territory covering Belarus, Moldova, and Ukraine, defined here as east-central Europe; the states of the former Yugoslavia and the Balkans, collectively termed south-eastern Europe; and the Trans-Caucasian states and central Asian republics that make up what is generally known as the "southern tier." The states that comprise these three areas are on the geographical periphery of the continent, and they lie along the lines that blur into Eurasia, Asia, and the Middle East. For this reason, the sense of being on the periphery of Europe has long historical antecedents in east-central Europe, south-eastern Europe and the Trans-Caucasus. For the most part, these areas have been on the periphery of the political and economic transitions that have dominated parts of the former Warsaw Pact territory for the past ten years, and they have not yet reached levels comparable to central, much less western Europe. They stand on the periphery of the security and stability that has benefited much of Europe after the end of the era of superpower confrontation. They remain, finally, on the periphery of the EU and NATO integration processes. These three areas could be described as the borderlands of the new Europe.

It is this "border" status that defines east-central Europe, southeastern Europe and the Trans-Caucasus and central Asia as particular subregions of the wider Europe. This collective identity is thus recent and highly ambiguous. In many ways what marks them are their differences, both from each other and among their constituent states.

**East-Central Europe**

Belarus, Ukraine, and Moldova taken together offer the most striking example of an area that has acquired its subregional status by virtue of NATO and EU enlargement processes. In other ways there is little basis for describing this space as a distinct area. The three countries lie to the east of what is generally regarded as central Europe; however, Ukraine, in particular, identifies itself as part of the latter. The alternative "eastern Europe" usually implies a larger grouping of states, including the three Baltic states. Moreover, Ukraine and Belarus are often identified as "northern" east European states, with Moldova grouped around "southern" east European countries. The term that most selectively refers to the three states as a group is "western Newly Independent States (NIS)," a description Ukraine vigorously rejects. For this reason we have elected to use the term east-central Europe to describe the three states that form the zone between Russia and the enlarging EU space.[5]

The fact that external political developments have increased the interdependency and sense of potential convergence of interest of Belarus, Ukraine, and Moldova, to the extent that the three states might be considered as a subregion, constituting a subregion does not automatically lead to subregional cooperation. Charles King explores why, despite sharing borders, trade, environmental problems, and external policy challenges, the three states have to date developed so little cooperation between them. He focuses on the political development of Belarus, Ukraine, and Moldova since independence and argues that domestic political factors are important determinants of external policy choices, particularly in the case of subregional cooperation. Oleksandr Pavliuk then examines the particular subregional initiatives in which the states of east-central Europe have become involved and assesses the future prospects for these nascent forms of subregional cooperation.

## South-Eastern Europe

South-eastern Europe represents, in many ways, the most discrete subregion of Europe's border zones. In this book it is taken to mean Albania, former Yugoslavia, Bulgaria, Romania, Greece, and Turkey. Although the frontiers of this area are not uncontested (particularly in the case of Slovenia), the term south-eastern Europe carries with it geographical, historical, and cultural connotations that contribute to a sense of interdependency among constituent states. The legacies of history and culture have also made south-eastern European states particularly resentful of peripheral status in the wider Europe, and they argue strongly that they are part of the "core" of western European civilization. There is a similar paradox in recent patterns of conflict and cooperation. South-eastern Europe has been the site of some of the most horrific inter- and intra-state violence in post-World War II Europe. Conflict and the threat of conflict still dominate the subregion, as the current Kosovo crisis all too convincingly demonstrates. At the same time, south-eastern Europe is also home to significant subregional cooperation processes that are far more developed than those seen in Europe's other boundary zones.

Sophia Clément and Plamen Pantev explore the interrelationship between conflict and cooperation in south-eastern Europe. Clément looks at how the international community has attempted to negotiate conflict resolution and post-conflict rehabilitation in the area through subregional cooperation. She assesses externally initiated cooperative processes in south-eastern Europe, identifying the somewhat paradoxical premises on which they have been elaborated. Plamen Pantev explores the evolution of attitudes among south-eastern European states toward subregional cooperation. States of the area are now beginning to take a more favorable approach toward cooperation, Pantev argues, precisely out of recognition of their security, economic, and political interdependency, and he examines the initiatives that have begun to develop as a result. Both writers emphasize the significance of the EU and NATO integration process for subregional cooperation in south-eastern Europe and call for clearer policies on the part of the EU in particular.

## Southern Tier

In many ways, the southern tier of the Trans-Caucasus and central Asia represents the most "problematic" subregion under consideration. Although formally part of the area known as the wider Europe, only the three Caucasian states, Armenia, Azerbaijan, and Georgia, can be described as a border zone of the enlarging Euro-Atlantic space. In many other ways, the Trans-Caucasus and central Asia represent two distinct subregions, geographically, historically and, arguably, culturally. In terms of interdependency, the states of the Trans-Caucasus and those of central Asia, Kazakhstan, Kyrgyzstan, Tajikistan, Turkmenistan, and Uzbekistan, represent two identifiable groupings.

In a number of ways that are important for subregional cooperation, however, the two areas constitute a single area. S. Neil MacFarlane demonstrates that from the perspective of a number of external actors dominant in the area—powerful states, international organizations and private economic actors—the Trans-Caucasus and central Asia form one subregion. This is likely to be increasingly the case as energy development in and around the Caspian Sea develops, linking producer and transit states across the southern tier. MacFarlane argues, therefore, that the policies of external actors not only determine processes of subregional cooperation, but also the very definition of the subregion itself, and he assesses the consequences of this dominance for subregional cooperation in the southern tier.

Arif Yunusov's purpose, however, is to look at the internal political developments of newly independent states and the effect of conflict between them for the development of subregional cooperation. He therefore examines the Trans-Caucasus as a distinct subregion and looks at the way in which the post-independence paths of Armenia, Azerbaijan, and Georgia have led them to confrontation, rather than cooperation. Interdependency between a group of states, Yunusov demonstrates, does not necessarily produce subregional cooperation.

The eight contributors to this volume tackle diverse geographical areas, actors, and issues. Two observations are made by all, however. The first is that subregional cooperation in Europe's boundary zones could facilitate the security and the development of the states that currently comprise Europe's peripheries. They are all also agreed, however, that the development of subregional cooperation in east-central Europe, south-eastern Europe, and the southern tier of the Trans-Caucasus and central Asia, faces significant obstacles and will be unlikely to blossom in the ways observed in other parts of Europe. The conclusion attempts to draw together the various themes addressed in the book and identify some of the principal determinants to successful subregional cooperation. It outlines the ways in which subregionalism might contribute to the particular challenges faced by Europe's boundary zones and how subregional cooperation might be negotiated in an enlarging Europe.

## Notes

1. It should be noted that the term has been also used to describe non-European cooperative processes, for example in southern Africa and south-east Asia. See G. Cawthra, "Subregional security: The southern African development community," *Security Dialogue* 28, no. 2 (1997): 207-18.

2. Barry Buzan, *People States and Fear: An Agenda for International Security Studies in the Post-Cold War Era*, 2nd edition (Hemel Hempstead: Harvester Wheatsheaf, 1991), p. 190

3. See discussion on systems in Tom Nierop, *Systems and Regions in Global Politics: An Empirical Study of Diplomacy, International Organizations and Trade*, 1950-91 (Chichester: John Wiley, 1994), pp. 17-35.

4. Andrew Cottey (ed.) *Subregional Cooperation in the New Europe: Building Security, Prosperity and Solidarity from the Barents to the Black Sea* (Basingstoke: Macmillan/EastWest Institute, 1999).

5. A recent study defined east-central Europe quite differently as the Czech Republic, Hungary, Poland, Slovakia and the three Baltic states. See Karen Dawisha and Bruce Parrott (eds.), *The consolidation of democracy in East-Central Europe* (New York: Cambridge University Press, 1997).

# 1

# Reflections on Subregionalism and Wider European Security

*Anders Bjurner*

The European security system has changed radically during the past ten years. The end of the Cold War opened up completely new opportunities, permitting a mixture of old and new options for security-building cooperation. This cooperation has gradually expanded to include new areas. Security is currently being established at all levels, ranging from the pan-European dimension to the local security environment. Security is being promoted at the central government level, by local authorities and by a wide range of nongovernmental actors. The impetus for this comprehensive security-building is, therefore, both a top-down and a bottom-up process.

A considerable number of "subregional cooperation arrangements" have been established in Europe, particularly in the north of the continent. At the intergovernmental level, the Council of the Baltic Sea States (CBSS) was established in 1992, the Euro-Arctic Council in 1993 and, most recently, the Arctic Council in 1996. Apart from different membership constellations, these arrangements have different functions, different organizational structures, and different aims. Yet, since they all contribute to security, they have a common objective, even if security (particularly military security) is not always explicitly addressed in their statutes.

This new subregional cooperation has helped to increase security by promoting confidence and trust between the states and peoples of the region, reinforcing mutual dependence, strengthening democratic structures, reducing economic differences, promoting economic and social development, reducing region-specific risks and threats, and promoting further regional integration.

Although subregional cooperation across the traditional east-west frontier is relatively new, it is achieving overwhelming results within the framework of formal intergovernmental structures, and perhaps even more in other quarters. The forces at work have varied. Generally speaking, the intrinsic potential of Cold-War eastern and western Europe, which could not be exploited in the past, has provided a powerful underlying impetus. Political and ideological confrontation have been replaced by consensus. Economic barriers and incompatible systems have been eliminated. The arms race has been replaced by cooperation and military contacts in various forms. At the personal level, sterile, formal contacts have given way to a plethora of meetings, exchange programs, and various forms of expressions of solidarity, confidence, and cohesion.

Subregional contributions to security are not absolute and isolated. They are part of complex processes. The strength and scope of these contributions vary according to particular circumstances and time. Since subregional processes affect each other and, to some extent, overlap, it is difficult to analyze each individual contribution in absolute terms. Nonetheless, they are generally all positive contributions to greater security.

**Different Subregions**

These security-building processes, however, are still in their initial stages. Baltic Sea cooperation, for example, has quite a way to go before it is comparable to the traditional and well-established cooperation between the Nordic countries. Integration takes time. Different systems have to be coordinated. Institutions have to be created. And, not least, it takes time for the real community of values to emerge. There are also a great many problems, old and new, which remain to be solved. Nevertheless, these active processes are in themselves security-building. It might be added that in the case of the Nordic cooperation versus Baltic Sea cooperation, a "gap-closing" process is taking place between these two subregional arrangements. The same goes for other parts of Europe.

Subregions and subregional arrangements that are geographically distant from "richer" cooperation arrangements, such as the EU, are obviously in a more difficult situation. It poses particular challenges to them to adjust their agendas and institutions to facilitate such links. It is equally a challenge for the EU and its members to cooperate substantially with countries beyond those that are now included in the enlargement process. That challenge is even greater if the countries in question are particularly short of financial resources.

It is almost axiomatic that cooperation leads to security. However, the converse also applies. If security prevails, cooperation will flourish. We can see this if we look at the areas in the new Europe in which subregional cooperation has made the greatest progress. The greatest successes have been achieved in more stable and secure regions, such as northern Europe. In such regions, there is a clearer consensus on the desirability of peace and an acknowledged common interest in the development of the region's potential, which serve to reinforce security and cooperation processes.

The different factors that positively influence cooperation in some parts of Europe are mirrored by various negative influences on subregional processes. The analyses in this book confirm this: War and other types of violent conflicts are certainly a negative force. All too often a vicious circle develops in regions where cooperation is limited and where there is a security deficit, either as a result of involvement in conflicts or various forms of crises.

Besides war and armed conflict, there exist other forms of disputes in a region that may preclude the success of subregional cooperation. The sources of disputes are sometimes deep-rooted and structural. Such conflicts are thus very hard to settle. Other sources of disputes or obstacles to cooperation are easier to solve, such as weak institutional arrangements, lack of information, inexperience, and meager financial and personnel resources.

This also implies that it is not possible to transfer a model for subregional cooperation directly from one subregion to another. Further factors that preclude an automatic process of this nature include different security environments, historical traditions, forms of government and societal organization, and differences in economic resources and development. As a result, there is considerable variation in the motivation and need for subregional cooperation from one region to another.

## Limitations

What are the security-building limitations to subregional cooperation, even where cooperation processes are working successfully?

By definition, a subregion is geographically limited and relatively small. In addition, a subregion has more limited resources than larger regions. This geographical limitation also implies that normative agreements have limited scope. Since neighboring areas are not included, this means that any normative security policy commitments between the governments concerned are of limited direct significance. Indeed, they may even be counter-productive, depending on their construction and their geopolitical nature. They may be seen as provocative toward one or more states in their vicinity, and their substance may violate the internationally-recognized principle of the indivisibility of security.

The inclusion of issues of military strategy in subregional arrangements is particularly serious given that such issues inevitably affect states outside of the subregion. Such interaction might also contravene the commitments of those states that are members of existing military alliances, or, at least, remain largely artificial, insofar as they only affect those states of the subregion that are members of a broader military alliance.

This geographical (and demographic) limitation also applies to the economic sphere and, in particular, to trade and fiscal policy areas. Agreements in these areas are clearly of limited importance for the national economies concerned and, hence, have limited impact on the security of these states. Here, too, there is the risk of negative effects on the outside world as such agreements may be contrary to global or regional trade arrangements.

Subregional cooperation cannot be regarded as a sufficient contributor to national security either from a subjective or an objective viewpoint. It is, rather, a very important supplementary contributor to security. What is referred to as "hard security" (rather inappropriately in my view) has to be supplemented in some way. Military defense, mainly providing security by deterrence, i.e., a "safety net," needs to be supplemented by nonmilitary cooperative structures. Cooperation engenders confidence and mutual interests as well as other dimensions of security not relating directly to the military dimension. That is the most important aspect of subregional cooperation. In this context, it may also be noted, military alliances are either inadequate, objectively speaking, or could sometimes even be politically questionable because they may create new tensions and sources of distrust between states. Sustainable common security is built on a bedrock of confidence and cooperation, not by deterrence.

## Wider Integration

In accordance with the inalienable right of every state to choose its own security policy arrangements, enshrined, for example, in the Charter of Paris (1990), most of the former Warsaw Pact states are currently seeking closer association or membership with the NATO military alliance. These states are, for economic, political, and security reasons, trying to strengthen their ties with the EU and the Western European Union (WEU) by entering into partnership or gaining membership. These efforts are based on historical experience, which must be taken into account in this context. At the same time, many of these states are active participants in a variety of subregional initiatives throughout central and eastern Europe and have benefited in a number of ways, including increased security and stability. The practical record demonstrates, therefore, the compatibility of subregional and wider regional engagement, including military engagement.

Subregional cooperation can promote wider regional integration, providing it is structured appropriately. The new subregional cooperation has been particularly fruitful where it has been linked with efforts to achieve integration, especially in connection with EU enlargement processes. Such links give confidence to those participating and those outside that the subregional initiative will be transparent, not directed at any other state/region and will not cut off states from their wider integrative goals. They will also help provide an agenda for subregional cooperation, based on EU integration objectives/criteria. Depending on the type of linking and the functioning of the subregional structures, they could encourage funding and other assistance from EU programs and institutions. Cooperation structures have also obviously benefited where the participants include members with adequate resources at their disposal.

Subregional cooperation clearly makes a positive contribution when it is based on the fundamental norms and specific rules that apply to a "wider" regional organization such as the EU. If subregional cooperation includes EU members, for example, this relationship facilitates integration into the EU framework. Solidarity between EU member states and nonmembers is strengthened by subregional arrangements of this nature.

Spheres of influence and dominance run counter to security. This historical lesson is currently making its mark on European security promotion processes. Subregionalism may also be relevant in this context. When a number of smaller countries join together in some form of economic and political cooperation, this reduces their dependence on larger and stronger (sometimes dominant) neighbors. This cooperation is not antagonistic as such toward their neighbor or traditional "protector." On the contrary, if subregional cooperation is based on sovereign equality, there is also scope for inclusion of the stronger power in different forms of cooperation arrangements. The benefits will depend on what sectors are included in that cooperation.

Universal norms and international law are particularly important for a small country that does not participate in military and/or political alliances. However, multilateral cooperation also helps to draw attention to a specific country or region. Nordic cooperation is an excellent example of the way in which small countries with different military and political alignments can, working together, attract international attention and also acquire a relatively greater measure of influence in larger organizations, such as the UN or the Organization for Security and Cooperation in Europe (OSCE).

In the case of subregions in which one state is particularly unstable and/or poses a threat to its neighbors, other countries in the region are faced with a choice: to isolate the state in question or include it in efforts to achieve wider cooperation. In many cases, inclusion in subregional initiatives is a significant factor in reducing tension, particularly if cooperation is based on universal norms such as the UN Charter or the principles promoted by the OSCE. If there are deeper affinities between the states concerned, or at least between their political leaders, there is also scope for various forms of conflict-prevention and conflict-management initiatives, such as mediation, arbitration, impartial monitoring, or even peacekeeping measures between the various parties, including internal measures within a given country.

**Inter-Institutional Relations**

Even where membership is not envisaged, either in the short term or the long term, larger organizations such as the EU, the Council of Europe (CoE), the WEU, and NATO have responsibilities toward countries that are seeking membership or close cooperation. That is the principle of the indivisibility of security. States that are currently not members of these organizations must be part of the process of sharing resources, disseminating norms and standards, and establishing greater understanding and trust designed to reinforce common security. On the other hand, the organization concerned also has a responsibility to its members and to the outside world to safeguard its own common values and resources in order to ensure that their "security-productive" capacity is not undermined. A weak EU is neither in the interest of EU member states nor of candidate countries. The political challenge lies in finding an appropriate balance between the interests of both parties.

The enlargement of the EU is perhaps the most important security producing process taking place in Europe today. It has the potential to reduce or even abolish dividing lines. It encourages political and economic reform processes that are important to greater security. It strengthens and widens the community of values within vital dimensions of security. However, it should be noted that there are risks of creating new dividing lines in the enlargement process if it is not pursued appropriately. It could make existing regional and subregional cooperation more difficult by creating new borders. Consequently, the EU must also deal seriously with neighboring states that are not part of the present enlargement. Cooperation with European countries that are not candidates should be strengthened. The EU should further develop its political, financial, and technical support for subregional arrangements affected by the enlargement. Specific attention should be given to new border arrangements resulting from enlargement. New measures might have to be considered by the EU so as not to unnecessarily create new obstacles to the flow of goods, people, and capital between states inside and outside the enlargement.

The responsibility of wider military alliances such as NATO toward subregional arrangements is different from that of political and economic institutions such as the EU. The main responsibility of military organizations lies in respecting, in its actions, the right and freedom of every state to choose its own security relations and arrangements. Second, the various cooperation (or partner) arrangements, such as the Partnership for Peace (PfP), should be offered to all individual members of a specific subregional arrangement without discriminating, while at the same time respecting the usually nonmilitary character of the subregional arrangement.

Today, cooperation in the security sphere between various institutions and organizations is growing rapidly in Europe. In practice, the principle of mutual reinforcement is accepted on an increasingly wider scale, although much remains to be done. An effort to establish a "Platform of Cooperation" within the framework of the OSCE's Security Charter is but one important and concrete expression of this endeavor, both at the normative and the operational level.

There is an increasing emphasis on the importance of subregional cooperation in this context, and the EastWest Institute has made significant contributions in this regard. The OSCE can assist subregional organizations by establishing norms, offering a meeting place, and providing a "toolbox." In practice, cooperation and interaction between the OSCE and the subregional arrangements should be developed, with the object of reinforcing comprehensive pan-European and common security. In principal, the concept of Article VIII of the UN Charter should be transferred to the OSCE and applied to its subregional dimension.[1] The OSCE should affirm subregional cooperation as an important element of common and comprehensive security in the region covered by the OSCE.

Subregional arrangements are, and should be, mutually reinforced by wider arrangements. That is the great challenge to governments in the future. The pan-European security architecture is just in the middle — or perhaps even at the beginning — of a promising construction process.

## Notes

1. Charter of the United Nations, Chapter VIII Regional Arrangements in Adam Roberts and Benedict Kingsbury (eds.), *United Nations, Divided World: The UN's Roles in International Relations*, 2nd ed. (Oxford: Clarendon Press, 1990), p. 514.

# Part I

East-Central Europe

# 2

# The Western NIS
## From Borderland to Subregion?

*Charles King*

Although the term is often used for lack of a better one, the "western NIS" is not a subregion in any meaningful sense. Since 1991 the three countries grouped under this label, Belarus, Ukraine, and Moldova, have not displayed a major desire for cooperation within a distinct subregional framework. Political elites in the three capitals do not normally conceive of themselves as having fundamental interests in common. All three are, of course, linked through strong interstate trade relationships and the cooperative political and economic arrangements of the CIS. But apart from the residual forms of economic integration inherited from the Soviet Union, there is little in Europe's eastern borderland to set it off as a region distinct from any other group of post-Soviet republics.

That this should be so, however, is perhaps surprising, since the three states share an array of policy challenges that would seem to create incentives for cross-border cooperation. This chapter assesses why, despite similar policy predicaments, there has been so little subregional integration among these three states. (The chapter by Oleksandr Pavliuk details the specific attempts at subregional cooperation in the western NIS, as well as the other forms of cross-border initiatives in which Ukraine and Moldova in particular have been engaged). Next, this chapter surveys political developments in Belarus, Ukraine, and Moldova, and examines the relationship between domestic politics and foreign policy orientations. Finally, the chapter assesses the areas in which some form of subregionalism would seem most desirable. These include: first, binding Belarus into a web of regional and subregional relationships, thus encouraging internal democratization and helping secure against its becoming a "rogue state"; second, untying Ukraine from dependence on the Russian Federation, embedding Ukraine in a framework of relations with its neighbors and with the west, and allowing Kyiv to play a more independent role in eastern Europe and the Black Sea zone; and third, making Moldova matter to neighboring states with a direct interest in Moldova's economic development and a resolution to the Transnistrian conflict.

More than anything, the western NIS provides a cautionary tale about the enthusiasm with which western governments and international organizations encourage subregionalism, as well as the real limitations on such forms of cooperation as a solution to common problems within transition societies. The cases below illustrate that, for all the enthusiasm for "medium-level" and "subregional" approaches to resolving transborder problems, thinking a region does not make it so. A real desire for cooperation at the national level, effective structures of local government to craft local solutions to cross-border problems, and a set of external factors that encourage multilateralism over bilateral approaches are essential to transforming subregionalism into something more than summit rhetoric.

### Common Challenges, Uncommon Incentives

The western NIS provides ample evidence that common historical circumstances do not automatically create common political interests. Indeed, one would be hard-pressed to find a more suitable set of candidates for subregional cooperation, since there are a range of historical circumstances and exigencies that bind the fates of these three states together. They would seem to have at least as much in common as states involved in the other existing subregional arrangements across eastern Europe and Eurasia, and in some important ways, rather more.

First, none of these three countries has a tradition of independent statehood in the modern period. All three claim lineage from particular historical antecedents, the Grand Duchy of Lithuania, Kievan Rus, the Principality of Moldova, and all existed as nominally independent republics in the chaos of revolution and civil war after 1917.

But there was nothing in these previous forms of statehood to give them the unique proprietary heritage of today's modern Belarusian, Ukrainian, and Moldovan states. As a result, all three countries are engaged in the same tortuous processes of redefining national identities and legitimating the independence that came largely as an unintended by-product of the demise of Soviet socialism.

Second, current state borders and the modern boundaries of ethnonational affiliation were each, in the main, creations of the Soviet system. The great irony of the Soviet Union was that a system founded on the obsolescence of nationalism set about, from its earliest days, to construct and formalize distinct ethnonational identities where only local or religious loyalties had previously dominated. Although intellectuals in Minsk, Kyiv, and Chisinau are loath to admit it, standardized languages, histories, customs, and the other desiderata of nationhood would not have existed but for the modernizing zeal of the Bolsheviks. Moreover, the borders of the Belarusian, Ukrainian, and Moldovan Soviet Socialist Republics were never intended as reflections of preexisting historical realities; they were drawn in the 1920s and again in the 1940s in ways that served the internal administrative needs and foreign policy interests of the Soviet government. The result of this tortured past is that each state must now wrestle with legitimating an identity that was in most instances self-consciously constructed under the Soviets while simultaneously shoring up control over territories to which most neighboring states such as Lithuania, Poland, Romania, Russia, could stake a reasonable historical claim.

Third, all contain large Russian or russified settler populations.[1] Collectively, these three states were in 1989 home to the largest absolute population of Russians of any subregion in the former Soviet Union: some 13 million, compared with 10 million in Central Asia, 2 million in the Baltic states, and less than a million in Transcaucasia.[2] These states were also the most culturally russified republics in the entire union; rates of linguistic assimilation to Russian, especially in the urban centers, increased more dramatically in these three republics than in any other area from 1959 to 1989.[3] Relations with the Russian Federation are thus of central concern, not only because of Russia's hegemonic position in Eurasia, but also because of the federation's special interest in the fate of "its" diaspora. Latvia, Estonia, and Kazakhstan have had complex relations with Russia because of the presence of sizable Russian communities in these states, but in Belarus, Ukraine, and Moldova relations are even more complicated since the lines between "Russians" and "indigenes" are still often indistinct. Defining who precisely counts as a "Russian" is notoriously difficult in eastern Ukraine, but even in Moldova, where the majority population is part of a separate language group, separating a uniquely Russian identity from a broader allegiance to the old Soviet system has been no less problematic.[4]

Fourth, all three are future front-line states with the European Union and NATO. This position gives these states distinct economic and security concerns. All are also the most immediate losers from EU expansion. As the EU "ins" and "pre-ins," from Poland to Hungary to Romania, begin to adopt strict visa requirements as signs of their commitment to the *acquis* on immigration, the people most immediately affected will be Belarusians, Ukrainians, and Moldovans. US and European rhetoric notwithstanding, "new dividing lines" already exist in Europe, and by the early part of the next century, this fact will become patently clear to Belarusians, Ukrainians, and Moldovans as the boundaries of "Europe" expand to – and perhaps stop at – their doorstep.

This common set of traditions and policy problems has not given rise to serious cooperation within the western NIS. One important reason is the fact that these states exist within a subregional environment that creates few incentives for multilateral cooperation. At least two of the three are concerned principally with shoring up independence and moving toward some form of integration with an expanding Europe. Both these goals, though, can run counter to subregionalism, which is sometimes seen by elites as either a consolation prize from Brussels or a mask for continued Russian domination. Moreover, there is little about Belarus, Ukraine, and Moldova that would seem to encourage cooperation in the areas most often addressed within a subregional context. They do not all share a common border, their trade patterns are determined largely by the residual relationships inherited from the Soviet system and their passport and visa requirements are likewise largely holdovers from the period when all three were part of the same state. Other issues, such as crime control and border security, are the targets of intense bilateral and multilateral cooperation (with Russia, the European Union, or the EU's future members such as Poland and Hungary), but as a result they are not issues that concern the states of the western NIS exclusively.

Beyond these external disincentives, however, all three states have taken rather different paths since independence, both in terms of domestic politics and in terms of each state's orientation toward the broader processes of European and Euro-Atlantic integration. The sections below briefly survey political developments in each state and account for the primary foreign policy orientations in each republic.

**Identity, Domestic Politics, and Foreign Policy Orientations**

For Belarus, Ukraine, and Moldova, independence came largely as an unintended consequence of the breakdown of the Soviet federation. From the onset of perestroika, political forces in all three capitals were deeply divided over the nature of the reform movement. Some saw the movement for reform as a genuine drive for national renaissance and eventual independence. Others saw the "informal" organizations and "popular fronts" in all three states as a handy vehicle for wresting control over local resources from Moscow, with little thought to a complete break with the center. Still others saw the movements as a chance for local ethnic majorities to gain control over institutions of power that had long been dominated by Russians or russified indigenes. While often portrayed today as movements of national renaissance, they were complex and multifaceted social movements composed of a plethora of competing, and often directly contradictory, interests. The struggle in the late 1980s was not between a popular "perestroika from below" and intransigent local communist stalwarts, but rather between competing visions of the relationship between the republics and the Soviet center.

These early divisions among the reformers themselves have continued to define the main fault lines within the domestic politics of each state since independence. These divisions have, moreover, been crucial in determining the foreign policy orientations of the three states. While the "domestic determinants" of foreign policy are a topic of considerable debate among international relations theorists, the three cases sketched below provide ample evidence that, especially in regimes in transition, the interests and ideologies of domestic actors play a dominant role in conditioning foreign relations.

## *Belarus: Defining and Redefining National Interests*

On the surface, Belarus's path from the Soviet Union seemed to follow the pattern of bottom-up calls for change seen in other parts of the federation. Beginning in the late 1980s, scholars, writers, and artists began to explore previously forbidden subjects in Belarusian history, especially the notorious "blank spots" in the historical record during the Soviet period. The position of Belarusian language and culture were also reexamined and members of the Belarusian Writers' Union began to argue for greater attention to local culture in education and the arts. This cultural movement among intellectuals received added public support after the fiasco surrounding the explosion at the Chernobyl nuclear plant in April 1986. Although located in Ukraine, the plant discharged some 70 per cent of its radioactive fallout on the territory of Belarus. The Soviet leadership's fear of the political fallout from the incident, however, prevented an adequate emergency response, leaving thousands of children and adults to become needlessly exposed.[5]

The cultural demands of Belarusian intellectuals and the popular discontent with the handling of Chernobyl found expression in the establishment of the Belarusian Popular Front in October 1988, the first local opposition movement founded outside the Baltic republics. Like its Baltic counterparts, the front was meant to provide a broad-based forum for the discussion of Belarusian history, to examine relations with the Soviet center, and to support Gorbachev's reforms against an intransigent and corrupt local leadership. Headed by Zianon Pazniak, an archaeologist who had earlier uncovered evidence of Stalinist mass graves in the Kurapaty Forest outside Minsk, the front became the forerunner of similar movements of national revival established later in Ukraine and Moldova.

Early on, however, the front ran into problems. Pazniak and other front supporters overestimated the ease with which dissatisfaction with the handling of Chernobyl would translate into dissatisfaction with the perilous state of Belarusian culture and channel a desire for national sovereignty. By mid-1989, the most important early supporters from the Writers' Union had already parted ways with the front and had made their peace with Conservative Party First Secretary Iafrem Sakalau. There was little grassroots support for the national ideals of the front, and because of the harsh restrictions on public demonstrations put in place by Sakalau, the front was forced to hold its first congress in Vilnius. Thus, unlike in Ukraine and Moldova, where reform communists, intellectuals, and local nationalists found common ground in the front movements of the late 1980s, hastening their republics' emergence as independent states, in Belarus Pazniak and his associates were from the outset largely voices crying in the wilderness.

The low level of national consciousness in Belarus is often cited to explain the lack of support for the national ideals espoused by the front. But the real question is not why there was so little sympathy for the Belarusian language and the old symbols of the medieval Grand Duchy that the front sought to resurrect, but rather why anyone expected that there would be any at all. All of the Soviet Union's fifteen republics were, in greater and lesser degrees, socially "sovietized" during the communist period. But the extent of sovietization, involving linguistic assimilation to Russian and the appropriation of a nominally transethnic identity associated with the struggles and triumphs of Soviet socialism, was perhaps greater in Belarus than in any of its sister republics. As Kathleen Mihalisko has reflected, "the engineering of a Russian-speaking homo sovieticus met with greater success in Belarus than in any other Soviet republic."[6] Belarus was in many ways the quintessence of Soviet socialism. A fifth of its entire population was lost during World War II, and its capital city, Minsk, along with its roads and railway lines, were utterly destroyed by the advances and retreats of the Wehrmacht and the Red Army. Upon this near *tabula rasa* was inscribed an image of a new, prosperous, and peaceful Soviet society. Investment flowed into Belarus from the center. The Soviet military, with the special privileges its members enjoyed, became a central part of Belarusian society. The standard of living was higher than in most neighboring republics and far higher than in the Caucasian or central Asian regions. Use of the national language was associated largely with the peasant past, not with the new, urban Soviet space in which a majority of Belarusians had come to live by the 1980s. Hence, the republic's true national heroes and the true flourishing of the Belarusian nation were associated exclusively with the Soviet period. Most Belarusians certainly did not come to consider themselves ethnic Russians, "but neither do many know what 'Belarusian' is outside a Soviet context."[7]

Belarus thus stumbled toward independence, but under circumstances far more accidental and far less promising than other republics. The actual declaration of independence on 25 August

1991 came largely as an effort by the local communist leadership to avoid the ban on the Communist party of the Soviet Union, enacted after the failed putsch in Moscow. Seeking to shore up their own positions, Belarusian party officials turned toward the small Front representation in the Supreme Soviet, coopting their motion to declare independence and thus avoiding the ban on the all-union party. The skillful handling of the August crisis by the new party boss, Anatolii Malafeeu, along with the weakness of the nationalist opposition, meant that independence was not accompanied by a broad grassroots movement for reform. The political structures of the state, and the elites who populated them, remained largely unchanged in the first years following independence; when institutional changes were introduced, they were almost always directed toward consolidating the power of those who had held office since the Soviet period.

The country's orientation in foreign affairs has followed a similar pattern. Although Belarus has developed some limited foreign policy autonomy and has even gone through periods of tense relations with Moscow, the country has remained more than any post-Soviet republic a virtual appendage of the Russian state.[8] Stanislau Shushkevich, who in autumn 1991 succeeded the former party leader as president of the Supreme Soviet and effective head of state, emerged as a centrist political figure, supporting the consolidation of independence within the context of strong relations with Moscow. But his lack of a clear political base, the growing strength of the renamed "Party of Communists" within the legislature and the machinations of rival politicians meant that his scope for action was severely constrained.

It was under Shushkevich's chief opponent and his elected successor, Alexander Lukashenka, that Belarus's retreat toward authoritarianism would be completed. A former state farm chairman with strong ties to the Belarusian countryside, Lukashenka stood in the summer 1994 elections on a populist platform of anti-corruption and the merging of the Belarusian and Russian economies. After winning some 80 per cent of the vote in the second round, Lukashenka set about implementing his program. Domestic opposition was stifled and regional government was centralized in the hands of the president. The new political system, validated in a controversial referendum in November 1996, further consolidated Lukashenka's powers by turning the newly created National Assembly into little more than a rubber stamp for laws prepared by the executive. Moreover, since deputies are allowed to hold simultaneous positions within the executive branch, the new system violates the most basic prerequisite for a genuine separation of powers.[9]

In the foreign policy arena, the most important of Lukashenka's initiatives was Belarus's reintegration into the Russian Federation, an agreement signed in April 1996. However, the Belarusian-Russian union (or "Union of Sovereign Republics," as it is officially known) was not originally intended by Lukashenka as a return to the Soviet fold. It was meant to be the exact opposite, an opportunity, bizarrely, for Lukashenka to gain control of a Russia that under Yeltsin had come to the brink of disaster. The Belarusian president was not interested in a mere confederation of newly independent countries; he had, in 1991, been the only parliamentary deputy in all of Belarus, Russia, and Ukraine to vote against the Belavezha Accord, the tripartite agreement that led eventually to the Commonwealth of Independent States (CIS). The union, in Lukashenka's mind, was not an Anschluss. It was to be a pan-Slavic Risorgimento, with Belarus playing the role of Piedmont. Since then, though, the union has turned out to be less than Lukashenka had imagined, largely because of Russian objections to Lukashenka's desire to recreate a "union of equal republics" under his own leadership. But the accord did formalize a relationship that most Belarusians seemed to desire and one that severely curtailed Belarus's autonomy in foreign policymaking. Although few of the more ambitious agreements on Belarusian-Russian cooperation have been fully implemented, the two states have actively collaborated in military training, air defense, border controls, and other military and quasi-military fields.[10]

Belarus does not suffer from the same ailments as many of its eastern European neighbors. Interethnic relations are generally good. It has no outstanding border disputes with adjacent states. Its political elites have no expansionist aims, nor is there an attempt to "nationalize" the state by adopting ethnically exclusivist symbols or restricting citizenship based on ethnic or linguistic criteria.[11] But equality in misery is no virtue. Since 1994, Lukashenka has created the last truly authoritarian state in Europe – and without the exigencies of war that his closest analogues, Franjo Tudjman and Slobodan Milosevic, might offer as an excuse. Political parties, while still nominally in existence, are weak and fractured. The president effectively rules by decree, with little thought to the demands of parliamentary democracy. He has created a praetorian guard of Interior Ministry troops that is perhaps twice as large as the Belarusian armed forces.[12] The KGB, the only security service in the former Soviet Union to retain the Soviet-era name, has the power to issue "warnings" to citizens without regard to individual rights or due process.[13] He has managed to gain for Belarus the distinction of being the only European state from which refugees have been granted political asylum in the United States, a state that has also effectively expelled foreign diplomats and that has even been refused admission to the normally forgiving Council of Europe.

It is difficult to see how this situation is likely to change, even if Lukashenka were removed from power (an outcome that will probably result more from palace intrigues in Minsk than from a rejection of the popular president at the polls in 2001). Political parties that seek some sort of openness to regional and subregional initiatives are few. Of the three states examined here, Belarus is the most unidirectional in terms of its foreign policy orientation and, as a result, the least inclined to cooperate subregionally. This does not mean, of course, that bilateral and multilateral arrangements do not exist. Cooperation with Poland has been at times profound, including the signing of an interstate treaty renouncing any mutual territorial claims in June 1992. In March 1995, Belarus signed a partnership and cooperation agreement with the European Union, the one form of integration with the west that many Belarusians seem to accept, but further cooperation was suspended after Lukashenka's moves against opposition parties and his wholesale control of the media.

Belarus does illustrate, though, that subregionalism need not always work the way we think. Indeed, in some ways, Belarus under both Shushkevich and Lukashenka has been an enthusiastic advocate of subregionalism – of a kind. It was a founding member of the CIS (the nominal secretariat of which is in Minsk), and in 1993 joined the six-state Tashkent Agreement on Collective Security. Three years later, Belarus signed the Quadripartite Customs Treaty with Russia, Kazakhstan, and Kyrgyzstan. Even the Russia-Belarus union is a subregionalism of sorts since it is open to further signatories, among which the unrecognized "Transnistrian Moldovan Republic" has expressed the most serious interest. Indeed, one might argue that few other states have so eagerly embraced subregionalism, just not of the sort that is often mentioned in the west. It is not only democracies, after all, that can cooperate.

### Ukraine: A Reluctant Subregional Leader

Like Belarus, Ukraine emerged from the rubble of the Soviet system primarily as a result of the collapse of power at the center and the effort by local elites to shore up their control in a disintegrating union. It was a region unprepared for independence, with neither a political elite committed and competent enough to build an independent state, nor a "politically usable past" upon which to construct the myths of nationhood.[14] Unlike events in Belarus, however, popular mobilization did play a significant role in Ukraine's exit from the Soviet Union, although the widely disparate components of that mobilization bequeathed serious difficulties to the political system after independence.

As in many republics, the earliest organized opposition to local communists came in the form of support for perestroika. The Popular Movement for Perestroika, later to become known as Rukh, sought to undercut the power of the Brezhnevite local leadership, headed by First Secretary Volodymyr Shcherbytskyi, by supporting the reform initiatives launched by Mikhail Gorbachev. Elections in 1989 to the Congress of People's Deputies, the new Soviet super-parliament, affirmed the power of anti-Shcherbytskyi forces and provided a broad platform for the articulation of discontent.

However, as with similar "front" movements in other parts of the union, Rukh was an umbrella organization that covered groups and individuals with hugely divergent interests, motivations, and goals. Ukrainian nationalists, mainly from western Ukraine and supported by the Ukrainian diaspora in the west, hoped to use the reform movement as a way of creating an independent Ukrainian state based on the model of the Ukrainian People's Republic that existed from 1917 to 1920. Democratic patriots in Lviv and Kyiv saw an opportunity to build a state more responsive to the needs of its citizens. Industrial workers, many either Russian or Russian-speaking, sought to have their salaries paid, their pensions secured, and their working conditions improved. And astute Communist party officials saw in the movement for reform an opportunity to secure their own positions in a crumbling system, primarily by co-opting the language of nationalism. When Ukraine declared independence on

August 24, 1991 in response to the Moscow coup, it was thus in the context of serious disputes among political actors over the meaning of reform and the future directions of the suddenly independent republic.

Since 1991, the central features of Ukrainian domestic politics have owed much to these fractious origins. Political parties have been internally unstable and their key constituents at best uncertain and at worst labile. The political elite, as in Belarus and Moldova, has remained largely unchanged since the late Soviet period, with nominally reform communists and quasi-nationalist members of the old nomenklatura moving into positions vacated by the old Communist party of Ukraine. It was not that there were no independent sources of political opposition in the republic; rather, there were perhaps too many, or at least too many with too many different agendas. Four churches, Ukrainian Catholics and three versions of Orthodoxy, vied for position as the single recognized national church. Rukh eventually split between two factions, a more moderate group focusing on democratization and another promoting a more ethnically exclusivist path. It is little wonder with such a divided political class that power should be retained by the amorphous array of factory managers, collective farm chairmen, government bureaucrats, politically astute party members, and nonparty technocrats who were able to see the writing on the wall before 1991. This group, often known generically as the "party of power" (*partiia vlady*) has, in various guises, remained at the center of the political system since independence.

Prohibitions on dissent and freedom of expression have, in great measure, fallen by the wayside since 1991, but good government has not followed the end of the bad. Independent Ukraine has been a state less governed than administered, a fact most evident in the utter failure of economic reform. The first post-Soviet parliament, elected in 1994, was unable to pass effective economic reform legislation, largely because of the strong representation by leftist forces who insisted on maintaining subsidies to defunct enterprises that annually created massive budget deficits and spurred hyperinflation.

President Leonid Kuchma, who succeeded Ukraine's first president, Leonid Kravchuk, in 1994, was verbally committed to serious reform. But the Verkhovna Rada, dominated by communists, socialists, and agrarian populists, effectively blocked any measures that seemed to cut into the "social protection" provisions of the constitution. The 1996 constitution copied virtually all the social protection clauses contained in the old Soviet one. While these provisions played well among the most conservative voters, industrial workers in eastern Ukraine, pensioners, and state bureaucrats, they proved to be a double ill for the political system and the economy. When the promises of state support were honored, they bankrupted the state budget; when they were not, they further cheapened the notion of basic human rights and led to still greater discontent with the idea of reform.[15]

The March 1998 elections changed little in the legislature's composition. Communist party candidates won 84 seats on party lists and another 40 seats in single-seat districts, giving the party once again the largest number of mandates in parliament. The elections also illustrated the fundamental importance of the division in Ukraine between the largely Ukrainian-speaking west and center and the generally Russian or Russian-speaking east and south. There are, of course, other salient divisions among the electorate, but the fact that the Communist party's base lies in the Russian-speaking east and support for the nationalist opposition mainly in the west is indicative of the sharp regional divide over the state's future trajectory. The communists and their supporters remain firmly committed to some form of reintegration with Russia, whether within the context of the CIS or within a new confederation on the Belarusian-Russian model. Such a notion, though, remains anathema to the nationalists and national democrats, from the more moderate remnants of Rukh and its successors such as the Democratic party, to radical pro-independence groups in the Congress of Ukrainian Nationalists and allied parties. As in both Moldova and Belarus, the future of the state is as contested as the future of its reform.[16]

Despite the rhetoric of the communists, full integration with Russia does not have the same base of support in Ukraine as in Belarus. The lines between "Russians" and "Ukrainians," especially in the east, are often indistinct, and in the west of the country there is a strong and vocal Ukrainian intelligentsia that keeps the spirit of Ukrainian nationalism burning.[17] Yet the key difference between Belarus and Ukraine is that local elites have firmly consolidated their positions in the Ukrainian economy and would be loath to lose it in any reconstituted union. It is a nationalism of the pocketbook, not a nationalism of the spirit, and since it is related to fundamental material interests, it may actually prove to be more powerful in the long run than the romanticism of Galician poets.[18]

Ukraine could, of course, play an important role on Europe's eastern borderland. Its size alone makes it a pivotal state and a potentially powerful subregional actor. However, in dealing with Ukraine the international community is often in a difficult bind. On the one hand, the high-level corruption, inefficient local administration, and anti-reform legislature create huge disincentives for the delivery of further development funds or foreign investment. On the other hand, Ukraine's strategic importance means that international lending agencies and western governments cannot simply turn their back on Kyiv, even though confidence in the Kuchma administration is practically nil.[19]

The conclusion since 1995 of a variety of interstate agreements with the other major states in the region, Poland, and Romania, indicate that at least some people in Kyiv are aware of Ukraine's potential role as an anchor of subregional cooperation. Still, the fractious nature of domestic politics in Ukraine, the strong regional and social divisions within the electorate, and the inability of the government to effect serious economic reform have all placed a check on Ukraine's ability to do more than stay the course (even though that course has led to hyperinflation, declining living standards, and continued dominance by the Russian Federation).

President Kuchma only belatedly articulated a clear position generally in favor of NATO enlargement, but he has long underscored his close relations with the west as a major foreign policy achievement.[20] There is no doubt that under his administration western governments, in particular the United States, have taken more seriously the idea of an independent Ukraine as the "keystone in the arch" of security in the western NIS and the Black Sea zone.[21] However, the degree to which Kuchma's views are shared by most Ukrainians is dubious. Ukrainians themselves are at best uncertain and at worst schizophrenic about their orientation and the future of an independent state.[22] An opinion poll taken in July 1998 showed that most Ukrainians saw Bill Clinton as their favorite politician, indicating a fundamental orientation toward the west, but coming a close second was Alexander Lukashenka, indicating at least respect for an iron-fisted leader and perhaps even a sense of nostalgia for the Soviet Union.[23]

## Moldova: Divided Elites in a Divided State

Since the late 1980s, Moldova has followed a pattern of political development similar to Ukraine's, but with two important differences.

First, Moldova was the only republic in the Soviet Union, the majority population of which shared a potential national identity with a state beyond the Soviet borders, Romania. It has therefore been faced with the task of defining its relationship with a state that has potential irredentist designs on it. Second, its titular nationality is divided over the fundamentals of its own cultural heritage. Even nearly a decade after independence, political elites remain sharply divided between those who think of the Moldovans simply as Romanians, a people who should one day be reunited with the country from which they were torn in the territorial changes of World War II; and those who think of them as a cultural group with its own traditions and historical destiny.[24]

As in Ukraine and Belarus, the most important "informal group" to emerge in late Soviet Moldova was the Popular Front. Established in May 1989, the Front was composed of two distinct wings, both associated with cultural and social movements that had formed the previous year. One wing sought primarily to support restructuring within the republic. Moldova had long been one of the last redoubts of Brezhnev-era corruption. While Semion Grossu, the local party first secretary, paid lip service to the need for economic restructuring, openness, and democratization, in practice the local party organization remained dominated by corrupt party bosses and industrial managers. The other wing had an agenda that focused more on national issues, in particular, the status of the Moldovan/Romanian language in the republic and the position of ethnic Moldovans within the state and party hierarchy.

After the formation of the front, these separate agendas did not disappear. Indeed, the fault lines that had existed early on in the opposition movement began to widen as the stakes rose in the struggle between opposition and party stalwarts. The Popular Front was able to remain relatively united from 1989 to 1991, enabling the passage of important legislation on the use of the Moldovan/Romanian language, local sovereignty, and eventually independence from the Soviet Union. However, in reaction to these changes, which augmented the relationship between the Moldovan majority and the Slavic and Turkic populations, local minorities developed their own countermovements.

By the end of 1991, Moldova had become, in both territorial and political terms, a divided state. The mainly Slavic eastern portion of the republic, Transnistria, had declared itself an independent

"Transnistrian Moldovan Republic," and districts in the south, populated in large part by Christian Turks (Gagauzi) and Bulgarians, had also effectively seceded. At the same time, in Chisinau the once united Popular Front had splintered into a variety of rival groups: ardent pan-Romanian nationalists, who supported the reintegration of Moldova and Romania; modern pan-Romanian patriots, who argued for a rebirth of Romanian culture in Moldova but at most a "cultural union" with Bucharest; a centrist bloc, upholding the multiethnic character of the republic; and opposing "Moldovan" nationalists faction that argued that Moldovans formed a nation separate from Romanians.

Disputes along these lines defined Moldovan politics in the early period of transition. The 1990 elections to the Moldovan Supreme Soviet (later renamed simply "parliament") allowed front supporters to come to power and, for a time, to control several important ministries. By the time of the 1994 elections, however, the tables had turned. Led by President Mircea Snegur, once a strong supporter of the front, the "Moldovanist" side of the political spectrum emerged victorious. The 1994 parliament included a plurality of seats controlled by the Agrarian Democratic party, a loose alliance of the former agricultural nomenklatura, united only in their desire to retain power in Moldova's extensive collective farm system and to undo many of the pro-Romanian cultural reforms instituted in the brief period of the front's ascendancy in 1990 and 1991.

The parliamentary elections in 1998 led to still further changes. The agrarian democrats, with no strong ideology or clear constituency beyond the collective farms, failed to gain representation in the new parliament, with most seats going to the newly resurrected Party of Communists and to the pan-Romanian remnants of the old front. The former were able to appeal to the discontent among both rural and urban citizens with the massive decline in living standards, while the latter were able to reorient themselves toward calls for quick privatization and integration in western security and economic structures. Thus, while the Moldovan political landscape has changed considerably since 1991, the fundamental dividing lines remain the same: a rightist pan-Romanian bloc composed mainly of ethnic Moldovan/Romanian intellectuals, an amorphous center populated by persons already in office and desiring to stay there, and a resurgent left of both Moldovans and Russian-speakers suspicious of the economic and social changes instituted since independence.

The foreign policy orientations among these various groups represent the standard range of choices in many post-Soviet republics. First, the political right in Moldova, primarily pan-Romanian parties such as the Christian Democratic Popular Front (the successor to the Soviet-era front) and the Party of Democratic Forces, continue to argue for cooperation with European and Euro-Atlantic institutions, the development of a "special relationship" with Romania, and the minimization of contacts with the Russian Federation. Second, centrist groups, such as the Movement for a Democratic and Prosperous Moldova (a party associated mainly with supporting President Petru Lucinschi), argue for a balanced foreign policy that recognizes cultural and historical ties with Romania, but also seeks to build bridges to other Soviet republics and to maintain a close link with Russia. Finally, the political left, primarily the Party of Communists, works to secure Moldova's place within the CIS, to limit contacts with Romania and to forge even stronger ties with the Russian Federation.

Moldovan foreign policy has emerged as an uneasy amalgam of all three positions. The country has actively participated in NATO's Partnership for Peace, even though it is a constitutionally neutral state. It has allowed the Russian Federation to take a controlling interest in its gas distribution network, even as it seeks to escape from Russian dominance. It sold nearly its entire fixed-wing air force to the United States, even though Russian troops remained temporarily stationed on its territory. And since 1991, it has had a passport-free regime with Romania, even though its parliamentary majority is viscerally anti-Romanian.

None of these foreign policy moves, of course, are incompatible, but they do illustrate the degree to which Moldova has tried to cover all its bases at once. It is difficult to see how it could be otherwise, given Moldova's size, the ongoing dispute with the Transnistrians, and the clear interests of far more powerful neighbors in its internal politics. At the same time, however, with such an incredible range of policy initiatives and orientations on the table – as well as the frequent parliamentary and presidential elections since 1991 – it has been difficult for Chisinau to articulate clear policy priorities.[24] While Moldovan policymakers across the board are committed to cooperation with neighbors, particularly in the context of Moldovan-Romanian-Ukrainian cooperation on the upper Prut and the lower Danube, it is unclear where subregionalism as such might fit into a foreign policy agenda that aims to be all things to all people.

## A Strategy for Subregionalism

It is unclear what subregionalism might be able to do to alleviate the policy predicaments in which Belarusian, Ukrainian, and Moldovan elites find themselves. Those predicaments, while owing a great deal to the regional environment, result most directly from the nature of domestic politics in each state. Still, at the most ambitious level, a strategy of subregionalism in the western NIS would seem to point toward the following:

### Binding Belarus

Belarus under Lukashenka is a state that has oscillated between being mildly unsavory to decidedly worrisome. It is not unthinkable that the country could become a more assertive "rogue state," especially once the regional implications of NATO and EU expansion are clearly felt by both citizens and political elites throughout the countries left out of the process of Euro-Atlantic integration. It is unlikely, however, that Belarusian opposition to western integration will translate into hostile foreign policy moves, if for no other reason than that the Belarusians themselves have so few foreign policy tools at their disposal. One can imagine a situation in which Belarus becomes a regional rogue, a conduit for the penetration of weapons, fissile materials, illicit substances, and even people into the heart of Europe. But in no sense is Belarus alone in this regard. For example, even with more cooperative states, such as Russia and Ukraine, the process of encouraging nonproliferation of nuclear materials and weapons technologies, from the level of the national government to individual enterprises, is fraught with risks and problems.[26]

But to secure against these and other potential threats, multiple and overlapping foreign policy relationships with Belarus are essential. Binding Belarus into a web of interlinked political relationships, particularly into multilateral initiatives that strengthen the country's presence outside the Russian-Belarusian bilateral relationship, may prove helpful in socializing the state's leaders, making them at most productive and at least nonobstructive members of a subregional, regional, and international community. Moreover, lower-level initiatives, from cooperation on border crossings to integration of crime-control strategies, are likely to be more palatable to Belarusian politicians than broad regional strategies. In many ways,

Belarus today still functions like the Soviet Union of the 1970s, and the informal contacts that paved the way for genuine reform later on in the Soviet case may be useful today in making Belarus an eventual good citizen of the wider Europe.

## Untying Ukraine

Security in eastern Europe depends upon a strong and independent Ukrainian state. However, serious economic problems and the uncertain orientation of the Ukrainian leadership have prevented the growth of a strong relationship between Ukraine and regional organizations, or indeed between Ukraine and some of its western neighbors. Ukraine can play a pivotal role both in east central Europe and further afield, in such organizations as the Black Sea Economic Cooperation (BSEC) and various trilateral arrangements with Poland, Romania, and Moldova. But its ability to do so is sharply constrained by its bilateral relationship with Russia. While relations between Moscow and Kyiv have improved considerably since their low point at the time of the Black Sea fleet dispute, the degree to which even the most liberal Russian politicians accept an independent Ukraine as a fact of international politics is still in doubt.

A web of subregional linkages, supported by the west, can play a role in untying Ukraine from its dependence on Russia. These linkages, again focusing on issues of direct interest to local policymakers, are likely to be less threatening both to Ukrainian politicians and to Russia than the broader processes of integration with NATO and the EU. There are a variety of concrete policy problems that concern Ukraine and neighboring states: pollution on the Dnestr, border crossings in the area of the northern Prut, environmental degradation in the Danube delta, port facilities on the Danube, crime control along the Odessa-Tiraspol corridor, development of the Transcarpathian zone, clean-up of the Chernobyl site, and a host of other vital but low-level policy targets. None can be handled exclusively within the context of a bilateral relationship, and moreover, few would be perceived as a potential security issue by Russia. These forms of cooperation, then, might allow Ukraine simultaneously to carve out a sphere of foreign policy activity separate from Russia, while at the same time not antagonizing policymakers in Moscow who are opposed to an assertive Ukraine.

## *Making Moldova Matter*

Moldova's foreign policy since 1991 has been of only marginal importance to western policymakers. The conflict between the Moldovan central government and separatists in the Transnistria region, although of some concern when war raged in 1992, never became a serious problem for European security. Western governments and international lending agencies generally praised the country in 1993-1994 for the swift pace of its reforms. However, problems with the privatization program and the unresolved nature of the Transnistrian dispute led to less sanguine assessments by 1996.[27]

Such oversight is unfortunate, for Transnistria in particular represents a problem of both subregional and regional importance and, moreover, provides a clear instance in which true transborder cooperation is essential. Since declaring autonomy from Moldova in 1990 and complete independence in 1991, the region has become part of an archipelago of unrecognized but de facto states stretching from the Transcaucasus to the Balkans. Abkhazia, south Ossetia, Adzharia, Nagorno-Karabakh, Chechnya, and Transnistria, among others, are areas that continue to represent major security threats to the countries in which they lie as well as to neighboring governments. They are areas in which no government's writ really runs, areas governed, in so far as they are governable, by a combination of criminal networks, corrupt officials, and transnational business interests. So far, however, apart from a standing offer for Ukrainian and Romanian assistance in mediating the dispute, there have been few major initiatives from neighboring states and even fewer serious attempts to make Transnistria and its attendant problems a focus of subregionalism.

## Conclusion

Although western governments often speak of the "western NIS" as a distinct entity, and organize aid programs and ministerial departments accordingly, there have so far been few real reasons to think of Belarus, Ukraine, and Moldova as a distinct subregion. Leaders in Ukraine and Moldova (but rarely in Belarus) have touted subregional initiatives as a desirable component of interstate cooperation, and Ukraine in particular has at times adopted the most activist stance with regard to trilateral and multilateral initiatives, both among states within the CIS and with external partners such as Romania and Poland. However, so far such initiatives have been more talked about than implemented.

It is worth making three final points about this state of affairs, points that perhaps reveal the real obstacles to subregionalism in the former Soviet space. First is the fact that subregional initiatives, like any other dimension of these states' foreign policies, are still largely driven by domestic political factors. Given the continuing uncertainties and rivalries within each capital, staking out clear and creative positions on cooperation with neighbors, other than in the most familiar form of bilateral treaties of cooperation and good neighborly relations, has been extremely difficult. Moreover, with rival elites jealous of their power, they are disinclined to allow, much less encourage, the loose transborder relationships that effective subregionalism entails. Subregionalism requires good and powerful local government but in all three states these two attributes do not normally go together. Where local government is good, its power is often restricted by central authorities, and where regional and local councils have managed to wrest power from the center, it has as often been to secure business interests and monopolize the local economy as to build good government.

Second, while both Brussels and Washington have hailed effective subregional cooperation as an essential first step toward eventual regional integration, to some extent, the two processes work at cross purposes. The easing of border restrictions among subregional partners, for example, runs counter to the strong border controls mandated by the European Union. Moreover, as enthusiasm for broader regional integration inevitably wanes once the problems of integrating the first contingent of new members into both NATO and the EU become apparent, it is worth asking whether similar enthusiasm for subregionalism can long endure.

Third, although few say it openly, subregional cooperation in eastern Europe and the NIS is, to some degree, designed to carve out a space independent of Russian influence. The most explicit example of this form of subregionalism is cooperation within the so-called GUAM group of CIS states—Georgia, Ukraine, Azerbaijan, and Moldova—countries that are the least enthusiastic about building the CIS into something other than an informal consultative body. However, for major subregional initiatives to work – from major environmental clean-up to crime control to immigration – Russia must at some level be involved. Its influence, if not interests, touches on virtually every major foreign policy issue from the Baltic to the Black Sea. It is for this reason that one must be rather sober in assessing the potential contribution of subregionalism, at least a subregionalism that does not include the Russians, to the broader strategic predicaments of Belarus, Ukraine, and Moldova. Good neighborly relations are to be encouraged, and promoting informal and low-level cooperation among groups of states is one way of achieving that end. However, the strategic challenges faced by the states of the western NIS are of a sort unlikely to be overcome without reference to Russia.

## Notes

I thank Renata Dwan and Oleksandr Pavliuk for helpful comments on a draft of this chapter.

1. For distinctions between "Russians" and "russified settlers," see Neil J. Melvin, "The Russians: Diaspora and the end of empire," in *Nations Abroad: Diaspora Politics* and *International Relations in the Former Soviet Union,* eds. Charles King and Neil J. Melvin (Boulder: Westview, 1998), pp. 27-57.

2. Russians, however, formed a much larger relative population in Estonia, Latvia, and Kazakhstan than in any of the western NIS states.

3. Jeff Chinn and Robert Kaiser, *Russians as the New Minority* (Boulder: Westview, 1996), p. 85.

4. On this problem, see David Laitin, *Identity in Formation: The Russian-Speaking Populations in the Near Abroad* (Ithaca: Cornell University Press, 1998).

5. See David R. Marples and Victor G. Snell, *The Social Impact of the Chernobyl Disaster* (New York: St. Martin's, 1988).

6. Kathleen J. Mihalisko, "Belarus: Retreat to authoritarianism," in *Democratic Changes and Authoritarian Reactions in Russia, Ukraine, Belarus, and Moldova,* eds. Karen Dawisha and Bruce Parrott (Cambridge: Cambridge University Press, 1997), p. 233.

7. Mihalisko, "Belarus," p. 236.

8. In autumn 1997, Belarus detained several journalists working for Russian state television, one of whom, Pavel Sheremet, spent over two months in prison. In response, President Lukashenka was banned from entering Russian territory, and his official plane was denied landing rights in Moscow. After Sheremet's release, though, relations improved considerably.

9. "Constitution Watch: Belarus," *East European Constitutional Review* (Winter 1997): 5-7.

10. Ustina Markus, "Russia and Belarus: Elusive Integration," *Problems of Post-Communism* (September/October 1997): 60.

11. On the perils of "nationalising states," see Rogers Brubaker, *Nationalism Reframed: Nationhood and the National Question in the New Europe* (Cambridge: Cambridge University Press, 1996).

12. Ustina Markus, "Lukashenka's proposed referendum," *OMRI Analytical Brief*, 2 August 1996, cited in Mihalisko, "Belarus," p. 257.

13. "Constitution watch: Belarus," *East European Constitutional Review* (Spring 1998): 3.

14. Ilya Prizel, "Ukraine between proto-democracy and 'soft' authoritarianism," in *Democratic Changes*, eds. Dawisha and Parrott, p. 331.

15. In early 1997, the debt to state employees stood at over $2.3 billion. "Constitution Watch: Ukraine," *East European Constitutional Review* (Winter 1997): 32.

16. See Paul S. Pirie, "National identity and politics in southern and eastern Ukraine," *Europe-Asia Studies* 48, no. 7 (1996): 1079-1104.

17. See Andrew Wilson, *Ukrainian Nationalism in the 1990s: A Minority Faith* (Cambridge: Cambridge University Press, 1997), pp. 117-146.

18. On the complexities of national identity in Ukraine, and its relationship to broader problems of identity along Europe's border regions, see Tim Snyder, "The Polish-Lithuanian Commonwealth since 1989: National Narratives in Relations Among Poland, Lithuania, Belarus, and Ukraine," *Nationalism and Ethnic Politics* 4, no. 4 (1998).

19. "Constitution watch: Ukraine," *East European Constitutional Review* (Spring 1998), p. 33.

20. Daniel Williams, "Ukrainian asks for more aid," *Washington Post* (22 July 1998), p. A22.

21. See Sherman Garnett, *Keystone in the Arch: Ukraine in the Emerging Security Environment of Central and Eastern Europe* (Washington, DC: Carnegie Endowment for International Peace, 1997).

22. For a helpful comparison with Belarus, see Stephen R. Burant, "Foreign policy and national identity: A comparison of Ukraine and Belarus," *Europe-Asia Studies*, Vol. 47, No. 7 (1995), pp. 1125-1144.

23. Daniel Williams, "Gore declines to back Ukrainian loan appeal," *Washington Post* (23 July 1998), p. A26.

24. See Charles King, "Moldovan identity and the politics of pan-Romanianism," *Slavic Review* 53, no. 2 (1994): 346-58.

25. Because of the sequence of events in the late perestroika period, Moldova's political institutions were reformed at different times. The country thus has a rather fractured election schedule, with local, parliamentary, and presidential elections all occurring according to different schedules. The result has been the holding of a major election almost every year. Since politicians are almost continuously in campaign mode, it is not surprising that few have staked out clear positions on foreign policy issues.

26. John C. Baker, *Non-Proliferation Incentives for Russia and Ukraine,* Adelphi Paper 309 (London: IISS/Oxford University Press, 1997), pp. 13-29.

27. Sally B. Donnelly, "Up from desperation," *Time*, 30 October 1995, 29.

# 3

# Subregional Relations and Cooperative Initiatives in East-Central Europe

*Oleksandr Pavliuk*

While the European republics of the former Soviet Union and now newly independent countries of east-central Europe, namely Ukraine, Moldova, and Belarus, do not constitute a separate subregion, all three states have, to varying degrees, become involved since their independence in what is for post-communist states a new phenomenon, subregional cooperation. This chapter assesses the engagement of these countries in various forms of subregional cooperation, their attitudes, priorities and agendas. Special attention is given to the participation of the three countries in smaller cooperative initiatives emerging in the area since 1997. Some of the initiatives are barely known, others are attracting increasing attention, curiosity and, among some, concern. This chapter addresses the rationale for their creation, the progress achieved so far, and their potential and future prospects.

The years immediately following the collapse of communism and the artificially created intergovernmental structures of the Eastern Bloc, the Council for Mutual Economic Assistance (CMEA), and the Warsaw Pact witnessed the emergence of a number of new subregional cooperative arrangements stretching from the Barents to the Black seas and encompassing post-communist central and eastern European states: the Central European Initiative (CEI) (1989-92), the Visegrad Group (CEFTA) (1991-93), Council of Baltic Sea States (CBSS) (1992), and the Black Sea Economic Cooperation (BSEC) (1992). All of these arrangements were established voluntarily and were based on geographical proximity and common sub-regional interests, mainly socioeconomic and environmental, rather than on ideological dogma or considerations of power politics.[1]

Post-communist central and eastern European (CEE) states, engaged in a complex process of internal transformation and search for new international roles, saw these new cooperative networks as useful tools for:

- providing an additional channel and a civilized framework for subregional dialogue;
- promoting economic, transborder, and environmental cooperation;
- enhancing subregional stability, security, and the solution of issues of common concern; and
- encouraging a sense of normality and community to dilute lingering Cold War divisions and suspicions.[2]

In the first years of their existence and development, these newly emerged subregional groupings tended to be overlooked and under-valued. Most observers and even participants were skeptical about their potential and future prospects. Yet, despite this skepticism and the existing political, financial, and organizational difficulties, the groupings have been gradually gaining ground, and some, like the CEI, have been expanding their membership.

Ukraine, Moldova, and Belarus joined almost all of these groups. Moldova and Ukraine were, in fact, among the eleven founding states of the BSEC, and in 1996, all three were admitted into the CEI. Ukraine has repeatedly expressed its interest in joining CEFTA and currently seeks observer status in the CBSS. In addition, Ukraine and Belarus have become involved in other forms of new post-communist multilateral cooperation, such as transborder cooperation and Euroregions. In 1993, Ukraine was a founding member of the Carpathian Euroregion, which also includes Hungary, Poland, Romania, and Slovakia; in 1995, Poland and Ukraine agreed on the establishment of the Buh (Bug) Euroregion, encompassing four Polish border regions (*wojwodztwa*) and the Ukrainian region (*oblast*) of Volyhn; western oblasts of Belarus have become a part of the Nieman Euroregion together with Polish and Lithuanian regions and the Kaliningrad enclave of Russia.[3]

For the three post-Soviet countries, these new subregional initiatives also represented a means of assisting the process of transition to independent, democratic, and market economy statehood, testifying to their "European" identity and vocation and enhancing their international positions and profiles. Subregional groupings, for some states, represented their first exposure to independent international politics on a multilateral level.[4] The voluntary, equal, and nondominant nature of subregional schemes were particularly appealing to the post-Soviet countries. Within these groups, Ukraine, Moldova, and Belarus favored the development of concrete activities and specific projects for pragmatic economic reasons. All three wanted to increase their export capacities, improve domestic and subregional transport, energy, and communication systems, promote foreign investment, and address environmental concerns. In the case of Ukrainian and Moldovan participation in BSEC, the quest for alternative energy supplies was another important consideration. [5]

Yet, while they might appear to share some common interest in the development of subregional cooperation, in practice the policies of Belarus, Moldova, and Ukraine within these groupings have been quite different. Ukraine, seeking to raise its subregional role and profile in central and eastern Europe and the Black Sea area, has been one of the main actors within the BSEC and was very energetic in gaining admission into the CEI. The Ukrainian president and prime minister have become regular participants in unofficial meetings of central European leaders. Kyiv was a strenuous proponent of the decision taken at the June 1998 BSEC summit in Yalta to transform the group into a formal subregional economic organization.

Initially, CEE subregional cooperation was also viewed from a security perspective by Kyiv.[6] The development of, and participation in, a system of subregional security represented one of the main pillars of national security-building. Ukrainian foreign policy thinkers argued that such subregional arrangements would enhance Ukraine's external environment, while at the same time maintaining the country's self-proclaimed nonaligned status. It was Ukraine's first president, Leonid Kravchuk, who, in early 1993, put forward the idea of the establishment of a central and eastern European "zone of stability and security," an appeal which failed to secure the support of other central European states. In 1994, Kyiv proposed another initiative on military and naval confidence-building measures in the Black Sea. Although Bulgaria, Georgia, Romania, Russia, and Turkey supported the initiative, the elaboration of a political document regulating military and naval activities was blocked by the Ukrainian-Russian dispute over the Russian military and naval presence in Crimea. The signing of the Black Sea Fleet agreements in May 1997 has opened the way for further progress on the document.

At the same time, the subregional involvement and contribution of Moldova and even more so of Belarus, have so far been very modest. Moldova's own economic problems have constrained its subregional activity and have encouraged it to view BSEC and CEI largely in terms of potential economic support and benefit. Belarus, while demonstrating some interest in subregional cooperation in 1992-94 that culminated in its accession into the CEI in 1996, has found itself on the margins of subregional cooperation in east central Europe. The November 1996 referendum held by President Lukashenka, recognized as illegal by most European states, including some of Belarus's immediate neighbors, has only increased this isolation.

## Subregional Relations and Enlargement

The debate over EU and NATO eastern enlargement has drawn additional attention to the development of subregional initiatives and their potential role. Subregional cooperation in CEE has started to be seen as not only an important element in stabilizing relations among neighboring states, strengthening democracy, and assisting transitions of the post-communist countries to market economies, but also as a facilitator of the process of wider European and Euro-Atlantic integration. As the NATO Madrid summit of 1997 approached, western states increasingly perceived subregional cooperation as a useful tool for "cushioning" possible new dividing lines between "ins" and "outs" and providing additional arenas for neighboring countries to meet and address mutual concerns. It was also hoped that such cooperation would help make NATO enlargement more acceptable to Moscow, especially as Russia is already involved in various subregional cooperative arrangements.[7]

For NATO and EU applicant states, active eastern policies and good neighborly relations have become an important element of accession strategies, as both the EU and NATO have made it clear that relations with neighbors and the ability to resolve existing problems in bilateral relations constitute important membership criteria. For nonapplicant CEE states, closer cooperative relations with their more advanced neighbors have become an additional chance to link them more closely to western structures and weave them into European and Euro-Atlantic integration.

In east-central Europe, the logic of subregional relations has been particularly linked to the logic of enlargement. It is in this area that an enlarging Europe meets and overlaps with the post-Soviet space.[8] On the one hand, the "subregion" is directly affected by NATO and EU enlargement. Ukraine, Belarus, and Moldova, whatever their national strategies, currently find themselves on the margins of European integrative processes, unlike their central European neighbors.[9] On the other hand, the three states each represent a central preoccupation of Russian foreign policy. As a result, their strategic situation becomes highly complex. The entire issue of whether security in Europe will be inclusive and transparent or exclusive and divisive depends to a large extent on the situation of these countries, and particularly Ukraine, the largest among them.[10] All this suggests a potentially profound impact on subregional relations in east-central Europe.

Contrary to the predictions of many critics, NATO eastern enlargement has so far not harmed relations between CEE states, but rather has facilitated subregional dialogue and helped to forge new partnerships. Basic political and border treaties were concluded between Hungary and Slovakia, Hungary and Romania, Ukraine and Romania, Ukraine and Belarus, and Ukraine and Russia after years of procrastination, while Ukrainian-Polish and Polish-Lithuanian rapprochements were further consolidated. This progress has been achieved thanks to the careful handling of the first wave of NATO enlargement. This has included the continuing transformation of NATO itself, the signing of the NATO-Russia Founding Act and NATO-Ukraine Charter, increased ties by the alliance with other "outs" through the Partnership for Peace (PfP), and strong emphasis on the development of close bilateral and multilateral subregional relations.

With most criticism focused on the potential dangers of NATO enlargement, much less attention was initially given to possible negative consequences of EU enlargement. Recently, however, fears have been growing in central and eastern Europe that a new EU boundary could become a "dividing line," potentially more dangerous than the security implications related to NATO enlargement. The introduction of new border regulations and stricter visa policies instituted by those CEE countries that join the EU in the first wave could seriously damage subregional trade and human contacts. Significantly, this concern is on the agenda of states on both sides of this "dividing line,"[11] EU enlargement also presents a serious challenge for the development and further consolidation of existing and emerging subregional intergovernmental cooperative ventures and Euroregions. The future of at least one central European subregional grouping, CEFTA, is already under question, given that most (if not all) of its current members are likely to join the EU.

The logic of enlargement also explains to some extent the different attitude toward subregional cooperation on the part of Ukraine, Moldova, and Belarus. After some initial hesitation, Ukraine has endorsed NATO enlargement and declared its strategic goal to be integration into European and Euro-Atlantic structures. Aware that this process will be long and complex, Ukraine has opted for two parallel and complementary avenues for accession. These consist of "direct integration" through development of closer ties with the EU, WEU, and NATO, and "indirect integration" through participation in various CEE subregional initiatives. As a result, Kyiv has primarily paid attention to bilateral relationships and forms of subregional cooperation, such as BSEC and CEI, which bring it closer to western integrated institutions, anchor it in central Europe and help to avoid the emergence of a new dividing line on Ukraine's western border.[12] At the same time, Kyiv has tried its best to stay away from, or prevent further formalization of, those intergovernmental structures that might distance Ukraine from its declared strategic objective. These include the CIS and the idea of a "Slavic Union" of Russia, Ukraine, and Belarus, promoted by Lukashenka. From this perspective, Ukraine is the east central European country most vulnerable to the consequences of EU enlargement as the closing of its western border could seriously endanger its efforts to build ties with its central European neighbors.

Moldova takes a similar approach. As Chisinau explores its own option for participation in European integration, membership in CEE subregional initiatives provides an accessible means of charting the general course of a gradual "return" to Europe. Official foreign policy, however, remains cautious, given Moldova's serious internal divisions, its heavy energy dependence on Russia, and the still unresolved Transnistrian problem. Moldovan officials stress the need for maintaining a balanced foreign policy and emphasize the country's constitutionally established neutrality.[13]

Belarus has found itself isolated internationally, largely as a result of its own policies, and excluded from most subregional cooperative networks. Under Lukashenka, Belarus has taken a negative stance on NATO enlargement and opted for closer integration with Russia and within the CIS. As a senior Belarusian official describes it, "Belarus is destined (in the best meaning of this word, because it is its historic destiny) to the Union with Russia. It corresponds with Belarus' national interests. This Union is as natural as the union of Belgium and Germany, or Holland and Germany."[14] The ongoing tension in relations with the west is periodically accompanied by the deterioration of Belarus's relations with its immediate neighbors. Participation in the CEI and the Nieman Euroregion has so far been mostly on paper, and its perspective on membership in the CBSS is problematic as well.[15] Far from being involved in the process, the "Belarusian factor" has rather stimulated ad hoc subregional initiatives.

## Emerging Networks of Cooperation

The climate of closer bilateral ties and mutual trust among CEE countries opened new prospects for the development of fresh subregional initiatives. In the course of 1997, several trilateral and multilateral cooperative arrangements were launched on an ad hoc basis, often within existing larger subregional frames, such as BSEC or CEI. These included Romanian-Moldovan-Ukrainian, Romanian-Ukrainian-Polish, and Polish-Ukrainian-Lithuanian "triangulars," the Tallinn summit and Vilnius forum, as well as quadrilateral cooperation between Georgia, Ukraine, Azerbaijan and Moldova (GUAM). Belarus was invited only to the Vilnius summit; Moldova takes part in two groups and was represented at the Vilnius forum, while Ukraine has been a central component in each of them. This section surveys the development of these networks and the progress achieved so far.

### *Ukraine-Moldova-Romania*

The emergence of trilateral cooperation between Moldova, Romania, and Ukraine has been one of the first results of the improved subregional climate in central and eastern Europe. The beginning of 1997 was marked by notable improvement in their bilateral relations. Moldovan-Romanian and Ukrainian-Romanian negotiations on basic political treaties were resumed in January, and

Moldovan-Ukrainian dialogue was intensified during the spring. On June 2, 1997, Kyiv and Bucharest signed a long-awaited basic political treaty recognizing territorial integrity and the inviolability of mutual borders. All this laid the foundation for launching a new trilateral venture for cooperation.

On July 3, 1997, presidents Kuchma, Lucinschi, and Constantinescu met in the Ukrainian port of Izmail on the Danube and signed a joint statement to boost cooperation among the three countries. The presidents resolved to convene regular trilateral meetings at various levels, including one summit per year, to support each other in the international arena, to hold consultations on issues of mutual interest. They also agreed to facilitate the strengthening of [sub]regional stability and cooperation and to foster joint positions and actions in relations with regional, European, Euro-Atlantic, and international organizations.

In addition, the statement called for the growth of trade and economic cooperation among the three states through the creation of a trilateral consultative mechanism in financial and economic spheres and the establishment of a free economic zone, Reni-Galats-Jiurjiulesti. Particular emphasis was laid on the need to develop transborder cooperation and create two new Euroregions, Lower Danube and Upper Prut, as a basis for the future free economic zone. Additionally, the three presidents expressed their "support for the development of direct contacts among people and NGOs."[16] Joint measures to combat organized crime, illegal migration, and weapons and drugs smuggling were also agreed to and followed by an interior ministers' meeting in Chisinau in November 1997.

Thus, the idea of Ukrainian-Moldovan-Romanian cooperation, initiated by Bucharest, received a promising start and even some unexpected enthusiasm in all three countries. However, the practical implementation of this network has turned out to be rather difficult. Common economic and political interest in promoting trilateral cooperation has been constrained by the three countries' limited financial resources, lack of proper legislation and infrastructures as well as the lack of experience in cross-border cooperation at the local level. For Moldova, in particular, the Lower Danube and Upper Prut initiatives represent its first direct experience of participation in the Euroregion framework for transfrontier cooperation. Common interests are, moreover, still overshadowed by scant mutual trust and confidence, the result of a complex history and remaining unresolved bilateral disputes. By 1998, progress in negotiations between Ukraine and Romania on the delimitation of the continental shelf and between Moldova and Ukraine on the demarcation and delimitation of the state border had slowed down again. Kyiv and Bucharest remain at odds on the treatment of national minorities. Chisinau and Bucharest have yet to sign a basic political treaty, a difficult task given Moldova's reluctance to recognize the "special" relationship between the two countries. Specifically, the Romanian treaty delegation insists on a provision that underscores Moldova's special relationship with Romania, something the Moldovans are not willing to accept. Given these contexts, both Moldova and Ukraine remain cautious of Romanian initiatives and often suspicious of the latter's subregional intentions.

After more than one year, an agreement on the establishment of the Lower Danube Euroregion was finally signed between the three countries in Galats, Romania, on August  14, 1998. The Odessa region (*oblast*) of Ukraine; Kagul Kantemir, and Vulkanesti districts of Moldova; and three Romanian regions (*judets*) Braila, Galats, and Tulcha make up this Euroregion. Nine commissions were created to deal with specific issues of cross-border cooperation, while work on the creation of the Upper Prut Euroregion, in which an Eco (ecological) Euroregion will be an integral component, has been intensified.

The second summit between presidents Constantinescu, Kuchma, and Lucinschi took place in Moldova on October 22,  1998. A statement on trilateral cooperation and a memorandum of cooperation on fighting organized crime were signed. The Chisinau statement reiterated the three countries' determination to strengthen trilateral cooperation within international and subregional organizations and to continue the development of the two Euroregions, and it called for the creation of a common information system on earthquakes and other extraordinary situations. The three presidents noted their concern at the lack of progress in the final settlement of the Transnistrian problem and supported the complete withdrawal of all Russian troops from the territory of Moldova in line with OSCE decisions. In an effort to contain competition, the three states agreed to coordinate their positions on energy transport projects, including the transportation of oil from the Caspian Sea.[17] Plans to establish a free economic zone (Reni-Galats-Jiurjiulesti) were discussed, and it was agreed that the necessary legislation would be elaborated and submitted to national parliaments by summer 1999.

The revitalized commitment of Moldova, Romania, and Ukraine to forge trilateral cooperation and the progress achieved so far deserve credit, particularly in light of the significant economic and political obstacles they have had to overcome. The hope is that this emerging cooperation will further enhance subregional confidence and facilitate the resolution of their remaining bilateral disputes.

### Romania-Ukraine-Poland

A second trilateral network encompasses Romania, Ukraine, and Poland. In contrast to the first, however, it has so far been marked by an absence of concrete projects and practical accomplishments. As in the previous case, this was also a Romanian initiative, put forward by President Constantinescu during his first official foreign visit to Poland in January 1997. After some consideration, hesitation, and mutual consultations, presidents Kuchma and Kwasniewski finally supported the initiative and gathered for an informal meeting in Bucharest on November 26, 1997.

According to news reports, potential areas for trilateral cooperation were discussed at the meeting. Romania and Ukraine showed interest in the development of economic cooperation, infrastructure, and transport and energy corridors from the Baltic to the Black Sea and on to the Caspian. The potential for cooperation within NATO's PfP program was noted, and the three presidents agreed on the need to jointly combat organized crime, terrorism, and drugs smuggling. It was also agreed that future trilateral meetings would take place in Bucharest.

No formal document, however, was signed and no specific joint projects were developed, since both Kyiv and Warsaw remain largely cautious, if not skeptical, in their assessment of the purpose and prospects of this trilateral initiative.[18] The Romanian proposal for the creation of a joint Romanian-Polish-Ukrainian peacekeeping battalion was not positively received in Warsaw.[19] Cooperation in the transportation of Caspian oil has, so far also been problematic, despite mutual assurances, as Kyiv and Bucharest are to some extent competitors in this undertaking. No date or location has been fixed for the next trilateral summit.

Although relations between Ukraine and Poland have assumed a strategic partnership status, bilateral relations with Romania have yet to reach the same high level of mutual understanding and trust.

As noted above, Ukrainian-Romanian relations are still overshadowed by the unresolved issue of delimitation and demarcation of the continental shelf and Ukraine's uncertainty about Romania's subregional goals. Polish-Romanian relations do not seem a priority for either side, with Warsaw far more proactive in forging strong cooperative ties with its Ukrainian and Lithuanian neighbors. A certain competition between Warsaw and Bucharest for subregional leadership can not be excluded as a factor constraining their cooperation within the Romanian-Polish-Ukrainian trilateral framework.

The short experience of Romanian-Polish-Ukrainian and Romanian-Moldovan-Ukrainian initiatives to date demonstrates that external factors can facilitate subregional cooperation. Both initiatives were inspired and pushed forward by Bucharest and were viewed within the context of a greater enlargement framework. Following the November 1996 presidential elections, Romania undertook unprecedented diplomatic efforts to boost its chances for early admission into NATO and the EU through the creation of a system of multiple trilateral subregional alliances. Bucharest hoped that these trilateral initiatives would serve as "an important signal to all of western Europe, NATO, and the EU that Romania supports all forms of cooperation that strengthen [sub]regional security."[20] The resulting arrangements have sometimes lacked a clear and strong enough "internally-driven" purpose to develop concrete projects, and in some cases they have remained largely expressions of good will. Their further evolution and ultimate success will remain problematic until existing bilateral disputes are settled and suspicions removed.

At the same time, Ukraine, Poland, and Romania are three large and geostrategically important states in central and eastern Europe with a total population of 120 million. Mutually beneficial cooperation among them would significantly enhance subregional and all-European stability and security and constitute a step toward their further integration into European and Euro-Atlantic institutions.

### Poland-Ukraine-Lithuania

The Polish-Ukrainian-Lithuanian triangular has developed on an ad hoc and largely informal basis. One may even question the very existence of such a triangular. Yet, mutual desire to forge trilateral cooperation is clearly present in all three capitals and is driven by shared interests and common positions on issues of European and subregional stability and their place in a post-Cold War Europe. The triangular is, apparently by common consent, heavily centered on Warsaw.

Breaking with historical grievances, Ukraine and Lithuania see a more advanced and friendly Poland as their key strategic partner and place much hope on Polish assistance in their efforts to join European and Euro-Atlantic institutions.[21] As Lithuanian Foreign Minister Algirdas Saudargas aptly put it, "Poland is a strategic Lithuanian partner, as both countries have sought to integrate into the European Union and NATO; therefore, integration via Poland would be easier."[22] In turn, Warsaw has eagerly advocated for the accession aspirations of both Kyiv and Vilnius.

The three countries also share an interest in a stable and secure subregional environment. From this point of view, the situation in neighboring Belarus as well as its growing isolation and its attempts to merge with Russia have become serious concerns for Lithuania, Poland, and Ukraine. The Trilateral Declaration on Belarus signed by presidents Kwasniewski, Kuchma, and Brazauskas in December 1996 reflected this and, in so doing, they marked the first practical manifestation of their emerging cooperation. The declaration expressed anxiety over developments in Belarus and condemned the unconstitutional disbanding of the Belarusian parliament by President Lukashenka. At the same time, Kyiv, Vilnius, and Warsaw constantly emphasize the danger of neglecting and further isolating Belarus. The idea of holding a Polish-Lithuanian-Ukrainian summit with Belarusian participation was actively discussed in January 1998. The invitation to Lukashenka to attend the Vilnius forum sponsored by presidents Brazauskas and Kwasniewski (see below) was an effort at maintaining political dialogue with Minsk.

A further example of Lithuanian-Polish-Ukrainian cooperation took place in May 1998, when the Polish-Ukrainian economic forum in Rzeszow, Poland, attended by presidents Kwasniewski and Kuchma, was joined by newly elected Lithuanian President Adamkus. The three sides once again noted the similarity of their approaches to transatlantic integration and subregional relations. Kwasniewski reiterated Polish readiness to help Kyiv and Vilnius in their process of integration into European and Euro-Atlantic institutions. The three presidents also declared that they had no intention of institutionalizing the triangular. The informal trilateral is likely to continue, however, and in the future could even develop into a "quadrate" pending political changes in Belarus.

*Tallinn Summit and Vilnius Forum*

The summit of five presidents that convened in the Estonian capital, Tallinn, on May 27, 1997 was probably the most direct cooperative response of east-central European countries to the first wave of NATO enlargement. The presidents of Estonia, Latvia, Lithuania, Poland, and Ukraine met on the same day as NATO and Russia signed the Founding Act on their relations in Paris. The first wave of NATO enlargement to Hungary, Poland, and the Czech Republic and tireless Russian opposition to the process, including repeated statements that Moscow would never agree to NATO membership of any former Soviet state, raised understandable concerns in Tallinn, Riga, Vilnius, and Kyiv. From this perspective, closer links to a NATO "in" Poland, and subregional cooperation among themselves was viewed as crucial. Of no less significance was the need to articulate jointly an east-central European position on central issues of European and subregional security in light of NATO enlargement.

The summit communiqué stressed that NATO should remain open to others in the future and underscored the importance of further cooperation within the PfP, support for the NATO-Russia Founding Act, the importance of signing a NATO-Ukraine Charter, and the need for closer subregional cooperation among the five states. The regional implications of Russian-Belarusian union were also discussed as well as the need to avoid the further isolation of Belarus.[23]

The practical attempt to engage Belarus in subregional cooperation took place in September 1997. On the initiative of presidents Brazauskas and Kwasniewski, Vilnius hosted an international forum/conference on "Co-Existence of States and Good-Neighborly Relations—the Guarantee of Security and Stability in Europe." The conference was attended by presidents of 11 states (Belarus, Bulgaria, Estonia, Finland, Hungary, Latvia, Lithuania, Moldova, Poland, Romania, and Ukraine). The Russian prime minister was also in attendance as were representatives of the OSCE, CoE, and the EU, and prominent academics and public figures. Subregional cooperation and the importance of reconciliation among states and nations were the primary themes for discussion. It was underscored that the countries of central and eastern Europe, while integrating into European and Euro-Atlantic institutions, need to develop cooperation with Russia. President Kuchma proposed a summit of countries of the Baltic and Black sea regions to discuss [sub]regional issues to take place in Yalta in 1999. It is hoped that this event might result in the conclusion of a charter on good-neighborly relations and partnership, which would serve as a code of behavior for the countries "between the seas."

### Georgia-Ukraine-Azerbaijan-Moldova (GUAM)

On 10 October 1997, a joint communiqué was issued, which had been developed at the periphery of the CoE summit in Strasbourg by the presidents of Georgia, Ukraine, Azerbaijan, and Moldova. The emergence of this subregional grouping did not come as a surprise to most interested observers. This de facto initiative had already been given the acronym GUAM by European diplomats even before its emergence.

The alignment between Georgia, Ukraine, and Azerbaijan, and later including Moldova, began to take shape in late 1996 on the basis of their joint approaches to modification of the 1990 Treaty on Conventional Forces in Europe (CFE). Proposed modifications, specifically the new Flank Limitations Agreement, addressed Russia's concerns and allowed it to maintain and even increase its military forces and weapons in the Caucasus and Crimea. GUAM countries were each experiencing tensions in their relations with Russia. They perceived that the new "Flank Document" ran counter to their interests because it actually condoned the stationing of Russian forces on foreign territories without host country consent.[24] All four states expressed reservations about these concessions and ratified the treaty only at the last moment as a result of stiff western pressure.

Cooperation in the CFE negotiations in Vienna has gradually been extended to other international arenas, mainly the CoE and OSCE, where GUAM states have begun to speak collectively and coordinate their positions on various international issues. In their October 1997 communiqué presidents Shevardnadze, Kuchma, Aliev, and Lucinschi declared their countries' intention to deepen political and economic ties and cooperation, and they affirmed their mutual interest in creation of a stable and secure Europe and [sub]region. They particularly noted the prospects for cooperation within the OSCE and other European and transatlantic structures, including PfP and the Euro-Atlantic Partnership Council (EAPC). The presidents spoke in favor of early peaceful settlement of unresolved conflicts and the need to combat "aggressive nationalism, separatism, and international terrorism." The statement also underscored the importance of cooperation to establish the proposed "Eurasian Trans-Caucasian transport corridor."[25] The meeting of the presidents in October was followed by consultations between their deputy foreign ministers in Baku in early November. Since then, GUAM has issued a number of joint statements within the OSCE.[26]

Cooperation between the four post-Soviet states is grounded in a number of mutually shared interests and goals. First, all four have declared their desire to be an integral part of the processes of European and Euro-Atlantic integration and are looking for optimal ways to weave themselves into those processes. Particular hope in this regard is placed on Ukraine and its experience. Baku, in particular, has begun to view the NATO-Ukraine Charter as a possible model for its own relations with the alliance. Second, and closely related to the first, is their common view of the mission, current state of development, and future prospects of the CIS. Ukraine, Georgia, Azerbaijan, and Moldova belong to those post-Soviet states that have successfully resisted attempts to turn the CIS into a closely integrated supranational structure. They view it, rather, as a loose consultative body facilitating the solution of existing problems and helping to improve bilateral relations. Again, Ukraine has played a leading role in this process, and many in Tbilisi, Chisinau, and Baku see Ukrainian sovereignty as a guarantee of their own independence and success.

Third, the national security and territorial integrity of each GUAM state has been threatened to varying degrees by separatism, often inspired and supported from abroad and leading to bloody armed conflicts. Some of these conflicts – Nagorno-Karabakh in Azerbaijan, Abkhazia in Georgia, and Transniestria in Moldova – have yet to be resolved. Mutual support against separatism and for territorial integrity is therefore a key element of GUAM's cooperation. Over the past year, Kyiv has expressed its readiness to become more actively involved in the final peaceful settlement of the situations in Abkhazia, Transnistrian, and Nagorno-Karabakh, including sending its observers and/or peacekeeping forces to those areas under UN or OSCE mandate. Ukraine's GUAM partners welcomed the decision, not least because of their dissatisfaction with Russia's track record as conflict mediator.[27]

Last, but far from least, is the search for alternative energy sources. It is this quest which brings Georgia, Moldova, and Ukraine closer to Azerbaijan with its estimated huge Caspian oil reserves. Moldova and Ukraine, in particular, count on being chosen as transit countries for the export of Azeri oil via Georgia to Europe. Some experts even believe that assurance of an alternative non-Russian oil transport route is GUAM's primary raison d'étre.[28] Caspian oil has significantly increased the role of Azerbaijan in GUAM, turning it into one of the informal leaders of the group. All four countries also display significant interest in development of the TRACECA transport corridor (Transport Corridor Europe-Caucasus-Asia) intended to establish an alternative transport outlet to Europe to complement the existing route via Russia.

So far, GUAM is an example of a rather successful newly emerging subregional initiative. Not institutionalized and without permanent structures, it remains a loose consultative and coordinating body, but one which is nonetheless proactive and visible. The grouping transcends natural geographical lines and brings together not the neighboring "ins" and "outs" of the enlargement process (as in the cases described above) but geographically remote "outs," which, however, share similar aspirations and attitude toward the process of enlargement itself. This quadrilateral initiative assists the four in consolidating their independent identities and statehood and in pursuing more efficiently their foreign policy agendas, including relations with Russia and policies within the CIS. GUAM emphasizes its openness to other countries, and it has not ruled out the inclusion of other countries in the future. Uzbekistan, in particular, is often seen as a potential member.

At the same time, GUAM's emergence was met with initial caution in the west and has raised a much higher degree of concern and alarm in Russia than have other newly emerging subregional frameworks. Despite reassurances by members that the grouping is not directed against Russia or any other state, Moscow tends to perceive GUAM as an alternative to CIS, a cordon sanitaire around Russia, or even an alliance that serves US interests.[29] Given Armenia's relations with Azerbaijan, Yerevan has also shown nervousness at GUAM's development. Some even suggest that GUAM's further evolution may facilitate the strengthening of another transgeographic axis encompassing Russia, Armenia, and Iran.[30]

It is increasingly believed that GUAM's future prospects will depend enormously on its ability to complement its political cooperation with a practical economic component, particularly in the field of Caspian oil transportation. As such, GUAM could become an example of a subregional grouping formed primarily along geoeconomic lines. So far, however, the grouping maintains its largely political nature, although at the October 1997 meeting in Strasbourg, the foreign minister of Azerbaijan underscored GUAM's economic potential.[31] There is, however, a certain divergence in GUAM members' views on this issue. While Tbilisi stresses the geopolitical role of the grouping because it sees the initiative primarily as a forum for political and security cooperation, Ukraine and Moldova, which find themselves far outside the picture of Caspian oil transport routes, emphasize that GUAM's full potential will be unrealized if it is not reinforced with strong economic substance.[32]

## Preliminary conclusions

The overall development of subregional cooperation in east-central Europe and the recent establishment of new trilateral, quadrilateral, and other cooperative networks is largely a logical and natural process still in its infancy. The newly emerging and interlocking ventures remain fluid and loose. None of them are formalized, and they do not currently envisage the creation of permanent secretarial or other structures; most have had few practical achievements; some lack regularity and operate on an ad hoc basis; while still others have unclear future prospects and may well remain "one-off" events. The potential and possible evolution of these emerging networks remain to be seen, and it would be premature to draw any final conclusions at this point. Still, some initial lessons can already be drawn.

Although significantly improved in the past year and a half, subregional relations in east-central Europe still remain in a fluid state. On the one hand, this suggests a certain demand for subregionalism and motivates calls for the consolidation of rapprochements and emerging partnerships that could facilitate the final settlement of unresolved problems. On the other hand, those remaining problems, historical grievances and sometimes divergent or even competitive national interests, overshadow bilateral relations and further constrain the mutual trust and confidence required for the development of subregional initiatives. The accumulated experience of subregional cooperation demonstrates that aside from the prerequisite of clear political will, countries involved must develop certain common practical interests and objectives. The smaller the initiative, the more coherence and convergence of domestic and foreign policy goals required for sustainable subregional cooperation. This is particularly important for the newly emerging cooperative arrangements in east-central Europe, given the fact that practically all of them involve only three to four states.

Subregionalism in east-central Europe is still centralized and remains largely the preoccupation of central governments. Very often, subregional initiatives are directly driven by, and depend on, individual national leaders, as is the case with Romanian-Polish-Ukrainian or Polish-Ukrainian-Lithuanian trilateral cooperation. In many cases, local and regional authorities still lack the necessary authority and freedom to pursue transfrontier activities. This, together with the lack of practical experience, often limits subregional cooperation, even after approval has been given at the national level. The lack of sufficient financial resources to allocate for specific cooperative projects is another serious weakness. Slow progress in economic and administrative reforms in Ukraine, Moldova, or Romania (to say nothing of Belarus) limits financial capacities, curtails the process of decentralization, and further constrains subregional cooperative potential.

The degree of participation of individual countries varies significantly at present. Ukraine is a key component in almost all newly emerging cooperative initiatives as well as the larger CEI and BSEC frameworks. Moldova has become much more active in its subregional policies as well. At the same time, the expanding subregional networks raise difficult questions about the role and place of Belarus. Although there is a growing realization among Belarus's neighbors of the need to prevent its total isolation and engage the country in cooperative ventures, the optimal mechanisms for doing so remain in question. Ukraine, many have felt, could play a particularly important subregional role, providing support to Moldova and demonstrating an alternative solution for Belarus. However, these leadership hopes have not, so far, materialized. Ukraine's domestic socioeconomic difficulties and the lack of a stable foreign policy consensus have so far prevented Kyiv from assuming a proactive subregional role. In most cases, Ukraine has found it easier, politically (and apparently less costly, financially), to cooperate with those CEE countries that have taken the lead in forging subregional partnerships. Poland's role in promoting such cooperation is particularly significant in this regard.

Subregionalism in east-central Europe develops in the framework of European and Euro-Atlantic integration and enlargement, and must be discussed within the broader context of subregional relations and cooperation in the wider Europe. In Moldova, and even more so in Ukraine, subregional cooperation, which ties them more closely to their more advanced central European neighbors, is seen as an important way of manifesting a European identity. Almost all the emerging cooperative initiatives covering east-central Europe were boosted by the first wave of NATO enlargement. At the same time, the close interrelationship between central and eastern European subregionalism and the process of enlargement constitutes a major weakness of the new cooperative initiatives. Experience to date has illustrated that the pragmatic objectives of some participating countries often overlap with largely political calculations designed for external consumption. The question of whether this cooperation will be sustained over the course of the enlargement processes remains open to doubt.

The fate and potential of subregional cooperation in east-central Europe will be determined to a large degree by the policies of the EU. In the last two years, EU interest in and support for subregional cooperation has increased substantially: In December 1997 the European Council adopted a specially commissioned report from the Commission, praising the role of [sub]regional cooperation and promising further political, commercial, and technical assistance to its development. At the same time, the report clearly states that the EU will support only those initiatives that demonstrate their internal strength and potential.[33] One issue, however, requires immediate EU action. This is the need to devise solutions to help allay the tensions engendered by the introduction of new border regulations and visa policies on the eastern borders of first round central and eastern European applicant states. These solutions may vary from the improvement of border infrastructures to the elaboration of long-term or interim visa regime modalities. If proper solutions are found and implemented in practice, the chances for the further consolidation of subregionalism in this part of the continent will be significantly improved.

It is also important that the new geometrical configurations developing in east-central Europe not be viewed as elements of old diplomacy and traditional power politics. Subregionalism in east-central Europe is a particular challenge for Russia. The newly emerging cooperative patterns are generally perceived in Moscow as elements of anti-Russian politics, especially when they include former Soviet republics and exclude Russia. GUAM is of particular concern to Russia. Russia's neighbors have yet to learn how to live with Russia, but Russia, in turn, has yet to learn that post-Soviet republics have a sovereign right to decide their own futures. And this includes the legitimate and natural pursuit of positive shared interests through subregional cooperation.

The interaction between wider and older subregional groups (BSEC, CEI, and others) on the one hand, and the newly emerging subregional initiatives on the other, also remains to be seen. Will these emerging groups complement and facilitate wider cooperative efforts, or will they fracture and disrupt the bigger initiatives? The membership of BSEC and CEI is diverse, as are the interests of the members. This fact, as well as their deliberate avoidance of sensitive political and security issues, poses the question of whether these groupings provide sufficient forums for subregional cooperation and meet the needs of all their members. From this perspective, the newly emerging smaller initiatives may add new value to larger groups, increasing their effectiveness and providing useful tools to link larger networks with each other. In this case, the larger subregional groupings could well serve as facilitators and umbrella organizational frameworks for smaller cooperative schemes: Ukraine, Moldova, and Romania, for example, could draw upon the financial capacities of the Black Sea Trade and Development Bank, established by BSEC, of which all three countries are members, to initiate cooperative projects.

If successful, the new interlocking networks could become an additional important factor in improving trust and confidence as well as in promoting subregional and all-European stability and security. They may help to bridge potential new dividing lines, address issues of practical regional concern, and stimulate internal transformation in each participating country. They may also facilitate human contacts, trade, and economic cooperation and possibly encourage the elaboration of joint approaches to various international issues. At the same time, their potential should not be overestimated. So far, the new cooperative initiatives are only beginning to develop, and their potential for evolution and sustainability remain unknowns. Their prospects will be affected by the pace and handling of European and Euro-Atlantic integration processes as well as by the subregional policies of western integrated structures. However, to become effective and long-lasting, the new subregional arrangements must develop into practical cooperative projects. Their survival and progress, thus, depend less on external factors and international politics than on the commitment and capacity of their members to initiate and implement concrete objectives for the benefit of all.

## Notes

1. Only the creation of the Visegrad group was motivated primarily by political considerations. Political cooperation within the Visegrad group was later transformed into trade and economic cooperation within CEFTA.

2. For more on the development and potential of these subregional groupings, see Andrew Cottey, ed., *Subregional Cooperation in the New Europe: Building Security, Prosperity and Solidarity from the Barents to the Black Sea* (London: Macmillan, 1998).

3. On the evolution of the Carpathian Euroregion see: Piotr Helinski, ed., *Carpathian Euroregion: Five Years of Dialogue and Co-operation*, 1993-1998 (Krasno: Secretariat of the Carpathian Euroregion, 1998).

4. Ukraine had at least some international exposure through the membership of Soviet Ukraine in the United Nations and its affiliated agencies; Moldova lacked even this experience.

5. For a Moldovan view on BSEC, see, for example, A. Nistrian, "The BSEC and Moldova," Background Paper prepared for ELIAMEP (November 1996).

6. According to President Kuchma, BSEC is "a very important component of a new European security system," *Zerkalo nedeli*, 6 June 1998.

7. Oleksandr Pavliuk, "Ukraine and regional cooperation in central and eastern Europe," *Security Dialogue* 3 (September 1997): 357.

8. Sherman Garnett, "Europe's crossroads: Russia and the west in the new borderlands," in Michael Mandelbaum, ed., *The New Russian Foreign Policy* (New York: Council on Foreign Relations, 1998).

9. Iris Kempe, *Direct Neighbourhood. Relations between the Enlarged EU and the Russian Federation, Ukraine, Belarus and Moldova* (Gutersloh: Bertelsmann Foundation Publishers, 1998).

10. On the subregional importance of Ukraine, see Sherman W. Garnett, *Keystone in the Arch: Ukraine in the Emerging Security Environment of Central and Eastern Europe* (Carnegie Endowment for International Peace, 1997).

11. Anatol Lieven, "EU accession raises visa worry in east," *Financial Times*, 26 February 1998.

12. See, for example, an article by Ukrainian Deputy Foreign Minister Borys Gudyma, "Modern priorities and the future of Ukrainian cooperation within the

framework of the BSEC," *Romanian Journal of International Affairs* 1 (1997): 106-7 and Andrii Kononenko and Andrii Yarmysh, "ChES: Nablyzhennia do novoi iakosti," *Polityka i chas* 9 (September 1997): 17.

13. See, for example, the interview with Deputy Foreign Minister Vasiliy Shova, *Nezavisimaia gazeta*, 4 December 1997.

14. Vladimir Konobeyev (Acting Head of the Foreign Policy Directorate of the Administration of the President of Belarus),"The Union of Russia and Belarus: New phase of cooperation in foreign policy," *Belarus in the World* 2 (July 1997): 51.

15. "Existing and Emerging Cooperation in New Central and Eastern Europe," Summary Report of an IEWS Workshop held in Kyiv, 18-20 February 1998, p. 13.

16. Statement of the Presidents of Ukraine, Republic of Moldova and Romania on Trilateral Cooperation, 3 July 1997.

17. The Chisnau Statement of the Presidents of Romania, Ukraine and Republic of Moldova on trilateral cooperation, 22 October 1998.

18. Author interviews with foreign ministry officials in Poland and Ukraine in May-July 1998.

19. Interview with the Romanian Defense Minister for *Rzeczpospolita*, 27 November 1997, p. 7.

20. Romanian Foreign Minister Adrian Severin, quoted by Ryszard Malik in "Pozyteczna wymiana pogladow," *Rzeczpospolita*, 27 November 1997, p. 7.

21. Wojciech Zajaczkowski, "Polish-Lithuanian relations: the complexities of geopolitics," and Oleksandr Pavliuk, "Ukrainian-Polish relations: a pillar of regional stability?" in Monika Wohlfeld, ed., *The Effects of Enlargement on Bilateral Relations in Central and Eastern Europe*, Chaillot Papers (WEU, Institute for Security Studies, 1997), pp. 26-62.

22. Quoted in Wojciech Zajaczkowski, "Polish-Lithuanian relations," p. 31.

23. During his visit to Kyiv on 12 May 1997, President Lukashenka tried to convince Ukrainian leaders to join the Russian-Belarusian union. *Vseukrainskie vedomosti*, 14 May 1997, p. 2.

24. Ukraine, for example, was at that time involved in difficult negotiations with Russia on the stationing of Russian military and naval forces in Crimea.

25. Joint Communiqué of the Presidents of Azerbaijan, Georgia, Moldova and Ukraine, Strasbourg, 10 October 1997.

26. Joint Co-Operative Action to Provide for Observance of OSCE Principles and Implementation of Commitments 14 May 1998; Statement at the Special Meeting of the OSCE Security Model Committee 3 July 1998.

27. Some in Tbilisi, for example, perceive Russian policy in Abkhazia as "armed interference in Georgian domestic politics." See David Darchiashvili, "Russian policy in the Black Sea area: Source of conflicts (Georgian case)," *Romanian Journal of International Affairs* 1 (1998), pp. 47-54.

28. Rostislav Khotyn, *Den'*, 12 February 1998, p. 3.

29. Oleg Rumiantsev, "Stanet li Armeniia uchastnikom novoho soiuza," *Nezavisimaia gazeta*, 6 March 1998.

30. "Subregional Relations in the Southern Tier: Prospects for Development," Summary Report of an IEWS Workshop held in Tbilisi, 17-18 May 1998, p. 13.

31. Elizabeth Fuller, "Interests converge among the members of the GUAM states," RFE/RL, 1 December 1997.

32. "Subregional Relations in the Southern Tier," IEWS Workshop summary, p. 14.

33. Report from the Commission to the Council on Regional Co-operation in Europe, Brussels, 1 December 1997, p. 1.

# Part II

South-Eastern Europe

# 4

# External Institutional Frameworks and Subregionalism in South-Eastern Europe

*Sophia Clément*

## Introduction

External institutional frameworks initiated by the international community to promote regional cooperation in south-eastern Europe are based on a host of paradoxes.[1] These paradoxes underscore the inherent limits of such an approach as well as the incentives to develop regional cooperation. First, there is a concern with the potential spillover of the instability in south-eastern Europe to the rest of the European continent. It is therefore agreed that appropriate ways must be found to ease current and future conflicts stemming from ethnic and political tensions (Bosnia, Kosovo) as well as successive economic crises (Bulgaria, Albania, FYROM) which have turned south-eastern Europe into one of the Europe's most troubled regions. At the same time, EU and NATO enlargement processes failed to expand to south-eastern Europe, the area that needs them most both in soft and hard security terms. The region thus faces marginalization from the broader European integration process as well as a "development discrepancy" *vis-à-vis* neighboring regions such as central Europe, which have already entered into negotiations for accession.

As a response, a range of top-down regional cooperative initiatives have been launched by both European and transatlantic organizations and south-eastern European governments.[2] Addressing political, economic, and military fields, these initiatives aim to provide frameworks to enhance good-neighborly relations and promote stability and security. Their scope also includes helping south-eastern European states catch up with overall developments on the European continent. NATO and EU enlargement has finally been redefined as an "open" process, accessible to all, provided certain sets of criteria are met, one of which is cooperative regional relations. There is, however, a lack of definition of the linkage between the enlargement process and a regional approach. Although the latter has been established as an inherent part of the enlargement approach, the practical implications of this remain unclear to the countries of the region. Subregional cooperation is still perceived by many as a potential alternative framework, 'waiting-room," or substitute to enlargement into broader European and transatlantic institutions. Countries are reluctant to further commit themselves and deepen such processes. This is intensified by the fact that most initiatives lack coordination, a strategic vision of the region, and a clear linkage to the broader European setting. Any attempt at defining regional cooperation and its relationship to broader integration, moreover, must take into account the particular conditions of each specific region.

Finally, subregionalism in south-eastern Europe reveals the interdependency between Europe's center and periphery. South-eastern Europe is linked to the north through a combination of direct and indirect interests as well as through geographic proximity and common shared history. It is the region where the main European and transatlantic international organizations regained their credibility and legitimacy through the redefinition of their functions, the testing of their decision-making and operational mechanisms, and the establishment of regional structures promoting an integrative approach to security. In the medium term, the level of conflict in the region implies the continued presence of external powers through intervention, implementation of peace, and internationalization of conflict. Thus, south-eastern Europe is understood here not as a mere boundary, but as a subregional system of Europe which cannot be addressed independently of the evolution and integration of the rest of the continent.

## The Security Paradox in South-Eastern Europe

South-eastern Europe, unlike central Europe, does not have the benefit of a fairly clear geographical and historical definition. The region may be defined in a variety of ways, and local and external actors use geographical, historical, or cultural attributes at their discretion. At the same time, south-eastern Europe is more than a collection of disparate states. There are a range of interdependent variables stemming from a recent common past as well as common security threats and concerns that make the region, if not entirely coherent, at least distinct.

South-eastern Europe is also one of the most diversified areas of the continent in terms of status within European and transatlantic organizations. The countries in the region were integrated to varying degrees into international groupings during the Cold War, with two NATO countries (Greece and Turkey), two Warsaw Treaty members (Bulgaria and Romania), and two independent countries (Albania and Yugoslavia). In the post-Cold War period, their membership status within western political and economic organizations such as EU, Western European Union (WEU) and NATO vary greatly (i.e., full members, associate partners and associate members, and those without any form of agreement). Further evolution is likely as Bulgaria and Romania have been included in the first round of negotiations for EU enlargement, and the latter could be eligible for future NATO enlargement. These processes will undoubtedly create new distinctions among countries of the region as well as with their central European neighbors.

In areas such as central Europe or the Baltic Sea area, parallel regional cooperative initiatives have been undertaken that have contributed to strengthening regional ties and have helped these countries meet western economic and political criteria. In south-eastern Europe, this process is still in the making. The political and economic development gap between the region and the rest of the continent means the potential for instability remains high in south-eastern Europe. The region does not have an appropriate "security umbrella" to manage and contain this instability, and this gap creates potential consequences for the rest of the European continent. Thus, the marginalization of the region from European political, economic and security organizations could result in a vicious circle that produces yet more instability.

## External Subregional Cooperative Frameworks

### From Negative Perceptions to Effective Cooperation

Perceptions of regional cooperation have evolved over the past few years. With the end of the Cold War, integration into western European political and security organizations such as the EU, WEU, and NATO has become the primary objective for most south-eastern European states. Political and economic instability as well as conflictual relations have created serious obstacles to a coordinated regional approach to this goal. The states of the region have been more inclined to get out of regional frameworks rather than to develop new ones. South-eastern European (SEE) states, moreover, have feared that a subregional framework might be considered by the west as an alternative to integration, and they are thus opposed to anything other than bilateral and loose multilateral ties. This tension between enlargement and regional cooperation remains a key factor in explaining the lack of internal regional initiatives.[3] Most initiatives, with the notable exception of the Conference of the Ministers of South-Eastern Europe, have been initiated from outside the region.[4]

More recently, however, SEE states have begun to perceive subregional cooperation as a means of filling the political and security vacuum in the subregion, avoiding further marginalization, and providing channels for closer cooperation and interaction with western organizations. Subregional economic, political, and security cooperation is increasingly seen as a way of helping states meet the criteria for accession into NATO and the EU. The development of close multilateral ties on a subregional basis is coming to be perceived as an integral part of the wider European integration process rather than a distinct and separate integration process. The evolution of EU and NATO enlargement strategies toward greater emphasis on the will and capacity for regional cooperation as a condition for membership is the primary determining factor here.

SEE states also have individual reasons for promoting regional cooperation. All support the goals of democracy and market economy, but they diverge on the role that regional cooperation can play in meeting them. Bulgaria, Turkey, and Greece, for instance, openly support the development of regional cooperation at the local level, independently of EU and NATO integration, as a means to building greater confidence and developing economic links between SEE states. Bulgaria, aware early on that it would not be part of NATO enlargement, supported all local frameworks aimed at enhancing confidence-building measures in the region.[5] Greece, as the only EU, WEU, and NATO member, saw regional cooperation as an opportunity to play a regional leadership role and improve its recent poor relations in the region. Others, like the Former Yugoslav Republic of Macedonia (FYROM), were initially reluctant to engage in regional efforts, perceiving that their national goals might be best achieved through unilateralism. The strong international presence in FYROM and the country's importance to regional security and stability further encouraged the FYROM leadership to dissociate itself from regionalism and promote the country's own western integration initiatives. Romania, and more specifically Croatia, dissociated themselves from the Balkans, claiming their place solely in central Europe on the basis of historical, cultural and, in the case of Croatia, religious criteria. Their stance was reinforced by the belief that their better economic situation and the support of historical allies, France and Germany respectively, would ensure their inclusion in the first waves of EU and NATO enlargement. The rejection of their NATO (and, for Croatia, EU) bids, the difficult access to the central European market, the conditionality of EU accession criteria, and US pressure convinced them to join south-eastern European cooperative frameworks.

For western European countries, the linkage between south-eastern European subregional cooperation and broader European integration processes was not initially envisaged. Regional cooperation only gradually came to be considered as an essential tool for confidence-building measures in south-eastern Europe. The absence of a strategic regional approach stemmed from lack of knowledge, geographical and cultural prejudices, and negative perceptions of the subregion, all of which were exacerbated by the violence of the Yugoslav wars, the complex minority and border issues, and the nationalism prevalent in south-eastern Europe.

The economic, political, and security consequences for the west of instability in south-eastern Europe, however, made the formulation of a more coherent approach necessary. The slow implementation of the civilian dimension of the Dayton Agreement in Bosnia, the internal economic and political crisis in Albania, the difficulty of democratization in Serbia, and the Kosovo issue, as well as strained interethnic relations in FYROM, constituted causes for concern which justified externally-led regional initiatives. Western European governments recognized the consequences that instability in south-eastern Europe could have for the EU's entire integration process: economic and human costs, as well as undermining the Union's internal cohesion and efforts to establish a common external policy. Concretely, Europeans would bear the main cost of conflict management and post-conflict reconstruction as was the case in Bosnia. Europeans, after all, were on the ground there alone from 1992 to 1995 and continue to contribute significant forces to UNPROFOR. The EU has been Bosnia's main financial donor in its reconstruction efforts. Further instability would necessitate increased economic and financial aid and signal the failure of EU policies initiated in the past few years. Germany, Italy, and Greece are particularly preoccupied with the waves of refugees from former Yugoslavia and Albania. Finally, it is tacitly acknowledged that SEE instability could weaken western organizations' internal coherence and cohesion at a time when efforts to consolidate decision making and institutional mechanisms are taking place. The difficulties in adopting common positions and implementing decisions have already weakened western European credibility and its capacity for effective action in the region. Divergences within the Euro-Atlantic community constituted the main stumbling block in the Yugoslav crisis and explain, in part, the failure of successive proposals to end the conflict.[6] Few are eager to put Euro-Atlantic unity through such a test again.

The lessons of the Yugoslav wars and the continued potential for instability in SEE, therefore, have led to a change of perception of the benefits of an emphasis on longer term commitment in the region rather than on ad hoc surgical approaches. Regional cooperation is perceived to be a vital component in this confidence-building approach, and the importance of externally-driven regional approaches has been acknowledged.

## Top-Down Initiatives

The EU General Affairs Council defined a regional approach for south-eastern Europe on February 26, 1996, which "should be directed primarily at those countries of the region for which the European Community has not adopted directives for the negotiation of association agreements. Neighboring countries which so wish should be able to be associated in the cooperation by appropriate means."[7] The countries involved are Albania and the successor republics of former Yugoslavia (with the exception of Slovenia): Bosnia-Herzegovina, Croatia, FRY, and FYROM.[8] A number of general conditions are applicable to all, such as the will to engage in transborder cooperation and grant similar advantages to other countries in the region. However, the nature and intensity of bilateral relations with the EU vary from country to country. Furthermore, specific conditions related to obligations within the framework of the 1995 Dayton Peace Agreement apply to Bosnia-Herzegovina, Croatia, and FRY. Ties between the EU and these countries are conditional on compliance with the Dayton Peace Agreement, particularly its civil dimension, such as respect for human rights, free movement of goods, people, and services as well as common democratic institution-building.[9] Annex 1-B (Agreement on Regional Stabilization) of the Dayton Peace Agreement contains specific provisions to establish a regional structure for stability and arms control through cooperation aimed at building transparency and confidence and achieving balanced and stable defense forces for the respective countries' security.[10]

The EU monitors compliance with the regional approach through six-monthly reports of the European Commission, which contain an additional section for each country on regional cooperation. On the basis of these assessments, the European Council has twice declared (April 1997 and October 1998) that the slow pace of economic and political transition in Bosnia-Herzegovina, FRY, and Croatia means that EU relations with them remain unchanged. Thus, these states will continue to receive special reconstruction assistance and are not yet eligible for the assistance programs (i.e., the PHARE program), through which the EU provides aid to associated partner states and Albania.[11]

The EU's Royaumont Process for Stability and Good Neighborliness in South East Europe was launched at the General Affairs Council of February 26-27, 1996, following the Royaumont Declaration by EU foreign ministers at the signing of the Dayton Peace Agreement in Paris. Its members are Albania, Bosnia-Herzegovina, Bulgaria, Croatia, FYROM, and FRY. While the EU's regional approach centers on established bilateral frameworks between south-eastern European states and the EU, the scope of Royaumont extends to cooperation with neighboring regional frameworks like the Central European Initiative (CEI) and the Black Sea Economic Cooperation (BSEC) and is open to the participation of nonstate actors. It deals with the financial implementation of a range of projects directed toward democracy and the development of a civil society in the region. In doing so, it follows closely the guidelines of the EU's regional approach.[12] Consequently, Royaumont process projects in FRY and Croatia take place at the nongovernmental rather than the state level, reflecting the EU's relations with these two countries. The Royaumont process is also related to the 1994 Stability Pact, the French initiative, now under Organization for Security and Cooperation in Europe (OSCE) auspices, which is designed to promote stability in central and eastern Europe by encouraging the conclusion of bilateral agreements on borders, minorities rights, and transborder cooperation.

The three main revenue sources for the Royaumont process are the EU, national contributions, and other sources such as foundations. The allocation of 1 to 1.5 million ECU has been under discussion, 200,000 ECU having been spent so far. Financing for projects has come from Greece, Luxembourg, the Netherlands, and the United Kingdom. The European Parliament has set aside 5 million ECU for this purpose, and from 1999, SEE governments (with the exception of Croatia and FRY) will be able to apply for funding for Royaumont process projects from the PHARE assistance program. In January 1998, the EU appointed a general coordinator to the Royaumont process, Ambassador Panagiotis Roumeliotis, who has the task of producing an action plan aimed at giving greater vitality to the process.[13] As a consequence, a range of events was launched and a series of projects initiated, which should lead to greater exploitation of these financial resources.[14]

It is envisaged that the Royaumont process will be incorporated into the OSCE and thus the Stability Pact as well once FRY's suspension from OSCE is ended. This, it is believed, would help coordinate EU and OSCE's politico-economic and security approaches toward south-eastern Europe and give the Royaumont process a concrete political as well as regional dimension. It could also enhance the regional stability and arms control provisions of the Dayton agreement, the implementation of which is under the auspices of the OSCE. France has been supporting the idea of creating an OSCE Stability Pact specifically for south-eastern Europe, which would pool all regional stability initiatives into a single pact under the auspices of the OSCE.[15]

The American-inspired Southeast European Cooperative Initiative (SECI or "Schifter Initiative"), established in December 1996, is based on the "Points of Common US-EU Understanding" to promote regional economic and environmental cooperation among the countries of the region. A statement of purpose was adopted at the inaugural meeting of participating states in Geneva on December 5-6, 1996.[16] A few days later, the OSCE chairman-in-office appointed Dr. Erhard Busek, former vice-chancellor of Austria, as SECI coordinator. Interestingly, SECI includes a wider range of countries than a narrow interpretation of what constitutes south-eastern Europe might imply, specifically Hungary, Slovenia, and Croatia. It should be noted that these countries were initially reluctant to join the initiative. Participating states comprise Albania, Bosnia-Herzegovina, Bulgaria, Croatia (as an observer), Greece, Hungary, Moldova, Romania, Slovenia, FYROM, and Turkey. The initial invitation made to the FRY was withdrawn in view of the political situation in the country. Italy and Austria are observers.

SECI is not an economic assistance program but focuses, rather, on self-help.[17] It is based on private sector financial commitments or loans from international financial institutions such as the World Bank, the European Bank for Reconstruction and Development (EBRD) and the European Investment Bank (EIB). Its primary focus is on economic issues, and it aims to promote better coordination of private sector aid and investment in the subregion. It avoids the more overt political dimensions. The SECI seeks to create a regional association aimed at encouraging cooperation among member states and to facilitate their integration in European structures. The initiative endeavors to facilitate closer cooperation and create new channels of communication between governments of the region. It is strongly oriented toward the development of the private sector in south-eastern Europe and principal areas of focus include facilitation of border crossings and infrastructure development and support for investment as well as environmental protection and energy.[18]

The US, Switzerland, Italy, Austria, and Germany have supported SECI activities with voluntary financial contributions totaling 300,000 USD for 1997. The US government provided a further 325,000 USD for travel costs and technical assistance.[19] Technical support is provided by the UN Economic Commission for Europe (ECE), which has the means to facilitate and simplify transborder operations and to provide mechanisms for solving problems through UN bodies and agencies. Although SECI is not part of the OSCE structure, it has developed close contacts with the missions and delegations of the participating states. The US had initially sought to merge SECI and the Royaumont initiative but this option was rejected by the EU due to the uncertainties related to private funding, fears of US interference in EU affairs and preference for closer coordination with the OSCE. Nevertheless, deliberate efforts have been made to coordinate SECI activities with EU programs. The SECI and Royaumont process coordinators meet regularly and have agreed to establish mechanisms for consultation and avoidance of unnecessary duplication. SECI also encourages cooperation with other regional initiatives such as the CEI and BSEC, among others.

The NATO Partnership for Peace (PfP) program, established in late 1995, provides a framework for military cooperation in southeastern Europe. The aim of PfP is to expand and intensify political and military cooperation throughout Europe, enhance stability and security, and build strengthened relationships by promoting practical cooperation and commitment to the democratic principles of the Alliance.[20] It focuses on defense-related cooperation and is addressed to all OSCE countries willing to contribute. The program provides assistance in military and broader defense-related fields to non-NATO member countries in order to facilitate transparency in national defense planning and budgeting processes; ensure democratic control of armed forces; maintain capabilities and readiness to contribute to operations under UN or OSCE guidance; and develop cooperative military relations with NATO for the purpose of planning, training, and exercise with a view toward participation in NATO-led peacekeeping, search and rescue, and humanitarian operations. However, PfP is not a multilateral or regional security arrangement, but is based on the development of bilateral relations between each participating state and NATO (the 16+1 formula). Each subscribing state develops with NATO an Individual Partnership Program (IPP) on the basis of individual requirements and priorities from a list of activities enumerated through a menu provided by the Partnership Work Program (PWP). NATO provides assistance, advice, and financing for activities (along with partner states).

Twenty-eight states have joined PfP, including south-eastern European countries such as Albania, Bulgaria, Romania (members since 1994), FYROM (1995). FRY, Bosnia, and Croatia do not participate. In early 1997 it was agreed to further strengthen PfP and give it a greater political dimension. The Enhanced PfP replaced the previous North Atlantic Cooperation Council (NACC) with a new cooperative mechanism, the Euro-Atlantic Partnership Council (EAPC), which aims to strengthen political consultation, decision making, and planning within the PfP framework. EAPC is intended to complement the work of other European organizations such as the OSCE, EU, WEU and the Council of Europe (CoE).[21]

The Enhanced PfP also aims at fostering improvements in good-neighborly relations through enhanced regional defense cooperation. Preparation of armed forces for peacekeeping efforts, joint civil emergency planning, disaster relief activities, and coordinated measures to strengthen environmental security form the main scope of this cooperation.[22] EAPC, as an element in this, is intended to be an inclusive multilateral framework with a significant subregional dimension. The EAPC's basic document aims to provide an overarching framework for political consultation and to promote practical cooperation on a range of political and security-related issues.

The need to build greater stability, security and regional cooperation between the countries of south-eastern Europe and to promote their increasing integration into the Euro-Atlantic community was explicitly recognized at the NATO Madrid summit in July 1997. The increased exploitation of the PfP framework to promote security and regional cooperation in south-eastern Europe is now under active consideration. Regional issues range from specific situations such as Bosnia and Kosovo to the eventual facilitation of the participation of SEE PfP member countries in a NATO Combined Joint Task Force (CJTF), at least during the early stages of a regional conflict.[23] The PfP framework also addresses arms control and nonproliferation issues, enhanced interoperability, implementation and verification of arms control agreements, and confidence and security-building measures (CSBMs). Although PfP is touted as being a flexible and non-institutionalized framework, the potential consequences of the Albanian crisis in 1997 led to the establishment of an "enhanced PfP" for the country, which included intensified cooperation and the creation of a permanent coordinating cell in Tirana.[24] The impact of the Kosovo crisis during winter 1998 and its potential consequences for regional stability led to the upgrading of PfP provisions for FYROM. Exercises among PfP partners in the region were organized in Albania and FYROM during the summer of 1998.[25] The PfP Action

Plan for 1998-2000 provides for enhanced political and military activities concerning transparency and confidence between members.

The WEU was the first western organization to enlarge to central and eastern Europe. It created a multiple-tier membership status: ten full members (EU and NATO members), three associate members (Iceland, Norway, and Turkey – NATO but not EU members), five observers (Austria, Denmark, Finland, Ireland, and Sweden – EU but non-NATO members, except for Denmark), and ten central and eastern European associate partners (countries with association agreements with the EU).[26] The latter take part in many of WEU's day-to-day meetings (except for institutional affairs and Article V matters) and have liaison arrangements with the WEU planning cell. They participate in the planning and implementation of WEU humanitarian, peacekeeping, and crisis management operations (so-called Petersberg tasks adopted in 1992) and have designated units of their armed forces that could be made available for that purpose.[27] WEU has undertaken a number of operations in south-eastern Europe, two of which have incorporated assets and personnel from associated partners Bulgaria, Hungary, and Romania: monitoring and enforcing Yugoslavia's compliance with the UN Security Council embargoes on the Danube and with NATO in the Adriatic, and police operations in Mostar and, more recently, in Albania.

The WEU has developed a certain degree of regional cooperation through the "Common Security Concept on European Security," adopted by its Council of Ministers in November 1995. This document provided an analysis of possible WEU responses to European security challenges and recommended a greater emphasis on regional cooperation through regional round table's dealing with CSBMs as well as environmental and economic issues. In 1997, the organization undertook a "Common Reflection on European Security Interests in the Twenty-First Century," which focused, among other things, on subregionalism and European security and the linkage between WEU and subregional frameworks, etc.

## Rethinking Top-Down Approaches

### *The Limitations of Top-Down Initiatives*

The plethora of initiatives outlined above cannot disguise the lack of an encompassing and coherent approach to the region. Some, such as Royaumont and SECI, gave initial priority to economic issues without defining common strategies and projects. All remain, to a certain extent, loosely defined and do not provide adequate goals or substantial financial means to address the real problems of the region. Most approaches are nonbinding and without clear linkage to wider integration processes, and they lack the main incentives for implementation and leverage. Furthermore, as most have developed on a bilateral basis between the relevant international organization and the country concerned, e.g., Royaumont or PfP, they do not contribute to a sense of regionalism. The implicit competitiveness of the various initiatives has not promoted complementarity or coordination between them. Finally, there is an imbalance between the involvement of certain countries and their commitment to regional cooperation.

NATO is one of the most prominent actors in SEE regional cooperation. The Kosovo crisis has increased NATO's presence in the region and put the United States at the forefront of regional cooperation. SFOR's role in Bosnia is central to south-eastern European stability. PfP, meanwhile, has been evolving toward regional cooperation with EAPC, while developing a subregional role that may have an increased impact in the future. There is an issue of potential duplication between NATO's PfP enhanced regional dimension providing for peacekeeping operations and the involvement of WEU associate partners in Petersberg tasks according to their status and their capabilities. PfP, however, incorporates a broader range of countries and issues than WEU. The particular advantage of the latter remains the strong link between EU and WEU as the defense arm of the European Union. Harmonization between the WEU and NATO initiatives might be facilitated with the implementation of the CJTF concept that would enable NATO assets to be used in WEU operations. The EAPC framework might also be useful in negotiation and effective implementation of the Dayton agreement's regional arms control provisions (currently the responsibility of OSCE) as it provides a forum for political debate and consultations as well as concrete military interaction through common PfP exercises.

The limits of Royaumont lie in the uncertain peace process in Bosnia, the Kosovo conflict, and the fragile economic transitions of SEE states. The process did not enjoy an auspicious start, with countries of the region regarding it as another conduit for EU financial assistance rather than as an instrument for promoting multilateral cooperation between them. The lack of implementation of the civilian dimension of the Dayton agreement and the Albanian and the Kosovo crisis further hampered regional reconciliation efforts. Furthermore, the differentiated relationship structures between the states participating in Royaumont and the EU make it difficult for the latter to develop a coordinated approach toward them. Certain countries, like Albania, FYROM, and FRY, assess the initiative positively. Others, like Bulgaria and Turkey, remain suspicious that their engagement might be considered an alternative to EU accession. Croatia and Slovenia continue to demonstrate reluctance toward deeper involvement in a "Balkan" framework. The European Commission, in its April 1998 report on the EU regional approach, stressed the need for most SEE countries to undertake further reforms.[28] However, the main problem for Royaumont is financial. Since it is not financed through the PHARE program, individual state or private funding has to be found for each proposed project. As a result, small concrete projects developed through NGOs, rather than coordinated intergovernmental initiatives, will be easier to sponsor and to implement. The eleven cooperation project proposals selected for implementation recently by the Royaumont coordinator were all initiatives of civilian actors.[29]

SECI had been cautiously perceived initially by some European countries, however, because it was a US-led initiative that was developed in the background and its private funding might raise issues of transparency and resource availability. Be that as it may, a convergence of interests over the past few years has led to greater coordination. This move has been encouraged by the shortcomings of both initiatives: The Royaumont process has an allocated budget but is burdened by bureaucratic procedures for the distribution of aid; SECI lacks funds but is flexible, can engage in short-term actions and has greater visibility. The recent implicit division of labor between the two leaves infrastructure projects mainly to SECI and democracy and civil society-related activities to Royaumont.

The WEU has tried to associate itself with the processes of other international organizations. However, while it declared associate partnership status to be complementary with NATO's PfP process, the latter opted for the wider OSCE framework of potential membership, instead of potential EU members.[30] Moreover, there was limited interest within WEU for further enhancement of regional cooperation. Associate partnership does not provide collective security guarantees and the ten associate partners have not been offered full membership. This is partly due to the existence of an alternative framework in PfP, the dominance of NATO and EU enlargements for most countries of the region, and the fact that prior membership in both of these organizations is a requirement for full WEU membership. WEU's rationale, therefore, has been to focus and develop cooperation with potential future EU members, and consequently, in south-eastern Europe only Bulgaria and Romania are associate partners. The eventual institutionalization of relations with Albania, Bosnia-Herzegovina, Croatia, FYROM, and FRY, perhaps along the same lines as the evolution of WEU's approach toward central European states (i.e., the creation of a consultation forum and later an associate partner status), remains an open question. WEU's capacity to act in as a stabilizer in south-eastern Europe cannot develop without a closer link between the EU's common foreign and security policy (CFSP) and WEU. The debate around a future merger with the EU might imply a further enhancement of subregionalism in the security and defense fields.[31]

In spite of efforts undertaken in south-eastern Europe by the EU, regional economic integration is limited by ongoing political rivalries, security risks, varying levels of economic development, and attitude toward economic integration.[32] At the economic level, broader relations might be possible only with the effective implementation of the common foreign and trade agreement and customs system in Bosnia-Herzegovina as well as an improvement in bilateral relations between Croatia and FRY. Both these states remain the main economic and political actors at the regional level. However, the prerequisite for economic integration is the settlement of regional security issues and political instability. The range and the depth of regional disputes in south-eastern Europe inevitably limit political flexibility and constitute barriers to effective regional cooperation. Cooperation in areas of low political salience cannot alone overcome these obstacles without the emplacement of a parallel confidence-building process and coherent conflict prevention approaches to each separate conflict as well as toward the region as a whole.

Most countries in south-eastern Europe, with the exception of FRY, are unwilling to develop multilateral economic and political relations with all of their neighbors for fear that the consolidation of regional cooperation would reconstitute the former Yugoslavian space. FYROM did not initially sign the Declaration of Stability, Security, and Cooperation, believing that local regional initiatives might delay its claims to EU accession. Bosnia-Herzegovina sent an assistant minister for foreign affairs to the 1997 meeting of SEE heads of state in Crete, indicating its reluctance to enter any local cooperative scheme which might result in the loss of political leverage for implementation of the Dayton Agreement. Greece did not at first join the Balkan Rapid Reaction Force, arguing that priority should be given to established western military alliances. Above all, regional initiatives might not be sustainable in the long run in the absence of FRY, a core regional country.

Economic cooperation has not been shown to spill over into the political sphere. South-eastern European countries are witnessing painful economic transitions with high inflation rates, a decrease in per capita incomes, and high unemployment rates. Trade relations are low, and western countries still remain the main trading partners. The countries of the region face enormous structural problems – average gross domestic product amounts to only 25 percent of the EU average – and a notable disparity in growth rates compared to central European countries. This discrepancy will in all likelihood increase further as the latter join the EU. Assessing the economic situation in south-eastern Europe in its report last April, the European Commission drew attention into the continued slow and differentiated pace of reform and development among the countries concerned.[33]

These development gaps between different subregions of Europe as well as within south-eastern Europe increase dependence on external assistance and constrain the development of regional cooperation that might help narrow such gaps. The EU, and countries which might have a more direct interest in the region (Austria, Italy, Greece), can play an essential role as south-eastern European countries do not yet have the economic means, the financial resources, nor the infrastructures available to invest in and promote transborder or regional projects. Therefore, further institutionalization of cooperative frameworks cannot alone compensate for the lack of resources and infrastructures. More importantly, countries of the region believe that direct links with western economic markets are more advantageous than currently weak regional economic relations.

The "attraction effect" of the western European subsystem hampers efforts at enhanced regional cooperation.[34] In other words, what makes subregional integration difficult is not only the problems coming from within the region, but also those that proceed from the very existence of a dominant system, namely the EU, within a broader regional one. The main goal remains to integrate within the main subsystem instead of creating a parallel one in the absence of concrete commitment toward enlargement on the part of western Europe. Given the asymmetry of the relationship, regional countries are convinced that, short of integration, a center/periphery relationship within the European system might emerge and create new dividing lines. Rather than trying to strengthen their own grouping through replication of the process of integration in western Europe, they opt for direct accommodation and integration into the core region. One could tentatively claim the following paradigm: The extent of regional cooperation is inversely proportional to the need for it. Consequently, a clear definition of integration is central to the dialectic between enlargement and regional cooperation. In the medium-term, protectionism in western European markets and a delayed integration process, ironically, might well bolster the development of economic and political links between and among the states of south eastern Europe.

**Prospects for the Future**

There are many arguments in favor of the development of regional cooperation in south-eastern Europe. The range and depth of internal conflicts and the lack of economic resources makes efforts toward a regional approach almost an imperative.

The emergence of common strategic concerns might, paradoxically, be one of the major incentives. In geopolitical terms, Albania, Bulgaria, FYROM, and Turkey on one side, and Greece, Bulgaria, FYROM, and FRY on the other, constitute the main transit corridors running respectively east-west and north-south. A number of countries, albeit for different reasons, have a strong interest in the maintenance of the regional status quo: FRY and FYROM fear a secession of their respective Albanian communities; Greece is unwilling to contemplate any further fragmentation along its northern borders, and Turkey fears autonomy movements that might intensify its internal Kurdish problem. For FRY, regional cooperation remains a unique opportunity to end the country's isolation. Finally, the common threat to security initiated by the Kosovo crisis has brought south-eastern European countries into cooperation with one another through joint declarations and the creation of a multinational peace-keeping force. Increased awareness of strategic interdependence has helped define a range of common principles (territorial integrity, border inviolability), similar internal concerns (borders, minorities), and common objectives (peaceful resolution of conflicts, no spillover effect). The emergence of common concerns might lead, in the future, to a degree of institutionalization, which could in turn contribute to the regional dynamic. This dynamic does not entail the emergence of a "regional identity" but may act as a forceful practical unifying factor.

The linkage of SEE states to broader European integration processes remains the main reason for participation in regional frameworks. External top-down initiatives thus play a central role in the build-up of regional cooperation. The enlargement door to European and transatlantic organizations should therefore be kept open for regional cooperation to work. The future effectiveness of regional cooperation frameworks, either top-down or bottom-up implies a clearer (re)definition of regionalism by western European countries and its linkage to the broader European security context. This clarification of the regional process (either as a substitute for, alternative to, or means toward achieving integration) would likely further enhance the linkage between enlargement and regional cooperation. South-eastern Europe, far from being marginalized at the periphery of Europe, would consequently be judged to be of direct interest to European organizations, which might then commit themselves to gradual integration of the region.

Most organizations have already made some first steps to compensate for this lack of definition. The EU Royaumont process has reiterated the openness of the EU's enlargement process and the existence of common objective criteria as well the conditionality of a regional approach toward enlargement. The EU's regional approach, however, could be regarded as a transitional process rather than a permanent framework, as the long-term objective of such a policy should be the gradual integration of the SEE countries into the EU. The EAPC has stressed that regional security cooperation and identity should be seen in the framework of the Euro-Atlantic integration process. It should not be seen as an alternative to NATO membership, but as a demonstration of the increased readiness of NATO candidates to undertake responsibilities and generate security for the whole region.

The conditionality of external activities in south-eastern Europe might then be reinforced to provide both incentives and obligations for the implementation of policies and reforms as a binding process. Regional cooperation could then be promoted and institutionalized, to a certain degree, within the framework of top-down initiatives. Complementary bottom-up initiatives could then be developed in accordance with these broader existing frameworks. Practically, EAPC might intensify regional cooperation by giving it a political dimension specifically linked to NATO enlargement. The OSCE might revise its regional provisions to enhance existing dimensions (borders, minorities, regional tables) and extend the Stability Pact to south-eastern Europe. Greater linkage between OSCE and the EU Royaumont process would help give the latter a more overt political rationale.

While in general terms, cooperation between international organizations at the institutional level has increased, a certain level of duplication in the different initiatives related to south-eastern Europe can be noted. The political consultative and regional arms control functions of the EAPC and the OSCE might lead to some competition. This is especially the case in the field of arms control and nonproliferation measures concerning implementation and verification, which has been, until now, one of the OSCE's principal tasks. Better coordination and division of labor between the two, such as that developed between the Royaumont process and SECI, might be appropriate in the future. The reinforcement of the OSCE/EU relationship would further enhance a European framework. In that perspective, more room might be left for subregionalism within the EU CFSP context. A better division of labor between conflict prevention (EU/WEU) and post-conflict resolution (OSCE) could also be thought through. However, in view of the depth of the problems in the region, a certain level of duplication between European and transatlantic organizations might be no bad thing, provided that the two organizations manage to coordinate their activities.

External cooperative frameworks also bolster internal regional cooperation such as the conference of ministers of SEE in Crete or the creation of a new multinational peacekeeping force for south-eastern Europe in September 1998.[35] European countries with specific interests in the region, such as Austria, Germany, Greece, and Italy as well as the Nordic countries and Turkey might take a particular lead. The task of external subregional frameworks would be to support, rather than duplicate, internal initiatives. Top-down initiatives could be encouraged to develop and extend their activities in the field of hard security (e.g., defense cooperation or arms control) under the aegis of NATO or OSCE.[36] If not, their agendas may not complement the different bottom-up regional initiatives, which essentially deal with "soft security," and could bring them into competition.

The major economic and security problems in south-eastern Europe require the substantial involvement of the major western organizations. However, the political and security vacuum in south-eastern Europe will not be filled by large numbers of interlocking networks of security arrangements unless they have political and economic coherence. International organizations could promote a better division of labor and coordination. The EU could focus on economic issues and reconstruction plans. The OSCE could address "soft" security issues, such as borders, minorities, transfrontier cooperation, and "new" security risks as well as softer arms control measures (such as transparency and advanced notification) and the extension of the CFE to the whole subregion. NATO could develop a "PfP Plus" for the region, dealing with military issues, interoperability and civil-military relations. This implies a combination of more traditional confidence and security building measures (such as partial disarmament and information exchange) as well as greater transparency in relation to political issues such as minorities and borders.

## Conclusion

The likelihood of south-eastern Europe becoming a region *stricto sensu* is not a basic precondition for regional cooperation to work. Flexible definitions based on interaction and proximate status prevail in this case. Deep economic, political, and social problems have prompted intergovernmentally-led regional cooperation without the existence of a real regional identification. Thus, regional cooperation in south-eastern Europe provides for alternative patterns of interaction at various levels and in different sectors. Regional cooperation in south-eastern Europe has, therefore, the potential to develop further, but in the short term it is bound to stay a noninstitutionalized, flexible process. It remains an open question whether institutionalization would better serve the purposes of regional cooperation or whether it might not be better to keep it to a minimal level, at least as long as the main problems in the area are unresolved.

Some European political leaders have advocated the necessity of collective regional security institutions for south-eastern Europe for a transitory period in order to avoid an unstable and dangerous security vacuum.[37] However, given the specific current conditions of south-eastern Europe, which is crisis ridden, economically backward, and has weak civil societies, external cooperative frameworks remain essential security-building mechanisms.

The success of regionalism, consequently, continues to be based on inspiration from outside interests. Since the driving force of regional cooperation remains integration within broader European structures, multiple memberships are not incompatible with subregional cooperation; nor is a combination and coexistence of top-down and bottom-up initiatives. In the process, the former should avoid further dividing the region by keeping certain countries out of regional cooperation, or by providing preferential treatment. This would harm the fragile coherence currently developing at the regional level.

For now, external regional initiatives should focus on security issues which are more likely to facilitate the development of common objectives, centering on the avoidance of further instability and fragmentation as well as the promotion of peaceful conflict resolution. Regional cooperation might be understood as a process for normalizing relations at the regional level to prepare for accession. They thus constitute a complement rather than an alternative to wider European processes. Locally-initiated regional cooperation is a precondition for the success of top-down frameworks. Externally imposed solutions can hardly be sustainable unless they are undertaken and promoted by the countries themselves. They might be clearly understood as part of a security-building process aiming to support and assist and to provide long-term solutions. For regional cooperation to work, a necessary balance between top-down and bottom-up approaches, their coordination, and transparency will have to develop. The existence or not of a south-eastern dimension to European security will depend on such endeavors.

## Notes

1. By "south-eastern Europe," we mean Albania, former Yugoslavia (except Slovenia), Bulgaria, Romania, Greece, and Turkey.
2. By top-down regional initiatives, we mean frameworks that have been pro-

posed by international organizations, external to the region, as opposed to bottom-up initiatives, initiated at a local level.

3. Sophia Clément, "L'Europe du sud-est après les élargissements de l'Union européenne et de l'OTAN," in *Les Balkans, deux ans aprés les Accords de Dayton*, Sophia Clément and Thierry Tardy (eds.) Relations Internationales et Stratègiques, Institut de Relations Internationales et Stratégiques, Paris, December 1997.

4. See Plamen Pantev's contribution on bottom-up approaches to regional cooperation.

5. Jeffery Simon, "Bulgaria and NATO: 7 lost years," *Strategic Forum*, no. 142, May 1998.

6. Sophia Clément, "Conflict Prevention in the Balkans: The Cases of Kosovo and the Former Yugoslav Republic of Macedonia," *Chaillot Papers* no.30, Institute for Security Studies, Western European Union, December 1997. See also Sophia Clément (ed.), "The Issues Raised by Bosnia and the Transatlantic Debate," *Chaillot Papers* no. 30, Institute for Security Studies, Western European Union, June 1998.

7. See "General Affairs Council Document," 26 February 1996. The Union defines political and economic conditions to be fulfilled as the basis for a coherent and transparent policy toward the development of bilateral relations in a series of areas identified for further action, such as trade, financial assistance and contractual relations.

8. The contractual relation of the EU with Albania and FYROM remain at an agreement level. EU has signed a commercial and cooperation agreement with Albania (December 1992) and a cooperation agreement with FYROM (January 1998).

9. See Annex III of the Council Conclusions specifically on former Yugoslavia adopted on 26 February 1996, *Bulletin EU* 1/2-1996. "The process of stability and good-neighborly relations in south-eastern Europe is to be seen in relation to the Peace Plan in for Bosnia and Herzegovina...the initiative could be incorporated into the wider context of regional cooperation, as approved by the Council on 29 January 1996.... The process of stability and good-neighborly relations in south-eastern Europe is to be seen in relation to the peace plan for Bosnia-Herzegovina.... This initiative should be incorporated in the wider context of regional cooperation...it follows the path of the Peace plan, the implementation of which it endeavors to facilitate."

10. See Annex 1-B of the Dayton Peace Agreement: Art. II on Confidence and Security-Building Measures; Art. III on Regional Confidence and Security-Building Measures; Art. IV on Measures for Sub-Regional Arms Control; Art. V on Regional Arms Control Armament.

11. On the conditionality approach, see the "Council Conclusions" on the principle of conditionality on relations between the EU and certain south-eastern European countries, *Bulletin UE* 4-1997 and Council Conclusions concerning the application of conditionality aiming at developing a coherent EU strategy for relations with the countries of the region, 29 April 1997 and October 1998. Bulletin UE 4-1998, and 10-1998.

12. See Annex III of the Council Conclusions on former Yugoslavia adopted on 26 February 1996, *Bulletin EU* 1/2-1996. See endnote 9.

13. "Le processus de Royaumont poursuit la mise en oeuvre de projets de coopèration," *Agence EUROPE*, no. 7245, 19 July 1998.

14. Events included the following: A media roundtable took place in Athens in March 1998, involving 60.000 ECUs; an NGO from the south-eastern Europe contact meeting in Thessaloniki set up an NGO network in July 1998 involving 60.000 ECUs; a meeting of the heads of local parliaments at the European Parliament in Brussels took place in September 1998; a meeting in Austria on education and cooperation in south-eastern Europe was organized by the Austrian government; and in March 1999 there was a formal meeting in Tirana on the NGO front to consolidate the creation of a network. As for projects, approximately 70 are planned, of which only a few have been financed and conceptualized. They mainly concern the media sector with 75.000 ECUs financed by Luxembourg; a workshop on media programs for ethnic minorities of 200.000 ECUs; the Halki seminar financed through the year 2000 up to 450.000 ECUs; a meeting organized by the Council of Europe on the legal status of NGO's; and 500.000 ECUs for the University of South-Eastern Europe, financed up to 90% by the Greek government.

15. "Mr. Védrine proposes a 'Stability Pact' for Southeast Europe", *Atlantic News*, No. 2988, 14 February 1998. See also "Reunion de suivi du 'processus de Royaumont'," *Agence EUROPE*, no. 7195, 4 April 1998.

16. From Ambassador Richard Schifter, President Clinton's political advisor

17. SECI-Southeast European Cooperative Initiative Activity Report 1997, Vienna.

18. It aims at developing the energy efficiency measures essentially at the municipal level of heat supply, and industry, source of major environmental pollution. SECI-Southeast European Cooperative Initiative, *Activity Report* 1997, Vienna.

19. SECI, *Activity Report* 1997, Vienna.

20. Communiqués of the Ministerial Meeting of the North Atlantic Council, NATO Headquarters, Brussels, 10-11 January 1994. "Partnership for Peace: Framework Document," Annex to M-1(94)2.

21. The EAPC meets in different configurations and at different levels and facilitates consultations on a wide range of subjects. "The Enhanced PfP Program," *NATO fact Sheet* no. 9, July 1997.

22. NATO/EAPC: Development of a politico-military framework for NATO-led PfP operations, *Atlantic News*, no. 2981, 21 January 1998. It provides for the development of rapid engagement procedures to involve partner countries that already play an important role in SFOR in the planning of such operations as well as in the preparation of politico-military guidance, as one of the cornerstone of an enhanced PfP. See also the Action Plan of the Euro-Atlantic Partnership Council for 1998-2000, Press release (98)2, 14 January 1998.

23. EAPC one-year anniversary press statement by the chairman, Luxembourg, 29 May 1998. *Atlantic News*, no. 3015, 3 June 1998.

24. George Katsirdakis (Senior Defense Partnership and Cooperation Directorate). "Albania: A Case Study in the Practical Implementation of the Partnership for Peace," *NATO Review*, Summer 1998.

25. Meeting of the Ministers of Defense of South-Eastern European Partnership for Peace participating States, Regional NATO member states Greece and Turkey, as well as NATO members Italy and the United States, Sofia, 3 October 1997.

26. Kirchberg Declaration, WEU Council of Ministers, 9 May 1994.

27. Erfurt Declaration, WEU Ministerial Council, Erfurt, 18 November 1997. See also Rhodes Declaration, WEU Council of Ministers, 12 May 1998.

28. To improve public order and security in Albania; public administration, Albanian rights, private sector in FYROM; Dayton provisions, democratic reforms and multiethnic reconciliation in Croatia; media and private property in Bosnia; and fundamental human rights in FRY. "Evaluation du Conseil de l'UE sur sa stratégie en matiére de conditionnalité et de son Approche régionale," Brussels, 10 November 1997. See also "Conclusions sur les pays concernès par l'Approche régionale," Luxembourg, 27 April 1998 and "South-east Europe: Commission recommends the council to maintain the status quo in bilateral relations with the five countries covered by the 'regional approach' —a warning for Croatia and FRY," *Agence EUROPE*, no. 7201, 16 April 1998.

29. "'Royaumont Process' pursues implementation of cooperation projects," *Uniting Europe Bulletin*, no. 14, 6 July 1998: 7.

30. Noordwijk Declaration, *Noordwijk*, 14 November 1994.

31. See WEU at 50, Institute for Security Studies, Western European Union (ed), October 1998.

32. It is interesting that most of the trade of the five countries participating to the Raiment initiative is oriented toward the EU. The FRY and FYROM still have important trade with Russia and central European countries. Regional economic cooperation, however, remains essential for them and has been relaunched for Croatia and Bosnia-Herzegovina.

33. *Agence EUROPE*, no.7201, 16 April 1998: 6.

34. Sophia Clément, "Subregionalism in south-eastern Europe," in Steve Calleya (ed.), *Regionalism in the post-Cold-War World* (Brookfield, VT: Dartmouth Publishing, forthcoming).

35. Common Declaration, Summit of the Heads of States of South-Eastern Europe, 4 November 1997.

36. Speech by Alyson Bailes, "Linking Subregional Cooperation to Wider Security Processes," Stockholm Conference on Subregional Cooperation: An Instrument for Modern Security Building, 13-14 October 1998, Stockholm.

37. Speech of the Greek Minister of Defense, Akis Tsohatzopoulos, at the WEU Assembly, May 1998.

# 5

# Legitimizing Subregionalism
## Evolving Perceptions, Initiatives, and Approaches to Subregional Relations in South-Eastern Europe

*Plamen Pantev*

## Introduction

European region-building is instrumental for the process of mutual adaptation by the more advanced and the less developed parts of Europe. It is also an element of European and Euro-Atlantic integration, whose momentum will be constantly reflected in subregion-building efforts. Alyson Bailes writes that subregional organizations "continue to make a contribution to the stability and security of the Euro-Atlantic area and that there is a strong synergy between the subregional process and integration."[1] In south-eastern Europe (SEE) this has particular resonance. The past four years have seen the beginnings of an effort to develop SEE cooperation emanating from the region itself. The legitimization of subregional relations stimulates the creativity and the initiative of local actors, and unites national politics with the practical aspirations of the peoples of the region. Higher living standards, modern economies, technology and infrastructure, peace and prosperity – these represent hopes that have often seemed distant, if not impossible for the region to achieve.

That these goals are now actively pursued through, among other things, the mechanism of regional cooperation, marks a new episode in the history of south-eastern Europe. This circumstance makes it important to examine how internal regional perceptions, initiatives, and approaches to the building of south-eastern Europe have evolved and what direction they are most likely to take. A second aspect is to explore the specific role of the emerging south-eastern European subregion in the broader processes of security and integration of Eurasia.

## The Legacy of Region-Building Efforts in the Balkans

The history of subregional cooperation in the Balkans is short and largely unsuccessful. In the first place, the Balkans did not emerge from the remnants of the Hapsburg and the Ottoman Empires as a "region." This had been the initial dream of nineteenth-century national liberation movements and freedom fighters. The latter were largely internationalist in outlook, aiming their efforts at the liberation and common future of all nations of the region. However, in practice, those who were first to be liberated with external support concentrated on their own national competitive goals, tacitly renouncing previous regional ideals. The Berlin Treaty of 1878, an international legal framework for the permanent fragmentation or "Balkanization" of the region, guaranteed this anti-regional behavior.

The political ideals of US President Woodrow Wilson and the practical designs of his post-World War I settlements in central, eastern and south-eastern Europe, based on national self-determination, did little to overcome this. The US was not yet a powerful enough diplomatic force to promote the normalization of ethnicity/nation and state border relationships in the Balkans. In the meantime, European powers exploited the internal regional divisions, conflicts and animosities as much as they could for their own ends. The result for the Balkans was opportunistic nationalist behavior under the umbrellas of alliances with external powers. The various inter-war pacts and alignments in the region amply reflected this, as did the region's economic retardation. The arrival of World War II did not fundamentally change this situation.

The Cold-War period froze and temporarily diverted conflicting attitudes along the axis of East-West polarization. Ex-Yugoslavia was the principal regional beneficiary of this divide, exploiting its nonalignment status both in the West and in the East. However, even ex-Yugoslavia could not adapt to the dramatic systemic transformations that took place at the end of the 1980s. Nor could the economic, transport, and communications infrastructure of the subregion change overnight as it had been constructed for decades to serve confronting rather than overlapping attitudes. For this reason, the vaguely perestroika-style multilateral meeting of the ministers of foreign affairs of the Balkan states in 1988 in Belgrade, initiated by Bulgaria, could mark only a modest attempt to depart from the formal Cold War division. Ambitious formulations for the development of multilateral regional cooperation were not backed by practical subregional projects. The 1990 Tirana follow-up foreign ministers' meeting preserved the political rhetoric but did not improve or subsequently continue the process due to the outbreak of war in the crumbling Yugoslav federation.

The lessons drawn by the states of the region from the horrific Yugoslav conflicts, however, became a major factor in the evolution of cooperation in south-eastern Europe. The nightmarish prospect of an all-out Balkan war in the early 1990s had a multiple effect both on politicians and on societies in the area. First, the Yugoslav conflict and its tragedies deterred others from seeking a nineteenth-century solution to twenty-first century problems; second, non-Yugoslav and many ex-Yugoslav SEE states realized that the wars were a major obstacle to much needed cooperation. Thus, a new conceptualization of the situation and activities in the region was motivated more by the negative experience of peoples and states of SEE than by a record of positive interaction and a tradition of regional cooperation inherited from the past. The early 1990s was a period in which most Balkan countries came to realize how much the region suffered because of the absence of a functioning common regional market and diversified cooperative relationships, and how much subregional cooperation was needed to prevent the expansion of ex-Yugoslav conflicts or the development of new ones.

The post-Cold War transformation of Europe introduced a new opportunity for south-eastern Europe to join in the enlargement of the security space and the integrated Euro-Atlantic community. This also motivated new perceptions of regional political behavior. The opportunity to join the modernizing democratic world by reinterpreting the lessons of history in the region strengthened the positions of those political actors favoring greater tolerance, reconciliation and rapprochement. The "silver lining" in the Yugoslav conflicts, if one can conceive of such a thing, was that the SEE states were brought into contact with major external actors who also demanded regional cooperation.

## Geoeconomics, Geopolitics and Geostrategic Motivations

There are geoeconomic, geopolitical, and geostrategic reasons for SEE states to become involved in political, security, and economic integration designs within post-Cold War Eurasia. The evolving interests of Europe after the demise of totalitarian socialism highlight the consensus arrived at by many in the area, i.e., that the Balkans must overcome old divisions and impediments and turn south-eastern Europe into a compatible part of the new Europe. This assessment has become dominant in the area and is conceived of as a basic prerequisite for the region's economic and technological modernization. Geoeconomic, geopolitical, and geostrategic opportunities are gradually coming to be seen as an alternative to the conflicts in the peninsula.

South-eastern Europe's position as a crossroads in energy transportation and distribution from Russia and the Caspian Sea to central and western Europe increases the importance of the region in the energy strategies of the US and the EU. This, in turn, increases the importance of the region to Russia, Japan, and China. The transport and communication opportunities of south-eastern Europe in the context of the larger east-west and north-south corridors also increase the economic attractiveness of the area. Its strategic economic outreach to the eastern Mediterranean, the Middle East, the Black and Caspian seas, Russia and Kazakhstan, as well as to the Chinese market, opens up private and government investment opportunities. Turkey's promising future in gas, oil, transport, and trade underscores another major US economic interest in south-eastern Europe. The potential for creating an open and functioning regional common market, in the mid- to long-term is thus conditioned by circumstances within south-eastern Europe and by the needs of the global economy.

The political challenges in this part of Europe are great. The transition to functioning market economies and pluralistic democracies, the battle for a secular and democratic Turkey, and proximity to the biggest European state, Russia, all focus the political interests of both the US and the EU on south-eastern Europe. These developments are perceived by most countries in the region as a unique historic opportunity to homogenize and stabilize the area politically and turn it into a vanguard of the expanding Euro-Atlantic civil and security space. The eastern opening of the EU has provided Bulgaria and Romania with the chance to become full members and, together with Hungary and Slovenia, to create an important link to Greece, an EU member state, and to Turkey, a member of the EU Customs Union.

A salient geostrategic motivation relates to the dangerous knot of conflicts in the post-Yugoslav space, the link between south-eastern Europe and the Black Sea, and its proximity to the southern borders of Russia, the Middle East, and the Gulf. The conflicts in ex-Yugoslavia will continue to require an international presence to prevent and/or to end fighting. Future military intervention cannot be ruled out. On the other hand, the rehabilitation of war-torn countries and the establishment of a workable peace entail a universe of difficult political, economic, and social considerations that can hardly be separated from the strategic ones to be addressed. The Bosnia precedent demonstrates the imperative of an interconnected strategic, social, economic, and political international engagement.[2]

The violent conflicts in Bosnia and Kosovo, the uncertainties in the Gulf, and the potential conflicts around the oil-rich Caspian Sea demonstrate the necessity for NATO and western Europe to apply a strategy of forward engagement and forward deployment to this key global strategic region. The strategic focus on the Balkans is already a security need for both western Europe and North America. Those countries in south-eastern Europe that exist between centers of instability share a common interest in bringing in external support for peace and security. This argument affects NATO enlargement policies, the Euro-Atlantic debate on the "new" missions of the alliance, and the attempt to find ways of adapting NATO and the Partnership for Peace (PfP) to the security needs of the next century. Local players perceive increasing opportunities for strategic cooperation with NATO and improved potential for the alliance to bridge the security interests of the European countries in the Organization for Security and Cooperation in Europe (OSCE) zone, including Russia, a traditional military player in south-eastern Europe.

## Conceptual Factors in South-Eastern European Region-Building

The concept of "region-building" may well be messy and loosely defined, but it nevertheless has a major appeal to the people of south-eastern Europe. Region-building, in this respect, offers a hope that south-eastern Europe is not doomed to be Europe's "litter-bin" and that its own initiatives and activities can improve its situation. This hope rests on a perception of south-eastern Europe as part of a wider European building process. Some writers have elaborated the concept of an "all-European neighborhood" as part of a strategy to stabilize the Balkans.[3] The first part of their argument is that this concept and the strategy resulting from it treat Slovenia, Romania, and Bulgaria as countries that, along with current member state Greece, will border states of the EU in the Balkans in the foreseeable future. Second, the OSCE and the Council of Europe (CoE) are expected to be directly involved in solving issues in south-eastern Europe. The third element of the concept is the development of regional cooperation as an instrument for tying the Balkans to the process of European integration. The fourth element is central and eastern Europe's bridging function between the EU and Russia. South-eastern Europe has the potential for playing the same role.

Other authors have tried for years to apply the concept of "security community" to the case of south-eastern Europe.[4] The basic premise is that relations within the Balkan security community should be aimed at prohibiting the very thought of using force in the case of a dispute among member countries. Both concepts have encouraged deeper understanding of the challenges faced by south-eastern Europe and have thereby assisted efforts to formulate more effective policies in and toward the region. The "Balkan security community" concept, in particular, focuses on region-building initiatives and therefore has the potential to influence practical policy actions.

### Recent Internal Region-Building Initiatives in South-Eastern Europe

Comprehensive multilateral cooperation in south-eastern Europe is still at an initial stage of evolution. The process to date has not yet matured enough to be institutionalized and remains dependent on the effectiveness of externally initiated, better subsidized and guaranteed politically subregional initiatives like Southeast European Cooperative Initiative (SECI) and the Royaumont process.

The Yugoslav conflicts, as already noted, have had a huge effect on region-building efforts. Not only did they represent the complete breakdown of stability and cooperation in the former Yugoslavia; they have shaped nation-state attitudes in ways that considerably complicate regional relations of any description. The repulsiveness of the wars in ex-Yugoslavia led some states to seek to create an entirely different international presence and project a new image, which, it is hoped, will lead to better economic and political opportunities, particularly integration in the EU and NATO. Slovenia, Croatia, and Romania, in particular, initially rejected the Balkan label, preferring to be treated as "central European" or "Danubian" states.

The 1995 Dayton Peace Agreement opened a new chapter for the subregional relationships, bringing the international community into the effort to establish stable regional relations. This coincided with Romania's subsequent new strategy of assuming fully the role of responsible player in south-eastern Europe, which was driven by their hope of joining NATO. Together with Bulgaria, Greece, and Turkey, Romania became one of the four states willing to initiate some cooperative processes among states of the region. Slovenia and Croatia also began to make bolder steps as observers or full participants in subregional activities, at the same time intensifying their bilateral relations with countries in the region.

Bulgaria, with support from Greece, Turkey, and Romania, was behind the first efforts aimed at reviving multilateral subregional cooperation. The meeting of the foreign ministers of SEE countries in Sofia on July 6-7, 1996 launched the process of comprehensive multilateral cooperation that some analysts have described as the "SEE cooperation process" or the "Sofia process." The Sofia Declaration on Good-Neighborly Relations, Stability, Security and Cooperation in the Balkans, signed by the ministers of foreign affairs and the heads of delegations of Albania, Bosnia and Herzegovina, Bulgaria, the Former Republic of Yugoslavia (FRY), Greece, Romania, and Turkey, marked their agreement to launch a process of an encompassing multilateral cooperation with a view toward enhancing stability and security.[5] The Helsinki principles of international relations and confidence and security building measures, the implementation of the Dayton Peace Agreement and support for a meeting of the defense ministers of the Balkan states to be held in Sofia were declared key aspects of this cooperation. The leaders also agreed to develop multilateral regional economic cooperation, especially cross-border cooperation; transport, telecommunications, and energy infrastructures; trade and invest- ment promotion; and protection of the environment. They also promised to cooperate in the fields of humanitarian, social, and cultural affairs and agreed to fight illicit drug and arms trafficking and combat organized crime and terrorism. Influential external actors, notably the US, Russia, France, UN, CoE, EU and the Central European Initiative (CEI), declared their support for this new process.

The second meeting of the foreign ministers of SEE states was held in Salonika, Greece, on June 9-10, 1997 as provided for by the Sofia Declaration the year before. The Salonika Declaration on Good-Neighborly Relations, Stability, Security, and Cooperation in the Balkans was signed by representatives of Albania, Bulgaria, the Former Yugoslav Republic of Macedonia (FYROM), FRY, Greece, Romania, and Turkey.[6] Slovenia, Croatia and Bosnia, and Herzegovina participated as "observers," alongside a number of interested states from outside the region. The major areas of coop- eration identified in 1996 were again underscored, with particular attention paid to cooperation in the construction of the pan- European transport corridors agreed to in Crete in 1994 (the latter, an initiative of the European Commission, was aimed at promoting south-eastern European integration and finding alternative trans- port routes to those forced to traverse the sanctioned FRY). There was also agreement on holding regular meetings of the political directors of participating states; to develop regionally applicable confidence and security-building measures jointly at a meeting in Skopje; to hold a defense ministers' meeting later in the year; to initiate regular meetings between trade ministers; and to establish a regional center for trade promotion in Turkey. Participating states agreed to participate in the Balkan Center for Cooperation among Small and Medium Size Enterprises in Bucharest and to establish a joint expert body in Athens within the framework of the Balkan Telecommunications Pool. Further agreement involved increased cross-border cooperation with a view toward implement- ing relevant EU programs at a more rapid pace. Ministers also invited the EU to further develop its policy toward south-eastern Europe in a manner analogous to policies toward other regions in Europe. Finally, SEE states noted their desire to convene summits of heads of state when circumstances required, the first of which was to be organized in Crete in November 1997.

This meeting took place on November 3-4, 1997 in Heracleion, Crete. The seven SEE leaders, along with an observer representative of the Bosnian and Herzegovinan government, issued a joint statement that outlined a framework for economic growth and political cooperation. The declaration noted the determination of participating states to work together to create conditions of prosperity for the nations in the region within a framework of peace, security, good-neighborliness and stability.[7] Several bilateral meetings also took place, including the first in more than half a century between the leaders of Albania and FRY. The leaders stated that they consider the European orientation of their countries to be an integral part of their political, economic and social development and declared European and Euro-Atlantic integration essential for promoting the objectives of economic growth, political cooperation, and prosperity. As in the case of the two previous foreign ministers' meetings, SEE leaders reconfirmed their support for already existing regional initiatives sharing the same ideals – the Royaumont Process, SECI, BSEC (Black Sea Economic Cooperation) and CEI. The leaders of south-eastern Europe invited their ministers of transport, energy, and communications to meet at least once a year to assess progress in the construction of their respective infrastructures and networks. Ministers of economy or finance, it was agreed, would meet to review cross-border cooperation, while foreign ministers would discuss the establishment of a joint secretariat to guarantee continuity between summit and ministerial meetings. There has been no unanimity on this issue to date: Greece favors a more institutionalized subregional approach with established coordinating bodies, while Bulgaria emphasizes substantial subregional projects prior to the elaboration of any institutional structures.

The third meeting of the foreign ministers involved in the "Sofia Process" was held on June 8-9, 1998 in Istanbul.[8] The seven regular and two observer participants from south-eastern Europe were again joined by representatives from external states, international organizations, and other subregional groupings in and around south-eastern Europe. This outside presence reaffirms that the SEE process is seen as a leading, internally-generated initiative, providing a comprehensive framework for cooperation and complemented in specific areas by other regional schemes. At the meeting, SEE ministers declared once again their conviction that Europe cannot be complete without their countries, each of which represent civilizations and historical traditions essential to the establishment of a contemporary European identity. They also agreed that European and Euro-Atlantic integration are essential in promoting common objectives. Turkey and Greece again expressed their support for an early extension of the NATO enlargement process to south-eastern Europe.

Foreign ministers agreed to convene Balkan business forums in parallel to their meetings and to provide an opportunity for business and professional organizations to exchange views and cooperate. They also agreed that bilateral and multilateral relations will stimulate the search for cooperative responses to stability and security problems in south-eastern Europe. The current network of regional bilateral relations is being supplemented by growing trilateral links such as those between Bulgaria-Romania-Turkey and Bulgaria-Romania-Greece.[9] Five of the participating states, Bulgaria, FYROM, Greece, Romania, and Turkey, had already issued a joint declaration expressing their deep concern with the situation in Kosovo in March. Further discussion of the rising violence in Kosovo took place in Istanbul (with the FRY foreign minister present), and the five, along with Albania, again issued a statement condemning the escalation of the conflict and making some recommendations for its peaceful resolution. These statements are without precedent in the diplomatic practice of the subregion.[10] The institutionalization of the SEE process was discussed again, and it was decided that until such time as a permanent joint secretariat is established, the country hosting the meeting of the ministers of foreign affairs will also assume secretariat responsibilities for that year.

The second summit meeting of countries from south-eastern Europe was held on October 11-12, 1998 in Antalya, Turkey, with the participation of the prime and foreign ministers of Bulgaria, FRY, FYROM, Greece, Romania, and Turkey as well as the foreign minister of Albania. A unique declaration on the Kosovo crisis was adopted upon a Bulgarian proposal. It urged the Serbs and the Kosovo Albanians to reach an agreement through negotiations and to implement the UN Security Council Resolution 1199, dated September 1998. For the first time, both FRY and Albania agreed to be part of such a declaration.

A significant aspect of the SEE process is cooperation in defense and security, an inescapable issue in the conflict-ridden Balkans.

Meetings of SEE ministers and deputy ministers of defense were initiated by Bulgaria in 1995 and supported by the US and Italy. They were intended to take the format of a specific subregional process in the framework of the broader SEE cooperation process. The first exploration of such a possibility was the March 1996 meeting of defense ministers of the region, the US, Italy, and Russia in Tirana. The fundamental principle of cooperation in the highly sensitive field of security and defense in south-eastern Europe is that it must be an "inclusive" and not an "exclusive" process and not be directed against one or more countries on the peninsula. Moreover, it must not be seen to be tied to any external "interference" that might disrupt the subregional balance of power and exacerbate existing divisions within the subregion.[11]

Though not originally envisioned as part of the PfP process, cooperation in defense and security has assumed a clear PfP/EAPC format, again as a result of a Bulgarian initiative. On October 3, 1997, the first meeting of the ministers of defense of PfP countries of south-eastern Europe that wish to become NATO members met in Sofia along with representatives from Greece, Turkey, Italy, and the US, as well as representatives from NATO headquarters, OSCE, and Western European Union (WEU). The remaining NATO member states and the three successful central European NATO applicants participated as observers. On this occasion, however, the Bulgarian organizers did not invite the Russian defense minister to participate in the Sofia forum, an unfortunate decision in light of the need for more partnership links with Russia in the field of security and defense. Russia participates in SFOR and is tackling other conflicts in south-eastern Europe. Its partnership in the Black Sea cooperation process and participation in PfP naval exercises there are important factors in bringing Russia into any cooperative security undertaking in the Balkans.[12]

On May 22, 1998, the deputy defense ministers of Albania, Bulgaria, FYROM, Greece, Romania, and Turkey signed a letter of intent in Tirana to create a SEE multinational peacekeeping force. The formal agreement was reached on September 26, 1998 in Skopje, FYROM. By September 1999, three NATO (Greece, Italy, and Turkey) and four PfP countries (Albania, Bulgaria, FYROM, and Romania) will form the rapid reaction force, which represents a major confidence-building step in the region. All able and willing NATO and PfP countries from the region are free to join this rapid reaction unit of 2,000 soldiers. It is expected to provide a contribution to NATO- or WEU-led conflict prevention and other peace support operations under the mandate of the UN or the OSCE. Enhanced contacts, cooperation, and efforts to increase the interoperability of the armed forces of these six countries are a contribution to collective peace-building and region-building. The inclusive character of regional efforts as well as the formulation of certain criteria for PfP and NATO membership, will determine the future of military and security cooperation in south-eastern Europe. It should not lead to the creation of "regional clubs" or "regionalized security," but rather should aim at the consolidation of democracy and stability in south-eastern Europe as well as to the creation of a broad coalition of states willing to act together in addressing specific security threats.

## Problems and Prospects for the Development of South-Eastern Europe

The region-building process continues to be dominated by a number of fundamental issues. These in turn, define attitudes and policies toward subregional cooperation.

The first problem is the definition of south-eastern Europe as a subregion. Regions are not a given; they are continually defined and redefined by the countries comprising them. Historical experience, coupled with positive political, economic, and strategic opportunities, have started to outweigh centrifugal tendencies traditionally nourished by external powers. Today, existing diversity is not perceived merely as an obstacle, but also as a great opportunity and challenge, especially if all the external influential powers assume a constructive region-building perspective toward south-eastern Europe and its states.

The second problem concerns the relative homogeneity of the countries in the area. Romania and Turkey are medium-size states, and the rest of the countries in south-eastern Europe are rather small. The state systems of Bulgaria, Greece, Romania, and Turkey are well established; Slovenia, and to a certain degree, Croatia, have also proved to be reliable international actors on a broad range of issues. The Albanian state's performance shows some fluctuations. The FYROM's relative stability to date, the product of domestic, internal, and external regional interactions, is good news for the area. Yet it has the potential to generate tensions stemming from its social and nation-formation immaturity and to violate human rights. Bosnia and Herzegovina and the FRY continue to face many serious internal issues that narrow their cooperation potential considerably. It would be misguided to expect all states to engage equally in cooperation-building processes. In this context, an inclusive approach with phased timing is the most realistic way of involving the diverse states of south-eastern Europe in region-building activities.

A promising tendency in south-eastern Europe is the gradual convergence of the value systems of the Balkan societies and their political elites toward democracy, market economy, respect for human rights and freedoms, and the rule of law. This influences civil-military relations, improves the chances for more effective democratic controls over governments and assists confidence and security-building measures in the region. NATO and WEU political and security cultures, as well as the EU environment and its *acquis communautaire*, play a major homogenizing role for most of the countries of south-eastern Europe.

The third problem is the existence of two types of relationships among SEE states: conflicting and cooperative. On the one side are the various conflicts in ex-Yugoslavia of the past decade. The Serbo-Croatian war and the wars in Bosnia and Herzegovina are essential parts of the new post-Cold War history of Europe and the world and have generated the region's post-war infamy. The conflict in Kosovo, which, has recently escalated into a dangerous crisis, is part of this trend. But there are other tensions of varying degrees between non ex-Yugoslav countries, for example, the Greek-Turkish dispute, which continue to constrain efforts at cooperation.

Even so, it is important to bear in mind what these regional conflicts have not done. First, they did not spill over and evolve into major regional disasters, but were stopped at the borders of the warring parties. Second, western Europe was not infected by these local wars. The influential external powers did not invest their own mutual tensions or rivalries in the area as sometimes happened in the past, tensions which in most cases have now abated. Third, four countries of the region, Bulgaria, Greece, Romania, and Turkey developed comprehensive bilateral and trilateral cooperative relationships: Bulgarian-Greek, Bulgarian-Romanian and Bulgarian-Turkish confidence and security-building measures extend beyond the formal requirements of the OSCE Vienna Document of 1994.[13]

Thus, the international community effectively constructed a "fire wall" around the hot ex-Yugoslav conflicts, and in so doing contained the further spread of war within and outside of south-eastern Europe.

The Bosnian experience gave birth to a methodology for coping with conflicts and region-building that might be called "the Dayton methodology," which consists of enforcing, keeping, and building peace as well as building up the region. International actors have had a crucial role to play here. The Balkan situation was rightly perceived by NATO and EU leaders as requiring a comprehensive approach and treatment in order to successfully contain its volatility. The methodology required a disaggregation of the issues in the region into two groups. The first consisted of coping with actual conflicts, and the second with supporting the integration of non-conflicting parts of the peninsula into European and Euro-Atlantic institutions.

This methodology stimulated bottom-up activity through top-down incentives by the EU and NATO. The European association agreements of the EU with Romania, Bulgaria, and Slovenia; its customs union with Turkey and various assistance programs; NATO's Partnership for Peace and Euro-Atlantic Partnership Council (EAPC) and the prospects for full membership; the membership criteria of the CoE and the OSCE and assistance in implementation within SEE states have all strengthened the local ambition to create a new atmosphere in Balkan relations. Within the region, the position taken by Turkey and Greece to extend NATO membership to Bulgaria and Romania; Greek support for Bulgaria; and Romania's EU membership have become crucial catalysts for strengthening Conference on Stability and Cooperation initiatives.

Another peculiarity of the interaction is that those countries that were not drawn into the conflicts in ex-Yugoslavia concentrated on their domestic problems, thereby improving their chances of overcoming potential ethnic issues and conflicts. The efforts to elaborate mechanisms and norms for the stable settlement of ethnic problems and to build up cooperative relations with ethnic kin states and/or common ethnic minorities offered a Balkan model for dealing with complex questions that differed markedly from the ethnic cleansing practices of ex-Yugoslavia. Nevertheless, it would be erroneous to presume that subregional cooperation has led to a new region-wide outlook. Most states remain firmly preoccupied with their own domestic and foreign policy challenges, and some perceive region-building exclusively in terms of promoting national aims. Thus, for FRY, subregional cooperation represents an opportunity to be recognized as the legitimate heir of ex-Yugoslavia and to be reintegrated internationally while FYROM views it as a chance to solve the dispute with Greece over its name in its favor. Albania regards subregional cooperation as a way of conveying a solution to the Kosovo issue, and even Greece and Turkey, two of the more active proponents of the process, perceive it as a chance to underscore their respective views about their bilateral conflict. Caution must be maintained, therefore, in describing the extent of the changes in perception that have taken place to date.

These three considerations raise two essential questions for an evolving SEE regional identity. The first is the relationship between internal region-building efforts and other European and Euro-Atlantic actors and, the second, the roles and tasks of subregional cooperation and the relationship of such cooperation to the development of south-eastern European states.

The SEE region bears special responsibility toward other neighboring regions and cooperative processes. The region covers the Black Sea Economic Cooperation (BSEC), the Mediterranean region, the Central European Initiative (CEI), the Central European Free Trade Area (CEFTA) and the states participating in Danubian Cooperation. Their functions and prospects depend on the direction that south-eastern Europe will take, either becoming a compatible subregion of the continent or turning into an obstacle to effective regional organization in Europe. South-eastern Europe is also responsible for the future stability of ex-Yugoslavia. The subregion is the test-site for the re-integration of FRY as well as Bosnia and Herzegovina in the international community, particularly in the UN and OSCE. It also has a role in bringing Albania, FYROM, and Croatia further toward meeting CoE, EU, and NATO membership criteria.[14] The stability of south-eastern Europe is also a major factor for the effectiveness of cooperation in the Black Sea region and the geoeconomic oil and transport network projects in this area.

South-eastern Europe is responsible for cleansing itself of the most repulsive violence seen in post-war Europe, in Bosnia and Kosovo. The legitimacy and respect accorded to SEE subregional cooperation will depend on its success in facilitating conflict resolution and stable settlements in south-eastern Europe. The involvement of Serbia and Montenegro in the international community will be virtually impossible until this task is fulfilled, and subregional cooperation will be an important first step.

SEE subregional cooperation has a specific dimension in relation to EU and NATO. EU and NATO interactions with the subregion require the countries of south-eastern Europe to be active as partners and prospective members. The subregion is in a position to contribute to the Union and the Alliance as a geopolitical, geoeconomic, and geostrategic crossroads of global importance. A specific responsibility is the search for effective formulas to involve Russia and Turkey in broad European and Euro-Atlantic projects in the subregion. Joint efforts in the Balkans offer means to ameliorate current tensions in the EU-Turkey relationship and to sustain NATO-Russia cooperation. SEE countries must therefore participate and cooperate in the elaboration of these relations. It would be counterproductive for subregional actors to try to exploit, for short-term advantage, diverging EU, NATO, Russian, and Turkish interests and attitudes in the region.

A second aspect is the role of subregional cooperation in the development of south-eastern European states. Regional identity will assume a real meaning only when it is associated with practical social roles and missions that contribute to the improvement of the region and benefit other international actors. South-eastern Europe, as a subregion, is expected to play a particular role in overcoming the effects of late modernization and the slow integration of its member states into the globalized economy. The Balkans need political, economic, and technological emancipation, and the regional civil society needs to enlarge.

It is widely acknowledged that in the long term, the entire Balkan region requires greater economic integration internally as well as with Europe if it is to grow and prosper.[15] If the region can lift itself out of its historical economic backwardness and poverty, the area could create an alternative to conflictual relationships and offer an example for those in the area still fixated on the past and on zero-sum reasoning.

The interaction between the cooperation process in the political, economic, transport, energy, communications infrastructure and environmental spheres and the cooperation processes taking place between security, defense, and confidence and security-building measures has special meaning. The interaction of these two process-es has been shown to have a reinforcing effect on the stability and improvement of the social and economic conditions of the subre-gion. However, modernization will not be attained unless all parts of south-eastern Europe abandon territorial claims and aggressive behavior. Conflict prevention and peacekeeping functions under the auspices of international organizations are significant elements of this stabilization.[16] The greatest challenge in this respect is breaking the vicious cycle of violent conflicts that produce bloodshed and refugees and are inevitably followed by efforts at remapping.[17] For that reason, SEE subregional cooperation must not focus only on economic development projects, but must equally address the cul-ture of conflict in the region.

SEE subregional cooperation is also expected to play an instru-mental role in the preparation of individual countries for full mem-bership in NATO, the EU, and the WEU. Regional cooperation is not perceived by local actors as a separate integration process but as part of the preparation for future NATO, EU, and WEU enlargements to south-eastern Europe. Participation in these cooperative processes is viewed as the most important engine for overcoming the belated modernization of the subregion mentioned earlier. Future joint EU/NATO memberships therefore strongly motivate bilateral rela-tions and the initial steps taken toward historical rapprochements in the Balkans. The window of opportunity for creating a region in the Balkans is directly proportional to the area's European and Euro-Atlantic integration.

South-eastern Europe currently lacks the resources needed for cooperative projects. EU and NATO financial and technical support are therefore crucial to the agenda of subregional cooperation. This, in turn, helps the EU meet its objectives by promoting stability in the area and providing a training ground for EU integration, thereby potentially accelerating the enlargement process. The interaction also makes multilateral forums for communication with SEE coun-tries possible, apart from the dominant bilateral partnerships.[18]

The NATO strategy of shaping the environment through a forward presence and forward engagement also defines specific interests for the Alliance in south-eastern Europe.[19] Again, subregional coopera-tion processes, particularly in relation to out-of-area peacekeeping and crisis-management tasks, can significantly assist NATO's own objectives and development. The debate over the costs of NATO and

EU enlargements often neglects these beneficial aspects. As one study has noted, "It goes without saying that costs and benefits of enlargement will vary according to area and time, and also in degree. Not all elements of the cost-benefit account are quantifiable. Qualitative elements in areas like politics, security or society may not be measurable in exact terms; they can, however, be just as or even more important than quantifiable indicators."[20] SEE subregional cooperation may be an important condition for security for the EU and for Europe in general.

Third, south-eastern Europe is in a position to involve Russia in building a comprehensive Euro-Atlantic security architecture. As NATO Secretary General Javier Solana noted recently, if this goal is to become a reality, a new partnership with Russia is needed. Solana pointed out that, "One cannot build such architecture without Russia, let alone against it. Bosnia and Kosovo made it crystal clear: If the international community is to act effectively in European crises, Russia must be on board."[21] South-eastern Europe is a very appropriate test-site for EU-Russia, NATO-Russia and US-Russia cooperation on the joint definition and treatment of the conflicts in the area. NATO-Russia cooperation in Bosnia has not been widely advertised, but it is one of the pillars of stability in the Balkans. The PfP is another sphere of cooperation with Russia for NATO and EAPC states in south-eastern Europe. Russia can do much to build up the subregion by implementing imaginative and positive economic and foreign policies. The regular contractual delivery of gas and oil to the region, for example, makes Russia a key actor in south-eastern Europe and does much to shape its perception in the region. Balancing the energy interests of Russia and the EU may be accomplished by means of large-scale energy projects.

The mutual dependence between south-eastern Europe and the BSEC is another area in which the interests of Russia and the EU must be balanced. South-eastern Europe can include Russia in the Euro-Atlantic civic and security space. Russia, however, must be open about its concept of region-building and underscore its rejection of all intimidation and exploitation of current or potential conflicts in the peninsula. SEE states will require that all influential outside actors, not simply Russia, state their commitment to this principle.

A fourth task for SEE subregional cooperation is linkage and support for the interests of the EU, NATO, and the US in the Black Sea and Caspian Sea regions, the Trans-Caucasus, the eastern Mediterranean, and the Middle East and Persian Gulf. This will inevitably focus attention on the sensitive relations between Turkey and the EU. The strategic position of Turkey and its huge internal market represent an opportunity to build a "win-win" situation for the countries of south-eastern Europe and outside investors by bringing external capital and expertise to bear on regional projects. The progress of the subregion toward a democratic civil society, a social market economy, respect for human rights and the rule of law, and secular statehood is the major argument for the effective implementation of this instrumental role. The interactive nature of subregional relations guarantees that nondemocratic tendencies in Turkish society can be critically assessed by its partners. Subregional cooperation can assist south-eastern European states to negotiate difficult democratic transitions and assist in the collective containment of extremist and authoritarian tendencies.

## Conclusion

It would be wise to avoid exclusion of any state in south-eastern Europe or to treat one preferentially and discriminate against others. At this stage, the core group of able and willing countries within the region, most of which are contenders for membership in the EU and NATO or are already members, is one of the keys to subregion-building. In the long term, a broader participation framework remains the best option for security, stability, and the development of south-eastern Europe. However, after almost a decade of devastating conflicts in former-Yugoslavia, the terrible image that the region now has, makes a gradual approach to cooperation in the subregion the most practical approach.

The "core group" mentioned above consists of Greece, Turkey, Bulgaria, and Romania. Bulgaria and Romania share strategic goals toward the EU and NATO. Romania brings an important strategic link with the EU and NATO enlargement process through its links with Hungary and Slovenia; Bulgaria has similar links with the two existing NATO members, Turkey and Greece. The core group, together with Hungary and Slovenia, constitute an "arc of stability" in south-eastern Europe, a stable link with Central Europe, and a barrier against processes of instability in the subregion and in the broader region of the eastern Mediterranean and the Black Sea.

The governments of these states are expected to expand their political, economic, and military cooperation and to consider those countries outside of the core group as partners and potential participants. Nongovernmental organizations and actors in these countries should be encouraged to develop networks of relations with a nascent regional civil society. Each of the core group states should be a reliable guarantor of the sovereignty and nonviolability of state borders in the Balkans and demonstrate a commitment to preventing the diversity of the region from becoming a source of conflict once again. They should also pledge their intention not use force to solve conflicts in their mutual relations. The core-group countries must rely on their own merits to gain entry into the EU and NATO; however, joint pre-accession strategies, i.e., con-joint efforts directed at integration, deserve encouragement.

This subregional core of countries must be supported by able and willing countries from the EU and NATO, and by other cooperative powerful actors like the US and Russia, in initiating stabilization and development projects in the region and in preparing individual states and the region generally for Euro-Atlantic integration. Countries in the region that fear the spread of the conflicts of ex-Yugoslavia should receive protection from more powerful international actors. The subregional core group of countries deserves full support in their goal of Euro-Atlantic integration, a basic motive for their subregional behavior. Support from NATO, the EU, and the west in general will be an important element in guaranteeing the effectiveness of SEE cooperative projects, such as the SEE Cooperation Process, the Royaumont Process, SECI, and the South Balkan Development Initiative (SBDI).

Finally, the SEE experience is helping to put in place a variety of relationships, interests, and strategies that will shape the future structure of international security. Acting locally really does affect thinking globally. Thus, the strategy of the US in the subregion will, in turn, influence its strategies to the east, south, and west of the region. In addition, the EU's relationship with the area will create the opportunity to integrate this part of Europe into the EU, and the potential for Russia to become involved in European integration processes and the chance for the US and EU to formulate another practical direction in transatlantic cooperation – all these strategic questions are affected by south-eastern European subregional cooperation.

# Notes

1. Alyson J. K. Bailes, "Sub-regional organizations: The Cinderellas of European Security," *NATO Review* 2 (March 1997): 27.

2. Christopher Lord, "An exit strategy from Bosnia," *Armed Forces Journal International* (March 1998).

3. Werner Weidenfeld, ed., *A New Ostpolitik—Strategies for a United Europe* (Gutersloh: Bertelsmann Foundation Publishers, 1997), p. 4.

4. Plamen Pantev, "Bulgaria and the European Union. The security aspect," *The Southeast European Yearbook 1993* (Athens: ELIAMEP,1994), pp. 55-63; *Coping with Conflicts in the Central and Southern Balkans* (Sofia: St. Kliment Ohridsky University Press, 1995), p. 37; *Strengthening of the Balkan Civil Society: the Role of the NGOs in International Negotiations, Research Studies* 4 (Sofia: ISIS, March 1997), pp. 10-13; John Roper, "Security Community," *Between Concept and Reality, Revue Roumaine d'Etudes Internationales, XXV*, 5-6(115-116)(1991): 315-316.

5. Sofia Declaration on Good-Neighborly Relations, Stability, Security and Co-operation in the Balkans, Sofia, 6-7 July 1996.

6. Salonika Declaration on Good-Neighborly Relations, Stability, Security and Cooperation in the Balkans, Salonika, 9-10 June 1997.

7. Joint Statement by the Heads of State and Government of Countries of South Eastern Europe, Heracleion, Crete, Greece, 3-4 November 1997.

8. Istanbul Declaration on Good-Neighborly Relations, Stability, Security and Cooperation in South Eastern Europe, Istanbul, 8-9 June 1998.

9. See, for example, Joint Statement, The Fourth Meeting of the Foreign Ministers of Bulgaria, Romania and Greece, Santorini, 10-11 April 1998.

10. Joint Declaration of the Ministers of Foreign Affairs of Countries of South-Eastern Europe, Sofia, 10 March 1998; Joint Statement of the Ministers of Foreign Affairs of Countries of South-Eastern Europe, Bonn, 25 March 1998; Declaration on the Situation in Kosovo by the Ministers of Foreign Affairs of Countries of South-Eastern Europe, Istanbul, 9 June 1998.

11. Ian Bremmer, Sophia Clément, Andrew Cottey and Thanos Dokos, "Emerging subregional cooperation processes: South-eastern Europe, the Newly Independent States and the Mediterranean," in Andrew Cottey, ed., *Subregional Cooperation in the New Europe: Building Security, Prosperity and Solidarity from the Barents to the Black Sea* (IEWS, Macmillan, 1998), p. 219.

12. For more on this approach to Russia, see Ambassador Alexander Vershbow, "The New NATO and the New Russia," speech at Chatham House, London, 11 May 1998 , *USIA Wireless File* (May 13 1998): 11-14.

13. "The Vienna Document 1994," *SIPRI Yearbook 1995* (Oxford: Oxford University Press, 1995), pp. 799-820.

14. It is an irony of history that at the beginning of the 1990s, Yugoslavia was the Eastern European country closest to the European Community's doorstep. For more, see Vladimir Gligorov, "The Price of Balkan Bluster," *Transitions* 5, no. 4, (April 1998): 70-74.

15. Barnett R. Rubin, ed., *Toward Comprehensive Peace in Southeast Europe: Conflict Prevention in the South Balkans* (New York: Twentieth Century Fund Press, 1996), pp. 8-9.

16. For more on this issue, see Michael S. Lund, *Preventing Violent Conflicts. A Strategy for Preventive Diplomacy* (Washington, D. C.: USIP Press, 1996); *Preventing Deadly Conflict, Final Report* (Carnegie Commission on Preventing Deadly Conflict, December 1997); Mark Eyskens, et al., "How can Europe prevent conflicts?" (PMI for Public Policy Research, November 1997); "Europe's role in the prevention and management of crises in the Balkans," Document 1589, 5 November 1997 (Assembly of WEU, 43rd Session); Sophia Clèment, "Conflict Prevention in the Balkans: Case Studies of Kosovo and the FYR of Macedonia" (Paris: Chaillot Papers 30, December 1997); Dan Smith, "Europe's Suspended Conflicts," *War Report, Bulletin of the Institute for War and Peace Reporting* 58 (February-March 1998): 11-16.

17. "The Balkans, Europe's roughest neighbourhood," *The Economist* (January 24-30, 1998).

18. "Executive Summary: Sub-Regional Cooperation and the European Union" (Ljubliana: IEWS/FIIA, 'Strategy Group' Series on Strengthening Cooperation in Central and Eastern Europe, supported by the Phare/Tacis Democracy Programme (25-26 April 1998).

19. "Remarks by Adm. T. Joseph Lopez, Commander-in-Chief, AFSOUTH at NATO Colloquy on ESDI in Madrid on May 7, 1998," *USIA Wireless File* (May 8, 1998), pp. 17-20.

20. Eric von Breska et al. "Costs, Benefits and Chances of Eastern Enlargement for the European Union," *Bertelsmann Foundation, Research Group on European Affairs,* eds. (Gutersloh: Bertelsmann Foundation Publishers, 1998), p. 11.

21. Javier Solana, "Keynote Address, XVth NATO Workshop: Confronting the Security Challenges of the New NATO," Vienna, 22 June 1998 (USIA Wireless File, June 24, 1998), p. 23.

# Part III

Trans-Caucasus

# 6

# External Factors Affecting Subregional Cooperation in the Southern Tier

*S. Neil MacFarlane*

## Introduction

The southern tier of the former Soviet Union (the southern Caucasian states of Armenia, Azerbaijan, and Georgia and the central Asian states of Turkmenistan, Uzbekistan, Kazakhstan, Kyrgyzstan, and Tajikistan) is an area that, for many reasons, would benefit from enhanced cooperation among its states and peoples. In the economic sphere, the states are small; the enlargement of market size inherent in subregional trade arrangements would therefore improve their prospects. This, in turn, would accelerate flows of investment into the region.

The states of the region are also highly interdependent in the area of transportation. In the environmental sphere, the countries of the region share several watersheds. Although the costs of the failure to develop sensible watershed management are most evident in the Aral Sea catastrophe, environmentally sustainable multilateral programming would carry benefits for all the countries of the subregion. Moreover, particularly in central Asia, disagreement over water policy carries some potential for interstate conflict.

The second set of incentives for subregional cooperation concerns regional conflict. Since independence, the internal politics and bilateral relations of these newly independent states have been troubled by a number of intrastate and interstate disputes.[1] The normalization of the subregion's politics requires the building of confidence, not merely at the state level, but between communities within states. Functionalist literature suggests that cooperation in practical and technical matters can have political spillover in terms of building trust between divided states and peoples, thus laying the basis for more positive political relationships.

Another major incentive for subregional cooperation lies in relations with external powers and the broader international society. All the states of the region are comparatively small and are surrounded by larger competitive regional powers. They are swamped by the power of the major international corporations with whom they must deal. The development of common cooperative perspectives would limit the capacity for external powers to transplant their competition onto the subregional terrain. Such cooperation could potentially enhance the states' bargaining power in discussions of major regional investments and with major donor states and organizations.

Many external states and institutions have ostensibly been attempting to promote such cooperation. Both the Organization for Security and Cooperation in Europe (OSCE) and the European Union (EU) have embraced the concept in their approach to this zone of Europe. The United States considers subregional cooperation to be a priority in its approach to development of the subregion's energy sector.[2] Turkey (through the Black Sea Economic Cooperation), Iran (through the Economic Cooperation Organization and various proposals for Caspian Basin Cooperation) and Russia (through the Commonwealth of Independent States and the Belarus-Russia-Kazakhstan-Kyrgyzstan union) have all sought to define cooperative subregional approaches that include some or all of the southern tier states.

Yet, despite all of these incentives and all this apparent effort, little cooperation has emerged between the states of the region as a whole. In the southern Caucasus, although there is limited evidence of cooperation between Georgia and Azerbaijan on both economic and political issues, there is almost no trilateral cooperation. The efforts of Georgian President Eduard Shevardnadze to construct a Trans-Caucasian zone of peace failed. In Central Asia, while there is greater evidence of institutionalization of cooperative arrangements, demonstrated, for example, by the Central Asian Economic Union, these arrangements appear to have had little effect.[3]

This rather depressing state of affairs can be explained in at least two ways. The first explanation focuses on processes within and between the southern tier states that affect the cooperative project. This aspect is treated in the companion chapter by Arif Yunusov. The second potential locus of explanation, treated here, concerns the roles of external actors as they relate to cooperation.

Many analyses of interstate cooperation focus on the incentives and disincentives for discrete groups of states to collaborate. From a realist perspective, limiting factors are generally analyzed in terms of the impact of anarchy, sensitivity to relative gains, and the dangers of defection.[4] A liberal institutionalist perspective generally focuses on the impact of interstate and multilateral regimes (with established sets of principles, norms, rules, and procedures) in mitigating the effects of anarchy on state interest in cooperation.[5]

However, subregions are embedded in larger regional and international structures and processes of conflict and cooperation. Cooperative decisions in a subregional context affect the interests of actors outside it. In turn, outsiders' pursuit of their own agendas can have profound effects on the prospects for, and the nature of, cooperation within the subregion. Consequently, cooperative processes in particular subregions cannot be fully explained in terms of the actors within the subregion itself.

In this chapter, after a brief discussion of subregional identity, I examine the geopolitical implications for the Caucasus and central Asia of the behavior of contiguous regional powers – Russia, Turkey, and Iran.[6] I then extend the analysis to include the role of United States as a key outside actor. This is followed by a discussion of China and Afghanistan and then by a discussion of the role of the international private sector. The final brief section concerns the role of international organizations, notably the EU, the OSCE, and the UN "family," in fostering or inhibiting the development of subregional cooperation.

Dr. Yunusov's chapter demonstrates that intraregional impetus for cooperation is weak in the southern Caucasus. The same holds true for central Asia, and this weakness plays a critical constraining role on the process. It also suggests that the voice of the region in discussions of regional cooperation is weak and is likely to remain so. As a result, discourse on regional cooperation is currently dominated by external voices, whose agendas are not so much based on a disinterested calculation of the interests of the subregion as on drawing the region into structures that reflect the interests of outside actors. In the absence of coherent and forceful intra-subregional agendas for cooperation, the southern tier states are objects rather than subjects in whatever cooperative movement occurs. There is no particular reason to believe that such movement will correspond to the real interests of the states of the region.

## Subregional Identity in the Southern Tier

It is worth dwelling for a moment on the meaning of the concepts of subregion and subregional cooperation as they are used here as well as on the issue of regional boundaries. For the purposes of this analysis, a subregion is a group of states or parts of states whose affairs (or perceptions of them) are more tightly intermingled among themselves than are the affairs of each with states or substate entities outside the area in question. The definition of regional boundaries is to some degree arbitrary, since its identity is likely to be less strong at the edge than at the core.[7]

Moreover, the intensity of subregional identity and the definition of subregional boundaries depends to a considerable degree on the issue area. The underlying theme of this book concerns the capacity and potential of subregionalism, as an idea and as an approach to institution-building, to make a contribution to conflict prevention, management, and resolution. In the realm of security and conflict, central Asia and the southern Caucasus have substantially different identities. The three southern Caucasian states form a "security complex," a group of states in which no member can construct its foreign and security policies without close attention to the others.[8] The intermingling of minority populations is a second factor creating a subregional sociopolitical complex in the southern Caucasus. It could be argued that central Asia (Kazakhstan, Uzbekistan, Tajikistan, Turkmenistan, and Kyrgyzstan) forms a comparable complex for similar reasons.

However, the security affairs of Georgia or Armenia can proceed sensibly without systematic reference to, say, Tajikistan or Kyrgyzstan, and vice versa. Likewise, there is little socioethnic connection between the two zones. In this issue area, therefore, separate consideration of the two areas of the former Soviet southern tier makes more sense than does an effort to cover both in a single analysis.

On the other hand, in the area of economics and, in particular, energy development, this division does not make much sense. The energy resources of the Caspian Basin are found on both the

Caucasian and the central Asian littorals, and future infrastructural decisions may produce an integrated Caspian Sea energy complex. Although the two areas of the southern tier do not constitute
a security complex, they do form a subregional economic complex.
If economic integration proceeds, and states become dependent on
linkages across the Caspian, this would foster the creation of a
broader southern tier regional security identity.

One final point bears mentioning in a discussion of subregional
boundaries of analysis. The growth of regional identity is dependent
not only on processes and perceptions within the space in question,
but also on how outsiders relate to that identity. Regional identity will
be affected by the extent to which others perceive the space as a unity
and deploy resources accordingly. As shall be seen below, in important respects all the major external actors treat the southern tier as a
single arena of policy. For these reasons, despite the obvious differences between the two areas, there is some sense in focusing on the
southern tier as a whole in consideration of subregional cooperation.

## Power Politics and Subregional Cooperation

Much recent commentary on the region has been dominated by com-
parisons to the nineteenth-century Great Game between Russia and
Great Britain for influence over the space between Russia and India.
This is not, however, a particularly helpful historical referent, as the current situation is multipolar rather than bipolar. Unlike in the nineteenth
century, the communities of the region today form internationally recognized states, entitled to the protections of international law. They are
substantially involved in international organizations. Finally, the current
involvement of outside actors in the region is not limited to states, but
includes the private corporate sector, particularly the energy sector.
Many of the energy firms involved are at least in part transnational. In
short, external agency is much more multifaceted than it was in the earlier period. The various levels of external engagement, i.e., state, multilateral, and corporate, interact in complex ways. The outcome, consequently, is harder to predict than a traditional bipolar game.

## Russian Interests and Policy in the Southern Tier

The first and arguably most important actor to consider in this context is Russia. The discussion of Russia is problematic, because its

foreign policy making process is ill-defined, poorly understood, and profoundly pluralistic. Russian policy in the subregion can be loosely divided into three phases. In the first (1991-92), the affairs of the other former Soviet republics were largely ignored by a government that stressed the need to sustain close relations with the west. At an unofficial or semiofficial level, various agencies (e.g., the military, left with a string of bases in the region and a strategic perspective that accentuated the southern Caucasus' central role in Russian security) and groups (e.g., the nostalgic nationalist component of the Russian Duma) were heavily involved in the subregion, largely in a more or less successful effort to destabilize Georgia and Azerbaijan.

By 1993-94, this pluralism had consolidated into a somewhat consensual view that the new states contiguous to Russia were too important to ignore and that the previous lack of policy had been detrimental to Russian vital interests. Russian parliamentarians, foreign ministry officials, military officers, and ministers came to the fairly unanimous conclusion that, for historical and geopolitical reasons, Russia had special responsibilities and rights in the region that should be accepted and respected by other states. Russia also had special interests that dictated preeminence in the former Soviet space and should retain its military presence in the other newly independent states (with the qualified exception of the Baltics).[9] The principal instruments in this endeavor were institutional, e.g., the CIS, and military, although there was an important economic component as well, with Russia attempting to maintain its control over the infrastructure, such as pipelines, upon which the states of the southern tier were dependent, and to prevent the development of alternatives.[10]

However, the fiscal, organizational, and personnel crises in the Russian military that developed in the mid-1990s, and the disastrous engagement in Chechnya, coupled with the deepening of western involvement in the development of Caspian energy, drew into question the feasibility of Russia's effort to maintain an exclusive zone of influence in the southern Caucasus. Moreover, the participation of Russian firms, notably LUKOIL and GazProm, in production and infrastructural consortia once again diversified the process of policy formulation. The result has been an increasing degree of uncertainty in a number of aspects of Russian policy in the region.

This is typified by the confusion over the issue of ownership of the Caspian Sea floor. The original position was quite clear. Russia, along with Iran, took the view that resources lying beyond the twelve mile zone of littoral states were owned jointly and should be developed cooperatively. On the other hand, LUKOIL has been granted shares in a number of production ventures that lie outside territorial waters but within the economic zone claimed by Azerbaijan. This led to the bizarre picture of then Russian Energy Minister Boris Nemtsov attending the opening of the Chirag field in 1997 at the same time as the Russian foreign ministry was claiming that the field had been developed illegally.

In late 1996, then Foreign Minister Yevgenii Primakov appeared to back away from the maximal Russian position on the sea floor by offering to extend the exclusive zone of exploitation of littoral states to forty-five miles. The bilateral agreement on the division of the Caspian Shelf negotiated between Kazakhstan and Russia in mid-1998 suggested a further Russian retreat, since the zone in question is now divided between the two states without obvious reference to previous Russian positions. If the agreement is replicated with other littoral states, it will produce a de facto sectoral division of the Caspian floor that has hitherto been strenuously resisted by Russian negotiators. This suggests that economic considerations, notably the profit motive of Russian energy producers, are playing an increasingly important role in Russian policy formulation in the southern Caucasian and Caspian littoral subregions.

Turning to the issue area of security there has been little evidence, despite the above, of change in Russian policy toward the major conflicts of the region, in particular Abkhazia in Georgia and Nagorno-Karabakh in Azerbaijan. Russia became involved in these conflicts, in part, because they could be used as leverage over these two states.[11] As long as the parties fail to translate cease fires into sustainable political settlements, they will remain an important source of vulnerability to Russian manipulation.

The picture of Russian involvement in the region is, thus, increasingly ambiguous. That said, certain principles appear to remain valid. The Russian Federation, and much of the foreign policy elite within it, seek to retain a position of military and political preeminence within the southern Caucasus.[12] In the energy sector, Russia seeks to obtain as large a share of production as it can for its energy industry and continues to resist a diversification of export routes that would reduce its dominance over the region's energy export infrastructure, which it inherited from the Soviet era. That there is a significant political motivation here is evident from the fact that Russia has persisted with this policy despite US offers of a share for Russian concerns in pipeline ventures (e.g., Ceyhan) that would bypass Novorossiisk, and despite the fact that the Russians as yet can provide no credible alternative for forward shipment of oil delivered to its terminal at Novorossiisk.[13]

What are the implications of the above for subregional cooperation? To the extent that efforts at subregional cooperation produce durable settlements to the subregion's two major conflicts, Russian leverage over Georgia and Azerbaijan would be reduced. In other words, such cooperation is inconsistent with one of the principal lines of Russian policy, and one would expect the Russian Federation to impede it. This is evident in the obstructive Russian approach to the Minsk process, with respect to Nagorno-Karabakh, and the Geneva process, with regard to Abkhazia.[14]

Moreover, any substantial normalization in the region would reduce Armenian strategic dependence on Russia, currently Russia's one reliable partner within the subregion. The development of a more positive relationship between Armenia and Azerbaijan and the normalization of Armenia's relations with Turkey would remove this dependence. More generally, for reasons already stated, disunity within the region makes Russian involvement and pursuit of its interests easier. Consequently, Russia would be predisposed to resist the evolution of any regional security cooperation that favored the development of a common perspective among the three states of the region. This explains Russian ambivalence to Shevardnadze's proposal for a Trans-Caucasian zone of peace. It also explains President Yeltsin's efforts to advance an alternative structure for regional security that placed Russia in a controlling role.

Similar geopolitical considerations underpin the development of Russian perspectives on the involvement of outside powers as they relate to subregional cooperation. As shall be discussed below, the economic and security involvement of other major external players have the effect of balancing, if not replacing, Russia's role in the southern Caucasus and central Asia. Not surprisingly, Russia continues to resist infrastructural options that tie the region to the west.

Russia is also deeply concerned about the evolution of political and security relations between the countries of the region and external states such as the United States and multilateral structures like NATO that do not include Russia and over which Russia cannot exercise a veto. In the realm of peacekeeping, Russia has consistently opposed the insertion of multilateral forces in which Russia does not have a leading role.[15] Russian foreign policy elites have expressed serious reservations about possible security roles for non-CIS multilateral forces in the region. In the Minsk Group context, it has sought to ensure that its own forces would play a dominant role in any peace force deployed in and around Nagorno-Karabakh.

The preferred framework for subregional cooperation in the southern Caucasus and central Asia is one that ties the region to its northern neighbor. This is evident, for example, in Russian proposals on joint air defense and border control. As already noted, it is also evident in Russian approaches to the question of energy export.

## Turkey

Turkey's policy is also strongly affected by power political considerations.[16] Turkey received a major strategic benefit from the 1991 collapse of the USSR in that its major contiguous security threat was removed from its borders. From a geopolitical perspective, its principal motivation in the subregion appears to be to prevent or to minimize any reconsolidation of the Russian position in proximity to its borders.[17]

The second geopolitical dimension of Turkey's motivations in the region is denial of influence to Iran, a concern reflecting both traditional rivalries in the pre-Soviet era, the clash of Persian and Turkic cultures in both parts of the southern tier, and Turkish concern over Islamic extremism.

Third, in the 1990s Turkey has also been forced to reconsider the strong European orientation of its foreign policies, since key members of the European Union are unwilling to give serious consideration to Turkish membership, while many of the transitional states of central Europe have been invited to begin the process of accession to the Union. As a consequence, many in Turkey have sought to reorient the country's foreign policy toward the larger Turkic community. An active policy in the southern Caucasus and central Asia fits well with any such reorientation.

The final aspect of Turkish preoccupations in the southern tier concerns economic interest. Turkey has a substantial interest in the region's energy development as it is a proximate source of energy for the Turkish economy and reduces dependence on Middle

Eastern energy resources. Turkish energy requirements are expected to grow extremely rapidly, particularly natural gas consumption in the power generation sector. The results are evident in the strong Turkish interest in access to Turkmen gas shipped via Iran. Turkey has also evinced a strong interest in becoming the major outlet for pipelines from the Caspian region to the world market. The other major consideration for Turkish commitment to overland routes across Anatolia to the Mediterranean is environmental concern over the Straits.

Outside the energy sector, the collapse of the USSR opened a wide new market in the southern Caucasus and also in central Asia. Turkey was well placed geographically and culturally to take advantage of the opportunity and did so. In the southern Caucasus, for example, Turkish trade with Georgia and Azerbaijan now exceeds in value the trade of either of those countries with Russia.

Turkish interests in the southern tier are also closely related to domestic political issues. Turkey is home to substantial diaspora populations from the northern Caucasus, Georgia, and Azerbaijan. This provides Turkish politicians with incentives to support the agendas of minorities in the northern Caucasus and Georgia. In the case of Azerbaijan, it promotes support for the Azerbaijani position in the Karabakh conflict.

More broadly, the concept of Turkic community has some resonance with Turkish nationalism. Turkey was formed in the context of a competition between two identities; that favored by Ataturk, which focused on the creation of a nation in Anatolia, and a broader pan-Turkic conception stressing Turkey's links to related ethnic groups in Azerbaijan, Turkmenistan, Uzbekistan, Kyrgyzstan, and Kazakhstan. Although Ataturk's conception of the nation has dominated Turkey's recent history, the collapse of the USSR and the liberation of the Turkic union republics have rekindled the pan-Turkic idea in Turkish politics.[18]

Economic and cultural considerations, therefore, give Turkey an interest in furthering cooperative initiatives in the subregion. This accounts, in part anyway, for Turkish leadership in the post-1991 effort to organize the Black Sea Economic Cooperation (BSEC). The same is broadly true of Turkey's political interests. From a geostrategic perspective, the southern Caucasus serves a useful role as a buffer between Turkey and Russia. The development of reasonably robust subregional structures of political cooperation and their linkage to the west through instruments such as NATO's Partnership for Peace (PfP) would enhance this role. This consideration also gives Turkey an interest of sorts in resolution of the Karabakh question. As already noted, the Karabakh conflict is a major source of Russian leverage in the subregion. Removing the question would diminish that leverage, allowing Armenia to play a more independent role in the subregion's affairs.[19] On the other hand, strong sympathies for Azerbaijan limit Turkey's capacity to promote settlement options that genuinely address the concerns of the Armenian minority in Karabakh.

Although Turkish interests in the region have tended to compete with those of Russia, this tension should not be overestimated. Turkish trade with Russia far exceeds in value its trade with the southern Caucasian states. The same is true of Turkish contracting and investment. And despite Russia's current weakness, the Russians are in a position to make life uncomfortable for Turkey, as was evident in the 1997-98 controversy over the sale of Russian air defense systems to the government of Cyprus. This suggests that any competition in the Russian-Turkish relationship in the southern Caucasus is likely to be significantly muted.

## Iran

Iran's political initiatives in the region have been limited largely to an abortive effort to mediate the Karabakh conflict in 1992,[20] and its involvement in the process of conflict resolution in Tajikistan. It is excluded from, or plays only a minor role in, the principal multilateral institutions involved in the region (OSCE, the CIS, and the UN). Its efforts through the Economic Cooperation Organization (ECO) and the Caspian Sea Cooperation have not amounted to much. Its policies in the region have defied the expectations of Washington Iranophobes in their moderate approach and pragmatism in implementation.

This is not to say that Iran has completely eschewed involvement in the region's politics and conflicts. As with Turkey, the collapse of the USSR held major benefits for Iran, since it removed a major contiguous military adversary. It also generated numerous new economic opportunities, while opening the field to Iranian cultural and religious assertion.

The change also contained several important dangers. Iran's most evident political interest in the southern Caucasus concerns Azerbaijan. The great majority of Azeris live in north-western Iran. Nationalist groups in Azerbaijan openly express irredentist designs with respect to Iran.[21] Partly in response to these factors, Iran has attempted to manipulate religious factions in Azeri politics and has proffered a degree of support to both Armenia and to Karabakh in their dispute with Azerbaijan. Such activities have the advantage of distracting Azerbaijani leaders from more ambitious nationalist agendas. They also serve as a form of deterrence by underlining Iran's capacity to inflict pain if necessary. Nor is Iran comfortable with the growth of Turkish influence on its northern border, in part for historical reasons and in part because of the close and deepening Turkish-American relationship in the region.

Iran's political agenda in central Asia is less defined, with the exception of the Afghan question. Here, ironically, the conservative secular leaders of central Asia and, for that matter, of Russia have a common cause with the Iranian leadership in resistance to the Taleban. This may explain, in part, their cooperation in the quest for a political settlement to the Tajik conflict.

Beyond this, Iran is an economic player of some note in the sub-region. Outside the energy sector, Iran has made significant inroads in trade throughout the southern tier. It is Armenia's largest trading partner and has significant trading relations with both Azerbaijan and Georgia. However, it has had considerable difficulty in consolidating these economic relationships because it is a weak producer of capital goods. It possesses few of the technologies needed by the new states for the exploitation of natural resources and for the reconstruction of industry and agriculture, and it has an inadequate domestic financial base for large-scale capital export.[22]

Nonetheless, it is an important player in the key energy sector. As a Caspian littoral state, it has a claim to the Caspian seabed, the sectoral division of which it has adamantly opposed, largely because the Iranian sector apparently lacks significant energy reserves. This stand on the seabed issue limits its potential for cooperation with the other major littoral states, other than Russia which takes a similar stand.

Second, Iran is the shortest route to the sea for both central Asian and southern Caucasian energy export. All other things being equal, Iran stands to gain significantly from the transshipment and processing of energy exports from the Caspian Basin, and its current policy aims to encourage the use of Iranian routes for such exports. It has had limited success in this regard, particularly with regard to natural gas exports from Turkmenistan. There is some prospect, moreover, of implementation of agreements between Kazakhstan and Iran regarding oil swaps. Finally, the Sino-Kazakhstani energy agreements of 1997 envisage the construction of pipelines not only to China, but also to Iran.

The problem, as already mentioned, is the profound hostility of the United States toward Iran and its opposition to any investment decision that might benefit the latter. This impedes Iranian efforts to realize its potential as an export route and limits the possibilities for Iranian participation in production consortia. This, too, has solidified the de facto Russian-Iranian alliance in the region. Both are deeply discomfited by the expanding role of the US and the US private sector in the region.

Iran, like the other contiguous powers, has an interest in orienting cooperative projects (e.g., energy infrastructure) toward the south. It shares with Russia an interest in impeding the development of east-west cooperative linkages that tie the region more closely to the west, increase the western, and particularly US, presence in the region, and maintain Iranian isolation.

**The United States**

US policy in the region reflects a broad array of strategic and domestic political and economic interests. At the strategic level, US policy has focused increasingly on the consolidation of the independence of new states of the southern tier, preventing the expansion of Iranian influence in the region, and tying the region's economies to the west. This general line of policy is constrained to some extent by Russian-US relations, as discussed below. It is also affected in important respects by domestic interests in the United States. Much of the recent evolution of US policy toward the southern Caucasus is not solely a result of an evolving understanding of the geopolitical significance of the region. It also reflects the increasingly intense domestic competition between the Armenian lobby and US energy firms seeking to deepen their involvement in the region.

One of the greatest uncertainties affecting the region at the time of writing is the direction of US policy. This is particularly true with respect to Iran. The United States, until recently, remained implacably hostile to Iran in general, and toward Iranian activities in the southern tier in particular. US policy makers consider Iran to be a state supporter of terrorism and an implacable opponent of US efforts to secure peace in the Middle East. In addition to applying sanctions directly against Iran, the United States has impeded Iranian efforts to participate in production consortia in the Caspian region by forbidding US firms to coparticipate and by putting pressure on the governments concerned to exclude Iran. This was evident, for example, in the Azerbaijani "deal of the century," where the Iranian National Oil Company (INOC) was originally allocated a share of ownership, but was then cut out as a result of US opposition.[23]

However, there is now some evidence of change in US policy toward Iran. Although congress remains unmoved in its antipathy, the executive branch is displaying considerable interest in evidence of growing moderation in Iranian foreign policy and domestic politics. The new Iranian executive has displayed interest in improving relations with the United States, which has to some extent been reciprocated by US executive agencies and spokespersons, including the president and the secretary of state. Such a shift appears to be favored by US business, not least by the energy sector, which stands to benefit from the diversification of export infrastructure options in the southern tier.

Thus far, however, change has been very tentative, as the administration is aware of the potential domestic political risks associated with a change of policy towards Iran. Moreover, the domestic balance in Iran remains unstable; it is unclear what the outcome of the power struggle between President Khatemi and more conservative clerical circles will be. Finally, despite the soothing rhetoric, there has been little evidence of substantial change in Iranian policy on the issues identified by Washington as crucial prerequisites for an improvement in the overall relationship. Statements by US officials responsible for central Asia and the Caucasus in the spring of 1998 indicate that there has thus far been little change in the general policy of containing Iran and excluding it to the extent possible from the development of the Caspian energy sector.[24]

A second major source of uncertainty in US policy in the southern tier is the US relationship with Russia and developments in the Russian Federation. In the 1990s, US interest in consolidating the new states' independence and expanding US influence in the area was constrained by the priority accorded to maintaining a stable and constructive relationship with Russia and not jeopardizing the political position of reformers within Russia. US interest in the strategic arms control process, weapons proliferation in the context of post-Soviet instability, maintenance of the conventional arms regime in Europe, and securing Russian acquiescence in, if not support of, US and western policy toward the conflict in the former Yugoslavia and sanctions against Iraq greatly outweighed any possible interest the United States had in the southern tier itself.

Moreover, US policy makers rightly perceived the new states to be prone to significant instability. The United States was itself unenthusiastic about taking an active role in producing security in the region. There was some hope in 1992-94 that the Russian Federation could play a constructive role in strengthening subregional security. This perhaps explains the lack of any substantial response to Russian intervention in Georgia and Tajikistan.

Three factors contributed to a shift in American emphasis in 1994-97. First, as noted, Russian regional policy tilted away from liberal internationalism and benign neglect of its neighbors toward a nationalistic and power-political effort to reassert Russian influence at the expense of the newly independent states of the region. In consequence, the policy of reliance on Russia to take the lead in the management of the security affairs of the southern tier was increasingly subject to question.

Second, the great instability and unpredictability of Russian domestic politics called into question the wisdom of sacrificing independence in policy to the sensitivities of Russian partners. If the outcome in Russia itself was to be the emergence of a revanchist semi-authoritarian regime dedicated to the restoration of the Soviet empire, then it made little sense to forswear an activist regional policy that might balance Russia.

The third major impetus for change was the growing realization of the dimensions of the region's energy reserves. When the states of the region gained their independence in 1991, little was known of the size of these reserves, although US firms (notably Chevron) had been active in negotiating entry into the Caspian energy sector well before the collapse of the USSR. As exploration proceeded on both sides of the Caspian in the early 1990s, it became clear that the region would become a major new player in world energy markets, with a likely impact roughly comparable to that of the North Sea.

This had two implications for US policy, the first of which was strategic. The United States was and is increasingly uncomfortable with the concentration of energy reserves and production in the Persian Gulf. The instability of the region carries the potential of significant interruption of global energy supplies. Excessive regional concentration of production gives Middle Eastern energy producers an uncomfortable degree of market power.

In the 1998 pricing context, this seems hard to believe. However, reserves outside the Gulf, such as the North Sea and the Alaskan North Slope, are being depleted fairly rapidly and few new energy reservoirs are coming on line. Demand, although temporarily depressed by the economic contraction in Asia, may be expected to recover as economic conditions improve. In the longer term, the growth of Asian demand, and in particular that of China, will make a significant difference in the balance between supply and demand in the global energy market. All other things being equal, this will have obvious effects on price. In such a market environment, the diversification of sources of energy is perceived to have considerable strategic importance.

From the perspective of US corporate interests, the Caspian Basin is a particularly attractive prospect despite its perceived political instability, and energy firms such as Chevron, Mobil, and AMOCO have become heavily involved there. US policy, responsive to these interests, has become increasingly active as well. This activism appears to be focused on enhancing the region's autonomy and tying it to the west. It retains the traditional emphasis on limiting Iran's involvement and relies quite strongly on association with Turkey.

This includes the subject matter of this study, namely subregional cooperation. The most significant components of American policy in this regard are energy production, transportation infrastructure, and security. In the first case, the United States has generally supported the Azerbaijani position on sectoral division of the undersea reserves of the Caspian Basin because this will enhance the autonomy of Caspian energy producers from both Russia and Iran.

With regard to the second, the United States has supported the development of multiple pipeline alternatives, balancing its residual desire to appease Russia with its increasing preoccupation with enhancing the autonomy of the states of the southern tier. As a matter of policy, the United States continues to resist transportation alternatives involving Iran, although American policy makers appear to accept that the cost of attempting to prevent European and other non-American firms from exploring of Iranian transportation alternatives exceeds the potential benefits. As an American spokesman put it recently when asked about the US attitude toward Shell's involvement in an Iranian option for the export of Turkmen gas, "They make decisions as they so choose."[25]

There is particularly strong US support for the Baku-Ceyhan alternative for the export of the major anticipated volumes of Azerbaijani oil, presuming this route is commercially viable.[26] This underscores the key role of Turkey in America's regional policy as well as the American commitment to Georgia's aspiration to serve as a transit corridor between Europe and Asia. The United States is also actively promoting the study of trans-Caspian options for the export of central Asia's oil and gas products, having recently funded a feasibility study for an undersea pipeline from Turkmenistan to Azerbaijan. If built, this line would contribute profoundly to integrating the southern Caucasus and central Asia into a single regional complex.

Despite the gradual evolution of American perspectives, the United States remains committed to the constructive engagement of Russia in the southern tier. It has not opposed the northern (Baku-Novorossiisk) variant for export of Azerbaijan's oil, and has supported publicly the Caspian Pipeline Consortium (CPC) variant for Kazakhstan's oil, arguing that the projected export volumes justify both Russian and western variants and that the principal criterion for any (other than Iranian) route should be its commercial viability. Moreover, American spokesmen have invited Russian equity participation in non-Russian pipeline alternatives, such as Baku-Ceyhan).[27]

In the area of security, the United States has sought to promote indigenous cooperative capacity for the management of subregional security, particularly in central Asia. In the PfP context, the United States has supported the development of the Central Asian Peacekeeping Battalion (CENTASBAT) and has financed and participated in joint training exercises. The hope is, apparently, that the development of this subregional capability will reduce the central Asian states' dependence on Russia in dealing with threats to regional security, a dependence recently underscored by the apparent victory of the Taleban in northern Afghanistan.

It is noteworthy, however, that the United States has taken no obvious position on proposals for subregional cooperation that originate within the region, or on institutions such as the Central Asian

Economic Union. This may reflect an assessment (probably accurate) of the prospects for their implementation. On the other hand, it may suggest a lack of interest in the development of significant independent regional capacity, as this might complicate the integrative agenda of US policy in the subregion.

## The Rest

In addition to these major players, there are a number of other state or quasi-state actors whose policies impinge upon subregional prospects for cooperation, two of which are contiguous. China has two principal stakes in the region. In the first instance, China's western province of Xinjiang evinces increasing instability, as the Uighur population asserts its claim to minority rights, if not to self-determination. There are significant kindred populations in both Kazakhstan and Kyrgyzstan, and there is significant sympathy for the plight of the Uighurs in both countries. This gives China a significant security stake in contiguous states of central Asia.[28]

In addition, China sees the central Asian zone as a potentially significant market for consumer and light industrial products. Third, as already noted, China is a major potential market for central Asian energy resources. China became a net importer of energy products in the 1990s, and as industrialization proceeds, its import requirements will grow rapidly. This explains the intense Chinese interest in eastward variants for the export of the region's energy resources, exemplified by the agreement for Chinese exploitation of one of Kazakhstan's major hydrocarbon basins and the construction of an oil pipeline from Kazakhstan to the Chinese pipeline head in Xinjiang.

China has expressed little interest in projects for subregional cooperation in the southern tier. This may reflect its apparent skepticism about formal subregional arrangements in east Asia itself. That said, the Chinese factor may have indirect impact on prospects for subregional cooperation. There is an historical legacy of Chinese efforts to dominate eastern Turkestan, and Chinese security concerns regarding Turkic minorities in Xinjiang may be translated into pressure on Kazakhstan and Kyrgyzstan. Furthermore, the great size and economic and demographic weight of China, when compared to its western neighbors, poses an existential threat to central Asia, occasioning considerable nervousness among elites of the region. This shared perception of threat may favor the construction of balancing subregional economic and security arrangements. It is noteworthy, however, that such cooperation would be of a distinctly realist variety, that is, of balancing against threat. It is not likely that this would produce functional spillover into other fields.

Finally, there is Afghanistan. The civil conflict in Afghanistan has had important spillover effects for central Asia since independence, in part as a result of the existence of significant Uzbek and Tajik populations in northern Afghanistan. The Afghan civil conflict merged to a considerable extent with the Tajik civil war in the early- and mid-1990s. The cooperative Russian/Uzbek/Kyrgyz/Kazakh peacekeeping effort in Tajikistan stemmed, in considerable measure, from the concerns of the Uzbek and other governments that the victory of radical Islamists in Afghanistan would destabilize more traditional areas of central Asia such as the Ferghana Valley, which is shared by Uzbekistan, Kyrgyzstan, and Tajikistan.

As the Taleban's hold on southern and central Afghanistan strengthened in 1996-97, the Uzbeks and Tajiks, presumably with Russian assistance, sought to sustain a buffer zone in northern Afghanistan. Taleban victories in mid-1998, however, suggest that this effort had failed. The relatively stable secular authoritarian regimes bordering on Afghanistan (notably Uzbekistan and Turkmenistan) now face a common threat, namely a reasonably consolidated Afghanistan governed by a hostile regime with a strong religious mission that challenges the legitimacy of neighboring governments. This, too, may favor subregional security cooperation as the states of the region balance against a common threat.

In this effort, the central Asian states are likely to make common cause with Russia and Iran. Russian elites remain seriously concerned about the threat of political Islam to the Federation itself. Iran displays little enthusiasm for politicized Sunni revivalism, particularly since the Taleban has specifically targeted Shi'a Muslims (e.g., the Hazara) who have long-standing and close ties to religious circles in Iran.

Religious links are one aspect of a broader phenomenon throughout the southern tier that significantly constrain the emergence of wide-ranging alignments that link subgroups of internal and external actors. To some extent, cooperation coincides in different functional areas and is mutually reinforcing. In other instances, alignments in one issue area contradict alignments in another. The principal example of the first is the emerging cooperation between Russia and Iran, embracing the regional politics of energy, concern with western involvement, and regional security. The obvious counterpart to this emerging alignment is the deepening cooperative relationship between the United States and Turkey which challenges the Russian geopolitical position in the region, aims to define energy exit routes from both the southern Caucasus and central Asia and, more broadly, the direction of economic development of the region as a whole. In addition, the alliance seeks to limit the influence and role of Iran in these areas. These two external powers are joined in this agenda, for the most part, by Georgia and Azerbaijan.

The reality in the central Asian sector is somewhat less clear. Here, for the most part, the principal states have sought to limit Russian influence and have explored, if rather diffidently, possibilities for subregional cooperation as a means of doing so. To some extent, the Central Asian Economic Union is a manifestation of a common understanding that the region faces significant external pressures, and that it may be better able to control these pressures as a group than the states of the region are individually.

On the other hand, their dependence on Russia remains intense, as does their vulnerability. This limits their capacity to strive unambiguously for dissociation from the Russian Federation. In some instances, states of the region have complemented the effort to construct autonomous subregional structures of cooperation with membership in political and economic structures that tie them to Russia (e.g., the Belarus-Russia-Kazakhstan-Kyrgyzstan union). And in the realm of security, the shared sense of threat emanating from Afghanistan has tied the "frontline" states closely to Russia. Moreover, the potential for the Central Asian Economic Union to become a real player is limited not only by the lack of complementarity between the region's economies, but also by the asymmetrical subregional balance of power. Smaller states such as Kyrgyzstan and Turkmenistan are tempted to use extraregional linkages to balance the intraregional preponderance of Uzbekistan.

The common characteristic in the above is the extent to which cooperative agendas in the southern tier reflect, in considerable measure, the overlapping and competitive interests of outsiders rather than any particularly strong definition of autonomous and shared subregional interest.

## The Private Sector

There is less to say here since, on the whole, involved companies have avoided taking public positions on political issues that carry potential for controversy. Analysis here must, consequently, be inferential. All other things being equal, energy corporations, like other private enterprises, balance profit against risk, both political and economic. The higher the potential profit, the greater the tolerance for risk.[29]

It is difficult to calculate risk and projected cost in unstable, under-regulated, and, consequently, unpredictable operating environments. Unpredictability in the southern tier reflects not only the weakness and lack of accountability of institutional and legal structures of the subregion's states, but also the fact that energy development is necessarily a multistate activity. Any export of an energy product requires the construction of infrastructure through at least one intermediate state. The multiplicity of conflicts in proximity to favored export routes (e.g., Karabakh and Abkhazia and Kurdistan for western routes, Chechnya and Daghestan for northern routes to Novorossiisk, Afghanistan for southern routes to the Indian Ocean) further complicates matters.

Another significant aspect of private sector calculation concerns relations with the home state. In the literature on transnationalism and globalism, international enterprises are frequently assumed to be autonomous actors, free-floating profit seekers. In reality, they are semiautonomous. Their pursuit of corporate objectives is affected in significant ways by the interests of the states in which they operate and/or are incorporated. For example of the effect of state interest on corporate policy, direct intervention by Samuel Berger, President Clinton's national security adviser, convinced British Petroleum to back away from its earlier support for a Russian route for new oil and to endorse a pipeline from Baku to Supsa, bypassing the Russian Federation.[30] British Petroleum's apparent preference for the northern route may reflect that company's deep involvement in the Russian energy sector and the consequent fact that BP must be attentive to Russian preferences.

On the other hand, corporate preferences may affect state policy. Policy makers and energy industry representatives interact continually and privately in the process of congressional and executive lobbying as well as at such public events as the annual Cambridge

Energy Research Associates (CERA) conferences and the May 1998 Crossroads of the World Conference in Istanbul.[31] The effects are clearly evident in the gradual shift of US policy with respect to Azerbaijan. The congressional ban on US humanitarian and development assistance to Azerbaijan has already been noted. However, since its initial adoption, the relevant section of US legislation (Section 907 of the Freedom Support Act) has been weakened by including a right of presidential waiver. There is considerable chance of its repeal. This evolution owes much to sustained lobbying on the part of US oil firms and their use of Washington influentials such as former national security advisers Brent Scowcroft and Zbigniew Brzezinski as well as Henry Kissinger to argue their case.

Private sector actors have also exercised considerable influence over more technical aspects of major state policies. It appears, for example, that the United States is now backing away from the idea of simultaneous construction of oil and gas pipelines under the Caspian Sea as a result of advice from the private sector to the effect that the technical difficulties of a joint oil and gas project were potentially insurmountable, while oil market conditions were sufficiently different from those in the oil and gas sectors to render a joint project problematic.[32]

Subregional cooperation is potentially significant for private international actors as a means of controlling or minimizing economic and political risk. This is true both for relations among firms as well as for private sector perspectives on diplomatic initiatives. In the former category, all major production and pipeline projects in the Caspian Basin are consortial, shared ownership being a means of reducing individual risk. Subregional cooperation among state actors has at least two significant potential impacts on corporate risk. In the first place, effective subregional cooperation in the area of security can reduce political risk. Second, the development of multilateral regulatory structures in the energy sector could greatly reduce uncertainty and unpredictability. The obvious example here is the Energy Charter sponsored by the European Union among others. The idea of this multilateral instrument is to facilitate trade and investment across state boundaries in the energy sector by establishing shared transparent principles on investment, taxation, and trade in energy. In this respect, private sector actors have a strong interest in the construction of an effective trading and investment regime to the southern tier.

### International Organizations

A wide array of international institutions have been active in the region. These include universal organizations (the United Nations and its specialized agencies, the World Bank, the IMF) and regional ones (the EU, NATO, the OSCE, and the CoE).[33] Their activities include humanitarian efforts, conflict management and resolution, economic development, and governance.

Since the role of international organization is covered in some detail in Andrew Cottey's chapter, I shall not consider this group of actors in detail. Instead, I limit myself to several general observations on their programming as it relates to subregional cooperation. First, given the multilateral character of these organizations, one might expect that there would be a strong subregional component to their programs. After all, many of them were founded to some extent at least on the basis of the proposition that regional and subregional functional cooperation is conducive to peace and welfare.[34]

It is striking, therefore, how little of their activity has a subregional cooperative component, with the exception of certain programs in the energy sector, notably, the EC's (European Commission) TRACECA (Transport Corridor Europe-Central Asia) and INOGATE (Interstate Oil and Gas to Europe) programs. In this latter context, it is noteworthy that the main lines and focus of such programming are designed not so much to foster durable subregional institutions in their own right, but to further the integration of the subregion into the broader EU-dominated regional economy, a process likely to culminate in a classic metropole-periphery pattern, whereby the EU states absorb raw materials and low value-added exports from the subregion and in turn export high value-added manufactured goods to the region. The terms of exchange in such circumstances may be better or worse. That depends, in part, on the negotiating strength of the parties. As already noted, the subregion shows little capacity to generate cooperation that might strengthen its hand in defining the terms of exchange. In such circumstances, whether or not this trend corresponds to the interests of regional states and peoples is an open question.

International assistance programs in the fields of governance and conflict prevention, management, and resolution activities similarly overlook cross-border linkages between ostensibly national conflicts and the potential for transboundary synergies in programming at the

regional level. The inaction and lack of initiative on the part of international organizations in the effort to stimulate viable subregional
cooperation in the sphere of security is paralleled by a degree of
indifference toward, if not active discomfort with, independent subregional initiatives in this area. The GUAM (Georgia, Ukraine,
Azerbaijan, Moldova) alignment, for example, was generally greet-
ed with considerable suspicion as an unwelcome expression of independence that complicated the renewal of the CFE (Conventional
Forces in Europe) arrangement and risked the alienation of Russia,
cooperation with which was necessary in the broader context of
cooperative security in Europe.[35]

To summarize, although international organizations have been
very active in the subregion across a wide range of functional areas,
little of their programming has addressed the question of subregional cooperation meaningfully. In this respect, the southern tier differs
substantially from the Balkans as is evident, for example in the
Royaumont process. The one significant exception is the energy sector. However, in this instance, the organizational agenda is dominated by the interests of the EU and may not adequately address the
interests of the subregional players. Owing to its selectivity, it may
degrade rather than ameliorate the regional security of the southern
Caucasian zone. Rhetorical commitments notwithstanding, international organizations have shown little commitment to capacity-
building for subregional cooperation, and have failed to explore in a
substantial way the limited potential that exists for such cooperation.

## Conclusion

The discussion above suggests several general observations. At the
level of external states, agendas for subregional cooperation do not
reflect particular sensitivity to the needs and interests of players
within the region, but rather the specific interests and calculations of
the external state in question. As these interests are competitive in
important respects, so, too, are the agendas for subregional cooperation. Subregional cooperation has become an instrument of state-
centric power-political competition.

To some extent, these conclusions are reflected in the activities of
international organizations that are, after all, composed of states. It
is probable that one reason the UN and the OSCE lack a clear agenda for subregional cooperation is that they include the competing

state interests within their membership. As for the EU, its activities directed at enhancing subregional cooperation thus far focus on the one issue area its members have no difficulty in agreeing upon, namely access to energy and trade in the southern tier. Both states and international organizations have displayed little interest in promoting indigenous efforts at subregional cooperation.

The third major category of external actor, the international energy corporations, to some extent reflects an agenda distinct from that of states. The geopolitical themes characteristic of state discourse are largely absent in the positions and activities of private firms. Moreover, their concern for commercial viability, profit maximization, and the dispersion or minimization of risk, can and do occasionally influence state policy and favor subregional structures that limit uncertainty. On the other hand, they depend to varying degrees on the good will of powerful state actors and are vulnerable to pressure from them. Again, their interests and actions do not necessarily correspond to what actors in the region would choose if they were in a position to determine the outcome.

The deep divisions among the states and societies of the region as well as their comparative weakness as agents in international relations suggest that they are likely to be more objects than subjects of the process, and that discourse on cooperation is likely to be dominated by external actors. The deep differences in interests among external actors suggest that the effort by any one or group of them to impose an agenda of subregional cooperation is likely to fail. In short, for both endogenous and exogenous reasons, prospects for meaningful subregional cooperation are slim.

## Notes

Much of the background research for this paper was conducted under the auspices of the Humanitarianism and War Project of Brown University. The author is grateful for this support, although the analysis is his own.

1. See S. Neil MacFarlane, "The structure of instability in the Caucasus," *Internationale Politik und Gesellschaft*, no. 4 (1995): 380-394.

2. On this point, see Nuzhet Cem Orekli, "U.S. foreign policy towards energy development," *Turkistan* 98, no. 2 (16 March 1998): 47.

3. See Shireen Hunter, *Central Asia since Independence* (Washington, DC: CSIS, 1996), pp. 1023 and 104-6.

4. See Kenneth Waltz, *Theory of International Politics* (Reading, MA: Addison-Wesley, 1979), passim.

5. See Robert Keohane, *After Hegemony: Cooperation and Discord in the World Political Economy* (Princeton: Princeton University Press, 1984).

6. For the purposes of this analysis, I take geopolitics to mean the relationship between space or location, power, and political behavior.

7. Cf. V. C. Finch, "Geographical science and social philosophy," *Annals of the Association of American Geographers* XXIX, no.1 (1939), p.14.

8. The term is from Barry Buzan, People, *States and Fear* (second edition), (London: Harvester Wheatsheaf, 1991), p.190.

9. On this point, see S. Neil MacFarlane, "Russian conceptions of Europe," *Post-Soviet Affairs* X, no.3 (1994), pp. 234-269.

10. On this point, see S. Neil MacFarlane, "The energy supply dimension," in Hans-Georg Ehrhart and Oliver Thrönert, eds., *European Conflicts and International Institutions: Cooperating with Ukraine* (Baden-Baden: Nomos Verlagsgesellschaft, 1998), p.163.

11. See Thomas Goltz, "The hidden Russian hand," *Foreign Policy*, no. 92 (Fall 1993): 92-116.

12. See, for example, "Vozroditsya li Soyuz? Budushchee Postsovetskogo Protranstva: Tezisy soveta po vneshnei I Oboronnoi Politike," *Nezavisimaya Gazeta* (23 May 1996).

13. This reflects Turkey's unwillingness to countenance any substantial growth of tanker traffic through the Bosphorus and Dardanelles.

14. See, for example, Elizabeth Fuller, "The Karabakh mediation process: Grachev versus the CSCE?" *RFE/RL Research Report III*, no. 23 (10 June 1994): 13-17.

15. 'Vozroditsya li Soyuz', p. 4. Russia did support Georgia's call for a UN peace-keeping force to manage the cease-fire in Abkhazia (interviews at the Mission of the Russian Federation to the United Nations, October 1995). However, given that after the Somalia events of October 1993 and the promulgation of Presidential Decision Directive 25, the probability that the United States would accept a substantial UN peace-keeping force was near zero, open opposition to the proposal was unnecessary. It was not going to happen anyway and Russia could be reasonably certain of American support for the CIS peace-keeping force it preferred, since the Americans needed Russian support for their proposed intervention in Haiti.

16. For a good account of the development of Turkey's strategic interests, see Graham Fuller and Ian Lesser, *Turkey's New Geopolitics* (Boulder, CO: Westview, 1993).

17. As Fuller and Lesser point out in *Turkey's New Geopolitics*, p. 66, the collapse of the Soviet Union seriously complicated Turkish-Iranian relations along at least four axes: Kurdish and Azeri nationalism, Islam versus secularism, and the contest for influence in central Asia.

18. On this point, see Fuller, *Turkey's New Geopolitics*, p. 67, and Shireen Hunter, *The Transcaucasus in Transition* (Washington, DC: CSIS, 1994), p. 45.

19. However, it is reasonably clear that normalization also requires a serious effort on the part of Turkey to address the historical record of Turkish-Armenian relations, a nettle that the Turks are understandably reluctant to grasp.

20. On Iran's diplomacy, see S. Neil MacFarlane and Larry Minear, *Humanitarian Action and Politics: The Case of Nagorno-Karabakh* (Providence, RI: Watson Institute, 1997), p. 31; and Lena Johnson, "The Tajik War: A Challenge to Russian Policy," *Discussion Paper* 7 (London: The Royal Institute for International Affairs, 1998), p. 38

21. Interviews in Baku, January 1998.

22. See Shireen Hunter, *Central Asia since Independence* (Washington, DC: CSIS, 1996), p.135.

23. Ebel, *Energy Choices*, p. 48.

24. See the remarks of Jan Kalicki (Counselor to the U.S. Department of Commerce), as cited in Robert Lyle, "U.S. wants multiple pipelines for Caspian oil," *Turkistan* 98, no 2 (16 March 1998): 47. The obvious exception was the spring 1998 waiver of sanctions against European companies investing in the Iranian energy sector. However, this had more to do with US-European relations than it did with US policy toward Iran. On the waiver, see the speech of Federico Pena at the May 1998 Istanbul Crossroads Conference, as reprinted in *Turkistan* (no volume or number) (6 June 1998).

25. Federico Pena, as cited in "Press Conference Transcript" (28 May, 1998), transmitted in *Turkistan* (no volume, no number) (3 June, 1998).

26. Pena, "Speech at Crossroads Conference."

27. Pena, "Speech at Crossroads Conference."

28. For general background on this point, see Hunter, *Central Asia since Independence*, pp. 126-7.

29. In this context, it is worth noting that current price trends have tended to depress potential profitability and this in turn, presumably, enhances short-term sensitivity to risk. It is probable, consequently, that the development of the regional energy sector will proceed more slowly than was projected in 1996-97. On the other hand, given the life of investment in energy production and infrastructure in a given region, the energy sector takes a longer term view of the problem of risk than do actors in many other sectors.

30. Dan Morgan and David Ottaway, "Power play in the Caspian," *International Herald Tribune* (5 October 1997), p. 15.

31. In 1996, for example, T. Don Stacy lobbied intensively and successfully for an official invitation for Heidar Aliev to visit the United States. The visit set the seal on several important oil deals between US firms and the government of Azerbaijan. Morgan and Ottaway, "Power Play," p. 1.

32. See Michael Lelyveld, "Azerbaijan/Turkey: Baku-Ceyhan oil pipeline likely to win approval," (from RFE/RL), in Turkistan, Volume 98-2-161 (30 September 1998).

33. Contiguous subregional organizations and proto-organizations such as ECO, BSEC, GUAM, and the CIS are treated in the companion paper.

34. On this point, see, for example, the remarks of James Joll on the European Coal and Steel Community, the precursor to the Common Market, in *Europe since 1870* (London: Penguin, 1976), p. 461.

35. Interviews with Georgian and Ukrainian officials, 1997 and 1998.

# 7

# The Southern Caucasus
## Cooperation or Conflict?

*Arif Yunusov*

In 1985, Soviet Prime Minister Mikhail Gorbachev announced the beginning of perestroika in the USSR, raising hopes for positive change across the enormous territory of the Communist empire. These hopes were thwarted when numerous, long smoldering ethnic conflicts reignited. The Caucasus was the first to fall prey, in 1988, with the outbreak of conflict between Armenia and Azerbaijan over the territory of Nagorno-Karabakh. Disputes in neighboring republics soon reemerged, making the Caucasus the most explosive region in the USSR.

The subsequent collapse of the USSR in 1991 heralded independence for the former Soviet republics and hopes for new change. Soviet totalitarianism and failed communist systems would be supplanted, it was believed, by a liberal model of social development, civil government, and economically prosperous democracies. The reality fell far short of this ideal. Formerly sporadic conflicts grew into protracted and bloody wars between newly independent governments, and the entire Caucasus was transformed into a crucible of international tension, eclipsing all other potential "hot spots" in the former USSR. The ideals of the first wave of democrats were quickly compromised, while the old communist nomenklatura gradually reemerged as a powerful actor in the new states. This was especially the case in the Caucasus, which in the post-Communist period was divided into two parts: the southern, comprising Azerbaijan, Armenia and Georgia, and the northern, which remained a part of Russia.

The present work focuses on these southern Caucasian republics of Azerbaijan, Armenia and Georgia (the northern Caucasus remains part of the Russian Federation) and attempts to examine why the post-Communist period has been so dominated by conflict in this area. Why do the numerous conflicts in the southern Caucasus seem beyond resolution? Is regional cooperation possible, and if so, in what form and on what scale? In exploring some potential answers to these questions, this chapter focuses on the internal developments and challenges of the southern Caucasian states and demonstrates how the domestic development of these states is a crucial factor for the potential of future regional cooperation among them.

## The Development of the States of Southern Caucasus

### Azerbaijan

Azerbaijan's journey toward independence began in 1987 as a reaction to crisis, rather than as a positive choice, when it was confronted by the problem of an influx of Azeri refugees migrating from Armenia. The arrival of refugees fueled the national movement that was beginning to emerge under perestroika. As in other Soviet republics, the earliest manifestation of Azeri nationalism was the formation of numerous clubs and societies aimed at the promulgation and revision of Azeri history and culture. By 1987-88, public and political organizations were also emerging. The official beginning of the Nagorno-Karabakh conflict on February 20, 1988, changed this drastically. Both Azerbaijan and Armenia were inundated with refugees: by the beginning of 1990, all of Armenia's 185,00 ethnic Azeris had been expelled. Similarly, 304,000 ethnic Armenians fled Azerbaijan to Armenia and other Soviet republics.[1]

It was under these circumstances that Azerbaijan nationalism began to coalesce into an organized movement, led by the Narodnii Front Azerbaijana, or Azeri Popular Front (APF). Initially, the APF advocated independence through the electoral process and other legitimate institutions and attempted dialogue with the Azeri Communist party. The latter's reluctance to negotiate enabled radical wings in the APF leadership to gain ground. This, coupled with the regime's failure to cope with the flood of refugees from Armenia, led to widespread public dissatisfaction with the Communist party and rising support for the APF. With victory of the nationalist movement in the parliamentary elections slated for early 1990 looking certain, Gorbachev sent the Soviet Army into Azerbaijan to forcibly prop up Communist rule in January of that year. Hundreds of Azeri civilians were killed in the ensuing violence and crackdown launched against the APF. This event was a watershed for it radicalized public opinion against the Soviet communist system. By autumn 1991, President Mutalibov had little choice but to disband the Communist party and allow the APF into the parliament. On October 18, 1991, Azerbaijan proclaimed its independence.

The worsening of the Nagorno-Karabakh conflict severely weakened the former Communist leadership of the country, however, and after the March 1992 pogrom and massacre of Azeris in the Nagorno-Karabakh city of Khodzhali, Mutalibov was forced to resign. The APF took control of the country and in June its leader, Abulfaz Elchibei, was elected president. The new government faced enormous political, social, and economic problems. Fighting in Nagorno-Karabakh dragged on, further weakening an economy in serious disrepair. Azerbaijan was one of the poorest of the former republics of the USSR, and the sharp break in trade with former Soviet partners was not followed with new relations with other regions or countries. However, Azerbaijan's wealth of raw resources, especially natural gas, the presence of highly-qualified specialists (*kadry*), and relatively well-developed heavy industry, instilled post-Soviet Azeri society with a certain degree of hope for economic improvement.

The APF government, however, failed to initiate widespread political and economic reforms. The promise to hold parliamentary elections never materialized, and the Elchibei government continued to rely on the old Soviet nomenklatura. Predictably, this alliance undermined prospects for economic reform. The Azeri defeat in Karabakh (and the ensuing influx of refugees) the following autumn precipitated internal political revolt that was only resolved when Gaidar Aliev, former party secretary in the Brezhnev era, took control of the government in Baku. The new president quickly managed to quell internal disorder, purging the army and bringing separatist elements in the south of the country under control. He was significantly assisted by the cease-fire signed with Armenia in May 1994, bringing an end to the Nagorno-Karabakh conflict that had left 11,000 Azeris dead and nearly 30,000 wounded (6,000 and 20,000, respectively, in Armenia). Armenia had annexed seven districts, comprising 13,000 square kilometers, or nearly 15 percent of the territory of the former NKAO (Nagorno-Karabakh Autonomous Oblast). The total number of refugees pouring into Azerbaijan had swollen to between 750-780,000.[2]

The popular hope was that a swift peace settlement would be reached in which the occupied territories would be liberated and refugees safely repatriated. Azerbaijan's entry into the CIS was viewed as the necessary price for these goals and did not, therefore, encounter strong popular resistance. The economic crisis was also a factor. Inflation, which previously had averaged 34 percent per month, rocketed to around 500 percent per month in 1994. Minimum monthly wages plummeted to US$2, while the per capita cost of living remained US$45.[3] The negotiation of the Natural Gas Contract of 1994 generated euphoria among the Azeri populace and raised expectations for the future.

This was slow to materialize, however. Azerbaijan waited until 1995 to initiate any sort of program for economic reform, and then only under pressure from the International Monetary Fund (IMF). Inflation was curbed and the currency, the manat, stabilized. Privatization began in 1996 and was enlarged a year later to include 59,000 enterprises, valued at US$15 billion. However, by the end of 1997, it was estimated that only 31 percent of these had been privatized (according to Gosizdat of Azerbaijan). Privatization of the industrial infrastructure has not yet taken place.

Formal economic indicators for Azerbaijan look optimistic, allowing the country's leaders to speak with legitimate confidence about the abatement of the crisis, and even the first signs of positive growth. Real growth is up 5 percent in 1998; inflation has nearly been halted, and the currency is strong. Most importantly, Azerbaijan has attracted US$1.2 billion in foreign investment, second in the CIS only to Russia. However, 90 percent of this investment is directed toward natural gas extraction, tying the whole economy to one product. Yet, even according to current production schedules, Azerbaijan will begin to see cash returns from the sale of natural gas only in the year 2010. In the meanwhile, official foreign debt stands at US$579 million.[4] Independent experts place the figure at $1.5 billion and expect that by the year 2010 it will grow to $10-12 billion.[5] Anticipated future profits will likely go toward paying off this debt, rather than toward positive development. Moreover, the vast majority of the country's wealth is concentrated in Baku. The economic situation in Azerbaijan's other cities is grim, and in rural areas nearly catastrophic. Even official sources admit that the agricultural sector remains severely depressed.

These factors are reflected in the living conditions of the Azeri populace. According to data compiled by the Confederation of Azeri Professional Unions, the monthly minimum wage remained unchanged at US$1.50 from February 1995 to September 1998, and the average monthly wage is approximately US$43.[6] High unemployment, especially in rural areas, has forced the Azeri people to seek alternative ways of making ends meet. Since 1993, a large number of Azeris, many of them former refugees, have migrated to other countries, principally Russia, but also to Turkey and Iran. According to the Azeri press, between 1993 and 1997, 1.5 million Azeri nationals traveled to Russia in search of seasonal work. Many of these migrants, of course, have remained for longer than a year – somewhere between 2 and 3 million Azeri citizens. However, 30 percent of the Azeri male population between the ages of 20 and 40 are illegally employed in Russia.[7] According to Russian statistics, the yearly cash flow from Russia to Azerbaijan as a result of this illegal migration equals US$2.5 billion, twice the amount of foreign investment in Azerbaijan.[8] Much of Azerbaijan's present social stability can be explained by this influx of money.

The political scene does not bode well for the wide reforms needed. Almost all power is concentrated in the office of the president and there is little practical delegation of authority. For all intents and purposes, the presidential apparatus is identical to the Central Committee of the Communist Party of Soviet times. The Cabinet of Ministers and the various regional governments play practically no role in the administration of the country. Serious changes in Azerbaijan's political structure are unlikely while Aliev remains in power. He alone defines and rules over the republic's political life. In his rise to power, Aliev has revived not only the old Soviet methods of governance but also the old systems of clan alliances and patronage. While the latter phenomenon has deep roots in all eastern countries, it had a unique history in Azerbaijan during the 1970s and early 1980s. Under Aliev's Soviet administration, the patronage system flourished and the financial underpinnings were laid for the rule of the so-called Nakhchevan clan, of which Aliev is a scion. The clan's position was seriously threatened in the first years of independence, but, thanks in part to the Karabakh conflict, which filled the clan's ranks with refugees from Armenia, it managed to reemerge. By autumn 1993, the Nakhchevan clan had organized itself into a network of seven small political parties aligned around Aliev's New Azerbaijan party. In November 1995, Aliev swept the last of his opposition aside, securing a majority for his constituency in parliament. This was the last hurdle that stood between Aliev and the establishment of an autocracy.

### Armenia

Armenia's attempts to form a new system of government have also been complicated by internal political and economic processes. There, as in Azerbaijan, Gorbachev's declaration of perestroika ushered in a proliferation of "unofficial" societies and organizations.

The primary factor influencing Armenia's development from 1988 onward was the movement to annex the Azeri region (*oblast*) of Nagorno-Karabakh. Political passions ran hotter in Armenia than in Azerbaijan, partly due to the highly politicized nature of ethnic identity issues in the country. The Karabakh question, with its association to the tragic massacres of 1915, galvanized the sense of identity of the almost ethnically homogeneous population and united Armenians across geographic and political boundaries. Another reason was the weakness of the Communist party in Armenia. Unlike Azerbaijan, Armenia never played an important strategic role for the Soviet Union, and the influence of Moscow was correspondingly weaker.

Both of these factors played a significant role in the formation of the Armenian National Movement (ANM) in the summer of 1988. The ANM grew out of the Karabakh Committee, effecting a marriage between the communists and the nationalists and was officially recognized by the former. The leader of the ANM, Levon Ter-Petrosian, began to participate in the republic's parliamentary affairs and when the ANM came to power, a great number of communists were invited to cooperate in government life.[9] The transfer of power from the communists to the nationalists was thus accomplished with comparative ease. To a great extent, this was due to the broad spectrum of membership in the ANM: in this respect, it resembled the national front movements in the Baltic republics more than it did Azerbaijan's APF or the nationalist movements in Georgia.[10]

In June 1990, the ANM easily defeated the communists in parliamentary elections, forming a new government in which the old communist elite was to play a fundamental role. It was under these circumstances that on August 21, 1991, Armenia proclaimed its independence and on November 11, 1991 inaugurated Ter-Petrosian as its first president. ANM leaders secured control of the country by moving quickly to restrict the activity of the numerous paramilitary groups that had become active in the country. A state of emergency was briefly declared in August 1990 which outlawed all illegal military formations. A significant constituency of these groups was absorbed into the regular army, while others disbanded. As a result, Armenia was able to avoid the serious internecine conflicts to which its neighbors fell prey. Furthermore, Armenia was able to raise and organize its military much sooner than Azerbaijan, giving it a distinct advantage in the Karabakh conflict.

Concurrently, the ANM government implemented a program of shock therapy to galvanize economic reform and privatize industry. Exceptionally poor in natural resources, Armenia relied heavily on the importation of raw materials (approximately 70-80 percent) from other countries of the CIS. This was all the more the case because the vast majority of fleeing Azeris had been rural dwellers and their deportation dealt a serious blow to agriculture. The blockade of Armenia by Turkey and Azerbaijan and the deterioration of ties with former Soviet trading partners drove the Armenian economy to the brink of collapse.[11] In March 1992, Ter-Petrosian introduced state-of-emergency measures. The government created a base of operations to direct economic policy, headed by the prime minister, whose decisions were binding. Leaders of the various executive organs were granted the authority to dismiss workers for low productivity. All activities that might possibly disrupt industry were forbidden. The justice system was charged with intensifying its crackdown on crime and given control over the most important industries. These austerity measures hearkened back to Stalinist times.

At the same time, Armenia was the first republic of the CIS to legally proclaim the right to private property, first and foremost, land. Many Armenians were unprepared for this, and consequently most livestock fell into the hands of the former agricultural administration, and the general level of agricultural production declined sharply.[12] Nevertheless, the move prompted steps toward agricultural self-sufficiency. Privatization of industry was initiated in 1992

through the conversion of industries into "closed joint-stock companies," entailing the distribution of shares to each industry's employees. This method of privatization allowed the old communist nomenklatura to amass colossal stock holdings.[13]

Until 1994, Armenia's internal political climate was intimately
bound to the conflict in Karabakh. After the cease fire agreement of
May 1994, however, the Karabakh problem receded somewhat in
Armenian political life. The most pressing issue became the economy, and on this point a change in the public's attitude toward
President Ter-Petrosian was apparent. Widespread criticism of his
policies and allegations of corruption became the norm. The opposition denounced the regime for retreating from the principles of
democracy and attempting to establish a dictatorship. In response,
Ter-Petrosian implemented a series of measures to liberalize the
economy and created a pro-government bloc, "The Republic," consisting of five parties and organizations, with the ANM at its head.
In December 1994, the influential opposition Dashnak party was
banned. Consequently, the pro-government bloc won the July 1995
elections with more than 70 percent of the vote (although with many
allegations of procedural violations).[14]

Still, the country's economy continued to worsen. Many factories
and businesses shut down, and unemployment increased sharply.
Foreign humanitarian aid was gradually replacing wages. According
to the UN, nearly 80 percent of the population today is living poorly or very poorly, with 13 percent below the poverty line.[15] These
conditions resulted in massive emigration. Official sources report
that by the beginning of 1998, 942,000 Armenians had left (a net
loss of 677,000), and other sources estimate the figure to be as high
as one million.[16] As in Azerbaijan, a significant part of the population (unofficially between 600,000 and 1 million) works illegally in
Russia, sending back to Armenia up to $100 million annually.[17] For
a country with a population of only 3.8 million, this carries grave
implications, particularly as the majority of émigrés are urban
males, many of them college educated.

Efforts to build a new system of government have also been difficult. The Nagorno-Karabakh conflict created an emergency situation
that was used to justify strict, centralized supervision of all spheres
of political life. The most important of these involved the distribution of the material, financial, and military resources, which entered
the country from Russia, as well as humanitarian aid from the west

and the Armenian diaspora. Although the clan system does not function in post-Soviet Armenia, devotion to the regime remains one of the chief criteria for professional advancement.

Ter-Petrosian's popularity declined further, and his narrow reelection as president in September 1996 led to serious allegations of election fraud. For the first time in Armenia's post-Soviet history, the government faced serious confrontation with the opposition, which attempted to storm the House of Parliament. Only the intercession of the ministers of Defense, Internal Affairs, and National Security prevented Ter-Petrosian from losing power. Troops were ordered into the capital, political assemblies were banned, and members of the opposition placed under arrest.

Aware of the precariousness of his position, Ter-Petrosian appointed Robert Kocharian, former leader of Armenian Nagorno-Karabakh, as prime minister in March 1997. Kocharian was popular not only among the armed forces and the Armenian diaspora, but also with the opposition. However, Ter-Petrosian faced further problems over statements on the Karabakh conflict. During his 1996 election campaign, Ter-Petrosian insisted that he would not agree to any compromise that would jeopardize the safety of the Karabakh Armenians. But as president, he understood that without the resolution of the conflict there would be no improvement in the country's economy. In an interview in May 1997, he stated that, "Armenia will continue to be unable to rise above its poverty if we do not resolve the Karabakh problem and tear the noose of the economic blockade from our necks." Otherwise, he continued, Armenia's "only alternative will be the politics of survival." He added, "The blockade itself can be overcome; Armenia [in some way] maintains a connection to the outside world through Georgia and Iran. But that amounts to a mere pittance; Armenia is deprived of its primary trading partner, Azerbaijan, from which, and to which, the widest variety of goods flowed before the conflict."[18] On September 26, 1997, Ter-Petrosian made the startling announcement that he would consider a proposal for gradual disarmament that had been drafted by mediators from the Organization for Security and Cooperation in Europe (OSCE) Minsk group, the body of 11 interested OSCE states established in 1992 to help settle the Karabakh question. He asserted that continuation of the conflict would have a damaging effect on Armenia's future development, and that the complete independence demanded by the leaders of Nagorno-Karabakh was unrealistic.

These pronouncements elicited a harsh response from the opposition. Yet more significant was the negative reaction of the leaders of the armed forces, whose political currency had risen sharply in contemporary Armenia, and whose ranks are dominated by emigrants from Nagorno-Karabakh. Indeed, observers today speak of the "Karabakhization" of Armenia, that is, the commandeering of the fundamental governmental structures by emigrants from Karabakh, bringing their own psychology to bear on Armenian politics.[19] On 3 February 1998, Ter-Petrosian appeared on television to announce his resignation, explaining that the protracted power struggle between the "party of peace" (the pragmatists) and the "party of war" (the radicals) had ended with the defeat of the former. On 30 March 1998, Robert Kocharian was chosen as Armenia's new president. Kocharian was, in Ter-Petrosian's terminology, leader of the "party of war," hard-liners in the Karabakh conflict. It was clear at home and abroad that a peace treaty would not materialize in the near future.

### Georgia

In Georgia, as in the other republics of the former Soviet Union, the beginning of perestroika legalized long-repressed nationalist sentiment. The first protest demonstrations began in the middle of 1987. By October of that year, the Ilia Chavchavadze Society had been established, uniting all opposition forces in Georgia. The society advocated the reformation of the Soviet Union into a federation and "the delegation of real economic and political power to all the republics."[20]

However, the Georgian national-democratic movement was dominated from its inception by a 'radical' flank. The radicals maintained that the independent Georgia internationally recognized between 1918 and 1921 still existed from the viewpoint of international law. All existing Soviet institutions were thus manifestations of an occupying government, and any kind of collaboration was amoral and politically unacceptable. Achieving independence by winning elections in an orthodox way and declaring, once in power, the Soviet political structure illegal (the "Baltic model") was, in their view, wrongheaded.

By the end of 1988, the radicals had left the Ilia Chavchavadze Society to form several parties and had gathered enough momentum to organize frequent mass strikes, pickets, and demonstrations. This wave of demonstrations reached its peak in April 1989, when the

Soviet Army killed 20 protesters outside the House of Parliament in Tbilisi. As in Azerbaijan, these bloody events galvanized the population. The Communist party of Georgia and Moscow lost control of the republic, ceasing to exert any real influence on its political processes. In turn, the opposition became even more radical. On October 28, 1990, Georgia held its first non-Communist elections, bringing victory to the Round Table, a radical coalition bloc led by Zviad Gamsakhurdia. Once in power, Gamsakhurdia began to establish an authoritarian regime. He fully monopolized the media and the legislative and executive powers of government and appropriated fledgling public social organizations. Until the very end of Gamsakhurdia's regime, not a single opposition leader had the opportunity to appear on television or publish in any official print media. Unofficial publications were banned. Similar tactics were applied to the government administration. Gamsakhurdia assigned local prefects to each of the republic's 74 districts. These prefects acted as his direct representatives, wielding unlimited and unchecked power and responsible only to the president of Georgia.[21]

In the economic arena, Gamsakhurdia's halted all reforms and privatization that had begun before 1990 (during the entire period of Gamsakhurdia's rule, only one business in Georgia was privatized). The result was catastrophic economic decline and the further deterioration of the internal political situation.

The worst for Georgia, however, was the deterioration of interethnic relations. Georgian radicals had been a principal source (in addition to Moscow's activities) of ethnic tension in 1988-89. At their assemblies, the radicals clamored for the abolition of the country's autonomous regions and claimed that resident non-Georgians were "guests who must be made aware of their place and know who their hosts are." Once in power, demands appeared in the official press calling for governmental regulation of the birth rates of non-Georgian population and proposing that resident non-Georgians opposed to such measures be granted the right to leave the country.[22] This contributed to a sharp rise in interethnic tension.

The most severe of these animosities erupted in Abkhazia, especially in south Ossetia, where a separatist movement, fueled by Moscow, demanded independence from Georgia. Georgian authorities attempted to suppress the separatists with force and in 1989-90, the conflict in south Ossetia intensified to the point of bloodshed. The Ossetians were brought under control only in 1991 and, for all practical purposes, the region now lies outside Georgian jurisdiction, its political status unresolved.

This unrest weakened support for Gamsakhurdia among the old communist elite and the military. In autumn 1991, public demonstrations against Gamsakhurdia's government began and by December had spiraled into armed confrontation, with two weeks of heavy fighting in the capital. On the night of January 6, 1992, Gamsakhurdia fled to Armenia, and from there to Chechnya. Power shifted to the hands of military leaders, but the military-established government exerted real control only in the capital. The economy was in a shambles. Lawlessness had risen to catastrophic levels, further complicated by the absence of any viable and legitimate police forces.[23] Military leaders called on the former head of the republic, Eduard Shevardnadze, who was popular in the west and to some extent in his own country, to return to take over power.

Such were the conditions that prevailed on August 14, 1992, when the Georgian Army advanced on the territory of Abkhazia, allegedly in order to combat banditry and protect the railway lines. Within three days the army managed to occupy the entire territory. In response, Abkhazia announced that it would mobilize civilians, and appealed to the other ethnic groups of the Caucasus and Russia for help. The conflict quickly assumed a panregional character. Throughout the republics of the northern Caucasus, protest meetings were organized and volunteers registered. One week later, the Conference of Caucasian Peoples (KNGK) declared war on Georgia.[24] Russian military units took part in operations on Abkhazia's side. The ensuing bloodshed resulted in the defeat of the Georgian Army. The Abkhazians took control of the region's capital, Sukhumi, on September 27, 1993. A month later, partisans aligned with Gamsakhurdia in western Georgia (known as 'Zviadists') laid siege to Tbilisi.

This was the nadir of Georgia's post-Communist history. A large piece of the country had been lost. As many as 300,000 refugees had fled Abkhazia, arriving mostly in the capital, Tbilisi, which was now under siege. With the country on the verge of total collapse, Shevardnadze requested help from Russia.[25] The Russians crushed Gamsakhurdia's supporters. In return, Georgia was forced to join the CIS and sign an agreement allowing Russian military bases on its territory.

The defeat in Abkhazia actually played out to Shevardnadze's advantage in as much as the population blamed the military leaders for the conflict. This enabled Shevardnadze to push the latter out of the power center and to strengthen his own power base. In order to achieve this, he made overtures to the former communist elite, the intelligentsia and certain quarters of the opposition. Finally, in autumn 1993, Shevardnadze created his own political party, the Union of Georgian Citizens (*Soiuz grazhdan Gruzii*).

Georgia's economy was an even greater challenge. By 1993, the temporary Georgian currency, the kupon, was practically excluded from circulation, and all trade was carried out in US dollars or Russian rubles. Between September 1993 and August 1994, the value of the kupon fell from 7,000 to 2,000,000 per US dollar. Almost all industrial production ceased. The government deficit reached nearly 98 percent of the budget. According to every economic indicator, Georgia came last among the republics of the former USSR. Furthermore, 80 percent of the population was living below the poverty line.[26]

In the summer of 1994, Shevardnadze changed his government, appointing reform supporters to key posts. With the recommendation and support of the IMF, Georgia embarked on a program of economic liberalization and stabilization. In September 1995, a national currency, the lari, was issued and remains stable today. Inflation was reduced to 3-4 percent per month and the budget deficit lessened. Privatization of small businesses has been nearly completed.

The success of this economic program allowed Shevardnadze to restore his political influence, and he easily won the presidential election of November 1995. The Union of Georgian Citizens became the leading force in parliament. In 1995, parliament approved a new constitution that significantly changed the power structure of the Georgian government. The presidential office was granted almost unlimited authority and in this regard resembles that of Azerbaijan. It is by no means a coincidence that in the recent past the Georgian opposition has become increasingly sharper in its criticism of Shevardnadze's style of governance, claiming that the president's close relatives control Georgia's principal sources of income. Georgian society, many argue, is succumbing to clan rule.[27]

## Commonalities and Divergences among the South Caucasian Republics

The three accounts above demonstrate the tortuous, disparate paths that the countries of the southern Caucasus have taken over the last ten years. External factors have played an enormous role in destabilizing the region and fueling its ethnic, political, social, and economic crises. The most significant of these factors has been Moscow, both in its Soviet and post-Soviet incarnation. Even today, the region's political stability depends greatly on the claims placed upon it by Russia, Iran, and Turkey as well as on the actions of leading western states, especially in regard to the question of oil resources.

However, as this analysis has tried to show, many objective problems in the region are rooted in the internal processes of the three states. Their different paths to independence, the conflicts that have embroiled them, the political and economic reforms they have undertaken, and the personal politics of their leaders have all had a significant impact on the stability of the region.

The transition to democracy and independence in the southern Caucasus began during Soviet times and resulted in the appearance of the numerous "unofficial" organizations that later served as the nuclei for political parties throughout the republics. From 1988, the fates of Armenia and Azerbaijan became interwined over the conflict in Nagorno-Karabakh. National-democratic movements which arose on the crest of this conflict, had secured control over the politics of their respective republics by 1989. The prospects for the development of civil societies out of perestroika-era activities were effectively limited.

Azerbaijan's oil resources and geopolitical significance made it the most strategically important republic from Moscow's point of view. Therefore, the Azeris were the first to bear the brunt of the Soviet crackdown, and the communists managed to retain power there until after the breakup of the Soviet Union. In Armenia, the leaders of the national democratic movement were able to attract the former communist elite into its fold. This allowed the national democrats to attain office in 1990 relatively peacefully, instituting a nationalist regime under the aegis of the Soviet system. Ter-Petrosian's election to president in November 1991 laid the groundwork for the country's first independent government. Events in Georgia took a different course. The nationalist movement here was, from its very inception, the most radical of the three republics. By the end of 1988, it had gained de facto control over the entire country. The Soviet clampdown of 9 April 1989 delayed the nationalists' official rise to power but did not undermine their general popularity. Finally, in the autumn of 1990, the

Georgian national-extremists came to power with their leader, Gamsakhurdia, elected president in May 1991.

Thus, by the middle of 1992, national democratic movement leaders had replaced local Moscow protégés and all three republics had embarked on a course toward independent, democratic governments. In the absence of a tradition of self-governance and stable sociopolitical structures, however, this proved a complex and difficult task. The governments of the southern Caucasus, like those of the other former Soviet republics, have been forced to compress the transition from authoritarianism to a centralized nation-state with a functioning market economy, stable infrastructure, legitimate system of government, and democratic political culture, a process that took at least two hundred years in the west, into in an extremely short time frame.[28] This requires a massive change in the social as well as political consciousness of nations where the population has habitually lived under foreign rule.

For all three southern Caucasian states, these processes unfolded amid uninterrupted ethnic crises, economic catastrophes, throngs of refugees, and the near-complete lack of executive leadership. Moreover, the Soviet method of solving complex problems through the use of force was still very much part of the traditional mindset. As a result, the Karabakh conflict, which smoldered during Soviet times, was one of the first conflicts to explode into a full-scale war between newly sovereign governments, with enormous losses to both sides.

Although Armenia incurred heavy losses in this conflict, the country's ethnic homogeneity enabled it to escape ethnic and separatist tensions within the country. Azerbaijan and Georgia were less fortunate, and the political and economic chaos that ensued gave way to bitter disappointment on the part of domestic populations. Older generations, in particular, longed for the order and stability of the Soviet era. This sense of general crisis that permeated the first years of all three republics encouraged the restoration of power in 1992-93 to former communist leaders and their attendant political elite in both Georgia and Azerbaijan.

Presidents Shevardnadze and Aliev, both experienced politicians, defeated their political rivals and managed to stabilize the economic crises in their respective countries, as did Ter-Petrosian in Armenia. With the help of the IMF and other international organizations, Georgia and Azerbaijan have managed to curtail hyperinflation, take steps toward liberalization of the economy and establish the basis for a market economy. However, many of these positive results have been possible because of foreign investment. Most industries and businesses are at a standstill and the privatization process remains incomplete. Armenia's semi-isolated status and lack of natural resources have made it particularly difficult for it to attract significant foreign investment. Economic stability there, as in Azerbaijan, is maintained largely by the influx of money sent from national laborers working abroad, mainly in Russia.

A degree of political stability and the Nagorno-Karabakh cease-fire have permitted governments to begin introducing tough economic reforms. On the outside, political life appears to be developing in all three countries. Opposition parties are permitted to function and an independent media, including television, is growing. Public civilian institutions are increasing, yet the leaders of all three countries have created harsh, highly authoritarian political systems in which parliaments have succumbed to presidential control and have ceased to play any real role in their respective countries' internal and external political affairs. Accordingly, popular support for the parliament as an institution of government has dwindled. Political parties are still fragile and lack stable bases of support among the general voting constituency. All administrative, legislative, judicial, and executive branches of government are increasingly appendages of the presidential apparatus. Most important, every stage in the formation of these new political systems has been managed by a single individual, particularly the case with Shevardnadze in Georgia and Aliev in Azerbaijan. A strong presidential presence was a positive influence during the initial stage of construction of these centralized governments. However, the presidents' intractability and the cult of personality are jeopardizing future reforms and the possibility of an open society in both countries. It remains to be seen whether these systems will function under subsequent heads of state. The "Karabakhization" of Armenian political life, meanwhile, in light of the country's grim economic situation, make Armenia's future similarly uncertain.

Yet at the same time, during the most recent presidential and parliamentary elections, voters in all three southern Caucasian republics rejected communist candidates, thereby demonstrating their wish to build a democratic, pluralistic society. In all three republics, the first signs of an emerging (albeit still weak) civil soci-

ety are visible. The press and other mass media enjoy relative freedom, and each country has several political parties. These facts, in
combination with recent economic progress, give some hope for the
further development of the countries of the southern Caucasus at the
turn of the century.

## Perspectives for Regional Cooperation

The current situation in the southern Caucasus seems in many ways
hopeless and the possibilities for regional cooperation extremely
limited in the short to medium term. Some argue that differences
between the three countries are simply too big to be overcome:
Armenia and Georgia, for example, are Christian, while Azerbaijan
is Muslim. Armenia and Georgia lack natural resources, while
Azerbaijan is very rich in them. Azerbaijan and Georgia define their
political identities in opposition to Russia while remaining receptive
to the west, whereas Armenia leans toward Russia and welcomes the
presence of the Russian military, both on Armenian territory and in
the region in general. Azerbaijan and Georgia suffer from ethnic
strife and consider closed borders to be a prerequisite for national
security and international cooperation. Armenia, on the other hand,
is ethnically homogeneous, contains no autonomous regions, and
advocates the principle of self-determination for all ethnic groups.

A more immediate obstacle to cooperation is the territorial claims
these countries make on one another. Further complications include
Russia's presence in the region and the unfolding geopolitical confrontation over the construction of oil and natural gas pipelines.
When one considers the relative lack of civil society actors who
could conceivably initiate cooperation at a bottom-up, people-to-
people, level, the overall situation appears extremely grim.

Nevertheless, the first "revolutionary" stage in the construction of
these new states, with all its attendant chaos, border repartition, and
precipitous violence has passed. Unresolved internal and external
conflicts are not only possible but, for the time being, inevitable.
The numerous mass migrations and deportations that have taken
place in the region during the past two centuries have resulted in
cataclysmic demographic shifts, making the entire area a cauldron of
ethnic and sectarian conflict. But in the future these conflicts will
bear a different character than that which they have at present; they
will be resolved through international law, or at the very least sub-

ject to the scrutiny and the involvement of the international community. In spite of their shared inclination toward authoritarianism, the presidents of all three southern Caucasian countries are extremely sensitive to censure from the west. All three leaders wish to present themselves as democratic statesmen. For this reason, they flirt with the opposition, push for liberalization of the political system, and engage in other quasi-democratic behavior that cumulatively contributes to the democratization of their respective countries. This sensitivity to international opinion provides one of the most important influences on future regional interaction.

Relations between Azerbaijan and Georgia offer the greatest hope for changing the region's political climate. Until the end of the 19th century, as well as during the communist era, Georgia dominated the southern Caucasian political and cultural scene, while Azerbaijan was the region's economic hub. Armenia, in its turn, has been Russia's traditional ally. For this reason, after the breakup of the USSR, Georgia came to be internationally regarded as the region's critical strategic link and the potential mediator among the region's mutually hostile ethnic groups, especially between the Azeris and the Armenians.[29] Georgia's conflict in Abkhazia, and the political and economic crises which it precipitated, noticeably diminished the country's place in the region, and Azerbaijan, with its energy resources, moved into the spotlight. This was short-lived, however. The continuing conflict over Nagorno-Karabakh severely weakened Azerbaijan. It also prompted the formation of two dominant alliances in the region: Russia with Armenia, and Azerbaijan with Turkey. The fact that both these alliances cut across the territory of Georgia, restored Georgia's role in the region.

During the first years of independence, the sympathies of both the Georgian political elite and the general populace lay with Armenia. In 1992, the Georgian president held meetings with both his Azeri and Armenian counterparts. While he described his visit with the former as a dialogue between "friendly neighbors," he received Ter-Petrosian as the representative of a "fellow Christian nation." But ethnic separatist conflict and tensions with Russia in both countries brought Georgia and Azerbaijan closer. Georgia's resentment at Russian involvement in Abkhazia and southern Ossetia was gradually transferred to resentment over Russia's support of Armenia's claims in Karabakh. Ethnic Armenian support for separatist movements within Georgia further fueled anti-Armenian sentiment. The

Armenian population in Abkhazia supported Abkhazian separatist efforts, while the Armenian minority in the Dzhavakheti region of southern Georgia has remained, in every practical sense, outside Georgia's jurisdiction since independence. Armenians there (90 percent of the population) refuse to serve in the Georgian army and between 1992-94 fought in Nagorno-Karabakh.[30]

The 1994 Natural Gas Contract that opened the way for the exploitation of Azerbaijan's resources offered further economic incentive for the development of Georgian-Azeri relations. As early as 1993, the governments of both countries had addressed the issues of the rights of Azeri and Georgian minorities in each country. They now moved to strengthen political and economic ties. The contract paved the way for both countries to focus their cooperation on the development of transport and trade. Delegations from the two republics began to meet regularly, negotiating agreements in nearly all areas of mutual concern. By autumn 1998, the leaders of Georgia and Azerbaijan had signed 69 official documents.[31] The planning of the Georgian section of the oil pipeline that will take Azeri oil to international markets, which was begun in 1995, further strengthened ties between Georgia and Azerbaijan.

This common practical interest has extended to the sphere of foreign policy. Azerbaijan and Georgia have increasingly aligned with Ukraine and Moldova on the international stage. GUAM, as this informal grouping has been called, developed in the context of the OSCE and speaks collectively in that forum. At the summit of CIS presidents in Chisinau, Moldova, in October 1997, Azerbaijan and Georgia combined forces to unleash a barrage of criticism that cast into doubt the very existence of the Russian Federation. The summit of GUAM heads of state, which followed soon after, declared their intention to develop political and economic cooperation, including possible assistance and cooperation to prevent separatism and regional conflicts.

GUAM member states underscore that the purpose of their organization is to provide a forum for consultation, rather than to organize a bloc or alliance against any country. However, it is plain to see that a central goal of GUAM members is to achieve greater independence from Russia. Predictably, this elicits concern not only from Russia, but also from other countries in the region, particularly Armenia and Iran. For this reason, there is no certainty that GUAM will succeed in bringing stability and peace to the southern

Caucasus, nor even that it will remain in existence as an active grouping. Much will depend on the relations of each of its member states with Russia: What was once the reason for unification may in the future become a reason for its disbanding.

A cooperative initiative with an explicit economic focus is the Black Sea Economic Cooperation (BSEC), which originated from a 1990 proposal by Turkish President Turgut Ozal. As early as December 1990, after the nullification of the Warsaw Pact but before the breakup of the Soviet Union, the leaders of Turkey, Bulgaria, Romania, and the Soviet Union met in Ankara to consider a proposal which would allow the free movement of people, goods, and capital across their borders. Other issues discussed were the creation of a Black Sea Development Bank and the multilateral development of telecommunication and transportation infrastructure in the region. The breakup of the Soviet Union changed the group's membership and scope of concern, and in June 1992, the leaders of Albania, Armenia, Azerbaijan, Bulgaria, Georgia, Greece, Moldova, Romania, Russia, Turkey, and Ukraine signed the Black Sea Economic Cooperation Treaty. This document, less ambitious than its 1990 predecessor, called for the development of a free trade zone in the region, but gave each member-state the right to designate the level of its commitment. The free movement of people was established as a goal and projects for cooperation in transportation, energy, and tourism, as well as environmental protection, were also discussed.

While financial and political difficulties continue to hamper the development of this regional initiative, BSEC has gradually become an accepted presence in the region and one of the few regional arenas in which the three southern Caucasian states interact with each other. All three states have shown interest in BSEC, although to varying degrees. Georgia is the most enthusiastic, seeing BSEC as a step toward greater integration in Europe and as a useful framework for assisting Georgia's development as a transit country. It is also one of the most active proponents of BSEC's extension into political and security issues, suggesting the possible establishment of a BSEC peacekeeping force for the region. Azerbaijan is also supportive of BSEC, given its interest in regional stability as a prerequisite to the successful pipeline exportation of oil from the region. Although Armenia remains suspicious of Turkish initiatives in the region, BSEC offers Armenia the potential for overcoming its current regional isolation and facilitating the opening of trade, which its economy desperately requires. In June 1998 BSEC heads of states agreed to transform the intergovernmental grouping into a formal regional economic organization. This raises the potential for the organization to develop active economic cooperation and opens the question of the extension of its agenda to political and security issues in the Black Sea region.

A cooperative initiative with a far longer history in the Caucasus is the concept of the "All-Caucasian Home." This idea first appeared in 1918 and advocated the creation of a union of all states and governments of the region under a federal aegis guaranteeing each member's autonomy. Between 1920 and 1924, Chechnya, Ingushetia, north Ossetia, Kabarda, Balkyria, and Karachai did form such an alliance, called the Mountain Republic. In 1919, Georgia and Azerbaijan signed a defense pact against Russia. These moves were undermined by Armenia, however, which rejected the idea of a confederation and claimed that orientation toward the Caucasus was not in its interest.[32] Nevertheless, efforts and dialogue toward the goal of a southern Caucasian federation continued under enthusiastic pressure from the west. As a result, in Paris in May 1921, representatives of Azerbaijan, Armenia, Georgia, and the Mountain Republics formed The Union of Independent Caucasian Republics, which served as the basis for the ratification of the Declaration of the Federal Caucasian Republic two months later.[33] However, this document was not legally binding, as the Soviets had already taken control of the Caucasus by then. In March 1922, the communists instated the Trans-Caucasian Federation of three republics that naturally became part of the Soviet Union. This idea of a Caucasian confederacy was strictly ideological and economic in character and therefore did not take hold. In 1936 this confederacy disbanded and Azerbaijan, Armenia, and Georgia came directly under the control of the Soviet Union.

The idea of a "Caucasian Home" became popular immediately after the fall of the Soviet Union, especially in the northern Caucasus. The most active proponent of this idea was Chechnya led by Dzhokhar Dudayev. The Caucasian Mountain National Confederacy (CMNC) was created on the basis of this idea. However, this organization did not find favor in the south, especially because of the north's support of Abkhazia in the war with Georgia, and because the CMNC was de facto a Muslim organization. Nevertheless, interest reemerged in February 1996 after Georgian president Shevardnadze proposed the creation of the "Peaceful Caucasus." Concrete results followed when on 8 March 1996, in the course of an official visit to Georgia by Azeri president Aliev, a joint Declaration on Peace, Stability and Security in the Caucasian Region was signed. This document was regarded by many as a breakthrough and a serious step toward the realization of an "All-Caucasian Home." Among the document's salient points was a call for combined efforts to provide safe transportation of goods and people.[34]

One potentially important consequence of the 1996 declaration was the decision to initiate cooperation between the Georgian and Azeri parliaments. This could be a first step in encouraging the Armenian parliament and other Caucasian governments to participate and create a "Caucasian Parliament," composed of deputies from the parliaments of participating countries as well as delegates chosen through direct elections.

Two countries alone cannot guarantee the security of the southern Caucasus, however. Only a union of three would make such a guarantee possible, and thus, without Armenia's participation one cannot speak of full regional cooperation. As long as the Nagorno-Karabakh conflict remains unresolved, Armenia's relations with Azerbaijan will continue to stagnate and effectively block practical cooperation between the republics. To a lesser, but nonetheless significant degree, Georgian-Armenian relations have been complicated by Armenia's support of Abkhazia as well as the southern Georgian region of Dzhavakheti and its ethnic Armenian majority. At the same time, Armenia is conscious of the economic costs of continued isolation from its neighbors. The continued development of oil and transport routes raises concerns that it will be left out of future economic development in the region. Regional agreement could be reached if Armenia gave up its territorial claims in exchange for access to oil resources. One analyst has suggested the creation of a regional consortium of southern Caucasian states for the export of energy. Such a consortium would oversee pipeline routes and the transportation of oil and gas, by which each country would receive its constant share irrespective of the means and route of transportation.[35] Such economic cooperation, in which three states benefit mutually, could promote the compromises necessary for the resolution of political disagreements, including ethnic and territorial disputes.

In this regard, it is important to note the signing of the Declaration of Inter-Ethnic Harmony and Peace, Economic and Cultural Cooperation in the Caucasus by the leaders of Azerbaijan, Armenia, Georgia, and Russia at a meeting in June 1996 in Kislovodsk as a welcome initiative in the direction of compromise.[36]

One important consequence of the 1996 declaration was cooperation between the Georgian and Azeri parliaments, which might inspire the Armenian parliament and other Caucasian governments to create a "Caucasian Parliament,", which would be composed of deputies from the parliaments of the participating countries as well as delegates chosen through direct elections. Otherwise, this parliament could consist of two separate houses – one for the government and one for the voting constituency.

The construction of a unified Eurasian transport corridor gives further hope for eventual changes in the region's political climate. In May 1993, the European Union (EU) drafted and ratified a plan to revive the ancient Silk Road by which goods were transported from China to Europe via the shores of the Caspian and Black seas. The Transport Corridor Europe Caucasus Central Asia (TRACECA) program of the EU is designed to realize this project through the provision of technical assistance to develop transit links. Azerbaijan and Georgia have been active in this project. Construction of a bridge on their shared border is underway with EU funds, and this bridge should become the primary transportation link between both countries. At the same time, both presidents began an active campaign to promote this project among the governments of central Asia and the countries of the Black Sea basin, and Turkey has also become active in the project. The heads of Georgia, Azerbaijan, and Turkey meet regularly to review and refine plans for the construction of an east-west transport corridor which would connect these countries via roadways, air routes, and railroads, and would also include oil and gas pipelines and electrical power lines.[37]

The need to incorporate the active participation of other Black Sea countries in these efforts led to President Aliev's initiative of an international forum in Baku in September 1998. With the financial support of the west and international organizations, the forum brought together representatives of 32 countries and 13 international organizations to discuss this gigantic project. At the conclusion of the summit, a multilateral agreement on the development of an international Europe-Caucasus-Asia corridor was signed. The document contains 16 points concerning the transportation of international goods, the guarantee of their safety, customs problems, tariffs, etc. In addition, the participants ratified the Baku declaration and created a higher body called the International Commission to oversee the revival of the Great Silk Road. Its executive offices are to be established in TRACECA headquarters in Baku.[38]

Perhaps, the most hopeful event of the Baku summit was Aliev's extension of an invitation to the president of Armenia. Unfortunately, President Kacharian did not take advantage of this promising opportunity and refused to visit Baku. Nevertheless, the Armenian delegation at the forum was represented by Prime Minister Armen Dabrinian, which may hold out some hope for a brighter future in the relations between the two countries.

Two other recent ideas that might increase cooperation in the region include a proposal for dual citizenship and the creation of a Confederation or Organization for Security and Cooperation in the Caucasus (K/OBSK), to be overseen by the UN Security Council and under the aegis of OSCE.[39] These have not yet been given comprehensive consideration, however.

Many obstacles still stand in the way of the realization of these ideas and proposals and some may well prove unrealistic. The resolution of the Karabakh conflict is essential for the stabilization of the southern Caucasus. This conflict remains the principal stumbling block on the road toward cooperation and the integration of the peoples of the region. But the first revolutionary stage in the construction of national governments is at least concluded and, most significantly, people in the region are tired of war and violence. The extent to which the focus of southern Caucasian governments and publics will center on the economic development of the region may well offer the best opportunity for regional cooperation.

## Notes

1. UNHCR. *Refugees and Others [sic] of Concern to UNHCR. 1996 Statistical Overview.* Geneva, July, 1997; "CIS Migration Report," 1996 (International Organization for Migration:Geneva, 1997) pp. 17, 23, 26.

2. A. Yunusov, "Azerbaizhan v postsovetskii period: problemy i vozmozhnye puti razvitiia." Severnyi Kavkaz—Zakavkaz'e: problemy stabil'nosti i perspektivy razvitiia," (Moscow, 1997), p. 145; "CIS Migration Report," 1996 (International Organization for Migration, Geneva, 1997) p. 23. Figures given by the government of Azerbaijan differ noticeably: Officially, there are up to 1 million refugees, and 20% of the country's territory is under Armenian control.

3. Zurav Todua, *Azerbaijan segodia* (Moscow, 1995), p. 14.

4. *Ezhednevnie novosti* (Baku), 24 April 1998.

5. See *Monitor* (Baku), 1997, no. 4 (January): 9, and no. 5 (May): 7.

6. *525 Gazeta*, (Baku), 10 October 1998 (in Azeri).

7. A. Yunusov, *Azerbaijan*, p. 146.

8. *Bakinskii rabochii* (Baku), 12 June 1998.

9. Ronald Grigor Suny, *Looking Towards Ararat: Armenia in Modern History*, (Bloomington: Indiana University Press, 1993), pp. 234-235.

10. Jonathan Aves, "Politika, partii i prezidenti v Zakavkaz'e," *Kavkazskie Regional'nye Issledovaniia* (Tbilisi) 1 (1996): 8.

11. *Aziatskii vestni* (Moscow), no. 2 (1992): 10.

12. Granush Kharatian, "Sotsial'naiia situatsiia v Armenii." *Zhenshchiny s universitetskim obrazovanie* (Yerevan), 1997, no. 1 (September), p. 28.

13. Jonathan Aves, *Post-Soviet Transcaucasia* (London: Royal Institute of International Affairs, 1993), p. 23.

14. *Nezavisimaia gazeta* (Moscow), 30 July 1998.

15. *Armenia: Human Development Report 1996*, UNDP, (Yerevan, 1996), p. 12.

16. Op. cit., p. 13; *CIS Migration Report*, pp. 11, 17.

17. *Segodnia* (Moscow), 30 September 1998

18. *Izvestiia* (Moscow), 13 May 1997.

19. G. Avakian, "Vliianie karabakhskogo faktora na formirovanie politicheskoi identichnosti v Armenii," *Severnyi Kavkaz – Zakavkaz'e: problemy stabil'nosti I perspektivy razvitiia* (Moscow, 1997), p. 177.

20. Jonathan Aves, *The Path to National Independence in Georgia, 1987-1990*, (London: School of Slavonic and East European Studies, 1991), p. 9.

21. Levan Tarkkhinishvili, *Gruziia: put' k demokratii?* (Warsaw, 1997), pp. 12-13.

22. O. Vasil'eva, *Gruziia kak model' postkommunisticheskoi transformatzii*, (Moscow, 1993), pp. 28, 45, 58.

23. Jonathan Aves, *Politika*, p. 15.

24. O.Vasil'eva, *Gruziia*, pp. 34-35.

25. David Darchiashvili, "Rossiskoe voennoe prisutstvie v Gruzii – pozitsii storon i perspektivy," *Kavkazskie Regional'nye Issledovaniia* (Tbilisi, 1997), vol. 1, book 2, p. 41.

26. *Obshchestvo i ekonomika* (Moscow), no. 2 (1998): 9-89.

27. *Nezavisimaia gazeta* (Moscow), 27 June and 12 August 1998

28. A. Iskanderian, "Stanovlenie politicheskikh sistem v stranakh Zakavkaz'ia: postsovetskii sindom i politicheskaiia kul'tura," *Severnyi Kavkaz – Zakavkaz'e: problemy stabil'nosti I perspektivy razvitiia* (Moscow, 1997), pp. 170- 171.

29. Aleksandr Kukhianidze, "Armianskoe i azerbaizhanskoe men'shinstva v Gruzii. O natsional'noi i vneshnei politike," *Etnicheskie i regional'nye konflikty v Evrazii*, book 1 (Moscow, 1997), p. 170.

30. Iskanderian, *Stanovlenie politicheskikh*, pp.172-180.

31. *Rezonans* (Baku), 8-10 July 1998. In *Azeri*.

32. Grant Avetisian, "K voprosu o 'Kavkazskom dome' i pantiurkistskikh ustremleniiakh." *Etnicheskie i regional'nye konflikty v Evrazii*, book 1 (Moscow, 1997), p. 149.

33. Grant Avetisian, "Ideiia konfederativnogo ob'edineniia Kavkazskikh respublik v

1918-1921 godax." "Caucasica." *The Journal of Caucasian Studies* (Tbilisi) 2 (1998): 49-51.

34. "Deklaratsiia o mire, bezopastnosti i sotrudnichestve v Kavkazskom regione," *Text in Kavkaz* (Baku), no. 2 (1997): 4-5.

35. Paul A. Goble, "Trevozhnaiia obshchnost' sudeb: geopolitika post-sovetskogo iuga Kavkaza." *Kavkaz* (Baku), no. 2, 1997, p. 15.

36. Medea Abashidze, "The Caucasus: Historical background," *Caucasia: The Journal of Caucasian Studies* (Tbilisi) 2 (1998): 21.

37. Aleksandr Atskvereli, "TRACECA: iz mifa v real'nost'," *Kavkaz* (Baku), no. 2 (1997): 12-13.

38. *Ezhednevnye novosti*, 11 September 1998, and Zerkalo, 12 September 1998.

39. Johann Galtung, "Nekotorye nabliudeniia na Kavkaze." *Kavkazskie Regional'nye Issledovaniia* (Tbilisi, 1997), vol. 1, book 2, pp. 85-86.

# Part IV

Interlocking Cooperation

# 8

# Europe's Security Architecture and the New "Boundary Zones"

*Andrew Cottey*

## Introduction

Subregional cooperation poses a major challenge for the countries of Europe's emerging "boundary zones," consisting of south-eastern Europe, the western Newly Independent States (NIS) and the southern NIS. Intensified multilateral cooperation could help the countries of these subregions to address the enormous difficulties they face in managing political change, promoting economic development, overcoming conflicts, and integrating themselves into the European mainstream. However, the very problems that would be mitigated by greater subregional cooperation – political instability, authoritarianism, nationalism, economic underdevelopment, internal and external conflicts, international isolation – also make such cooperation difficult to achieve in practice. This tension raises the question of how far external actors, particularly the main European and international organizations, can and should play a role in promoting multilateral cooperation in these subregions.

The main European and international organizations – NATO, the European Union (EU), the Western European Union (WEU), the Organization for Security and Cooperation in Europe (OSCE), the Council of Europe (CoE), and the United Nations (UN) and its various functional agencies – are already heavily involved in south-eastern Europe, east-central Europe and the southern NIS. NATO, the EU, and the WEU are actively involved in these subregions as a result of their outreach and enlargement related activities, including the Partnership for Peace (PfP), the WEU's Associate Partnership, and the EU's Association and Partnership and Cooperation Agreements as well as their conflict management efforts, particularly in the former Yugoslavia. The political, economic, and military power of NATO and the EU give these organizations substantial influence, as illustrated by the desire of many "boundary zone" states for membership of NATO/EU. The OSCE, the CoE, and the UN are actively involved in the three subregions through various democracy and human rights support, economic and environmental development, and conflict management and resolution activities. However, they lack the more direct influence that NATO and the EU have over the countries of these subregions.

Despite the strong presence of the main European and international organizations in Europe's new "boundary zones," their policies have only begun to develop a significant subregional dimension. NATO, the EU, and the WEU's outreach activities have, until recently, been either bilateral in character or "partnership-wide," i.e., focused on NATO/EU/WEU's overall relations with all of their partners. Enlargement policies have been based on the premise that while states may join in groups, membership decisions will be based on the merits and preparedness of individual applicants. This approach did not encourage subregional cooperation between the partner states and sometimes intensified competition between them in developing ties with the west. The OSCE, the CoE, and the UN have similarly focused on activities either in one member state (e.g., election monitoring) or more general organization-wide activities (e.g., OSCE arms control commitments).

Since 1995-96, there has been a gradual recognition that the main international organizations should do more to encourage multilateral cooperation in the various subregions of central and eastern Europe and the former Soviet Union. NATO has made efforts to encourage subregional activities within the PfP framework and, since its creation in 1997, within the Euro-Atlantic Partnership Council (EAPC). The EU has encouraged multilateral activities between its partners and supported existing subregional groups such as the Council of Baltic Sea States (CBSS) and the Central European Initiative (CEI). The OSCE has initiated discussions on its own role in subregional cooperation. International organizations have acknowledged the contribution of subregional cooperation to security and development and have sought to support existing subregional efforts. However, it is also recognized that defining a subregion is a sensitive issue and that it is difficult, if not impossible, for international organizations to encourage subregional cooperation where no basis for cooperation exists. International support for subregional cooperation is growing, therefore, but is still at a relatively early stage in its development. How far NATO, the EU, the OSCE and other such organizations can promote subregional cooperation, particularly in the difficult circumstances of Europe's emerging "boundary zones," remains unclear.

The divergent geopolitical situations of south-eastern Europe, east-central Europe and the southern NIS have major implications for international efforts to promote multilateral cooperation in each. With the demise of the Warsaw Pact and the Soviet Union, south-eastern Europe has effectively become NATO and the EU's "backyard." Although Russia retains historic and cultural ties with Serbia, residual economic links, and a veto over UN Security Council decisions, it is no longer a major player in the subregion. The proximity of NATO and the EU and the combined political, economic, and military power of their member states gives both organizations enormous influence. At least some south-eastern European states (Slovenia, Romania, and Bulgaria), moreover, have prospects for joining the EU and/or NATO at a future date.

Since the mid-1990s, there has been a growing recognition in both south-eastern Europe and in the west, that subregional cooperation could play an important role in helping to overcome the subregion's many problems. The result has been the establishment of the Balkan Conference on Stability and Cooperation (BCSC), the EU's Royaumont Initiative, the United States' Southeast European Cooperation Initiative (SECI), and other NATO and EU efforts to promote subregional cooperation in south-eastern Europe. The wars of Yugoslav secession and Serbia's growing authoritarianism, nationalism, and self-imposed isolation, however, have fundamentally undermined the prospects for subregional cooperation and posed major challenges to the credibility and will of the west. Thus, while NATO and the EU have substantial potential to promote subregional cooperation in south-eastern Europe, the prospects for such cooperation cannot be separated from the wider challenge of managing Yugoslavia's disintegration.

In east-central Europe, NATO and the EU are major actors, but given the proximity and continuing close engagement of Russia, the subregion will for the foreseeable future be defined by its position between Russia and an enlarging west. Although neither Ukraine, Belarus, or Moldova appear likely to join NATO or the EU for at least a decade, relations with these organizations are already sensitive issues, and the issue of Ukraine and Moldova's membership in the EU and/or NATO may emerge more substantively. However, the divergent political and foreign policy paths of Ukraine and Moldova on the one hand, and Belarus on the other, mean that east-central Europe does not constitute a coherent subregion. There is, therefore, no real basis or rationale for trilateral cooperation between Ukraine, Moldova, and Belarus.

Nevertheless, given the important geostrategic location of the three and the many common political, economic, and security problems they face, there is a case for encouraging flexible, multilateral cooperation between the western NIS and their neighbors, both as a means of addressing specific functional problems and as a means of promoting confidence in the subregion. Some limited progress has been made in this direction within the context of the Central European Initiative (to which all three belong) and via NATO's PfP. International efforts to promote subregional cooperation between Ukraine, Belarus, and Moldova, however, are likely to be constrained by the absence of any sense of a shared subregion and by Russia's troubled relations with the west.

In the southern NIS, the geopolitical situation is defined by the weakness of the states of the subregion, latent or on-going conflicts, the existence of large oil and gas reserves, and competition for influence between Russia, the US, the EU, Turkey, Iran, and China. There is also competition with such countries as India, Pakistan, and Saudi Arabia as well as with major (primarily western and Russian) energy companies.[1] The influence of NATO and the EU is thus less than in south-eastern Europe or east-central Europe, and none of the Caucasian and central Asian states have prospects of NATO or EU membership in the foreseeable future. While the southern NIS share certain generic common interests, such as political stability, economic development, managing environmental problems, and developing transport infrastructure, they have many conflicts with one another. Their interests in how common problems are resolved are not necessarily the same, and there is no consensus on the extent to which a shared subregion exists. International organizations have begun to provide support for subregional cooperation efforts in the

Trans-Caucasus and in central Asia (e.g., NATO PfP support the central Asian peacekeeping battalion, OSCE initiated discussions of central Asian environmental problems, CoE efforts to promote dialogue between the three Caucasian states). Given the political and geostrategic realities of the southern NIS, however, international efforts to promote multilateral cooperation in the subregion are likely to be constrained by the competing interests of both the southern NIS and the external powers.

The divergent geopolitical situations of south-eastern Europe and east-central Europe as well as the southern NIS suggest that while the main European and international organizations can develop general policies to promote subregional cooperation, they will also have to tailor specific strategies to meet the circumstances of each subregion. This chapter examines the issues for international promotion of subregional cooperation in these areas.

### South-Eastern Europe

In the first half of the 1990s, the Yugoslav conflict fundamentally undermined the prospects for subregional cooperation in south-eastern Europe. The international community's failures in Croatia and Bosnia reduced what little leverage the west might have been able to use to promote multilateral cooperation in the area. The use of military force to enforce a settlement in Bosnia toward the end of 1995 and the conclusion of the Dayton Peace Agreement in November of that year greatly improved prospects for subregional cooperation and restored western credibility.[2] Thus, it is no coincidence that several regional initiatives, namely, the Balkan Conference on Stability and Cooperation (BCSC), the Southeast European Cooperation Initiative (SECI) and the EU's Royaumont Initiative, all emerged at this time.

The Dayton Peace Agreement gave international organizations' engagement in south-eastern Europe an increasingly subregional dimension. Within the framework of PfP, NATO is engaged in a wide range of "16+1" cooperation activities with Romania, Bulgaria, Slovenia, Albania, and Macedonia.[3] Although Bosnia has not yet joined PfP, NATO's involvement there has involved supporting reform and cooperation between the armed forces of the various factions.[4] NATO has sought to mitigate the bilateral character of PfP by encouraging multilateral PfP activities in south-eastern Europe as a means of building confidence and cooperation within the subregion.[5] This has included military exercises involving various southeastern European countries and NATO members, as well as other multilateral training, defense education, and dialogue activities. Subregional cooperation in south-eastern Europe and the Trans-Caucasus has been one of the main areas of discussion within the EAPC since its inauguration and the establishment of a PfP peacekeeping training center and a multilateral south-eastern European peacekeeping force is under consideration.[6] NATO has also been engaged in efforts to promote bilateral confidence-building measures between Greece and Turkey in order to avoid the escalation of tensions between them.

Given the enormous problems facing the countries of south-eastern Europe and the fragile relations between them, there is a strong case for NATO to intensify its multilateral outreach activities in the subregion. The alliance could, for example, provide greater financial support for PfP/EAPC activities and encourage dialogue on nonmilitary aspects of security (such as economic and transfrontier cooperation and the management of ethnic tensions). It could also offer more practical support for the establishment and implementation of bilateral and multilateral confidence-building measures (such as hotlines between political leaders and between armed forces and reduced force deployments in border zones). As far as possible, such efforts should be undertaken on a subregion-wide basis and, where possible, incorporate existing cooperative efforts.

The EU, after its failed efforts to intervene in the Croatian and Bosnian conflicts in the early 1990s, has gradually come to assume a crucial role in south-eastern Europe. The EU and its member states are among the major aid donors to the Bosnian peace process. Through its association agreements with Slovenia, Romania, and Bulgaria and its lesser cooperation and trade agreements with the other south-eastern European states, the EU is also involved in extensive bilateral cooperation with individual states.

Nevertheless, the EU's efforts at promoting stability and subregional cooperation in south-eastern Europe have met with only limited success. The EU has been only partially successful in using its economic and political leverage to encourage domestic reform and foreign policy moderation. Although Slovenia has been included in the first wave of countries invited to join the EU, the economic circumstances of all other south-eastern European states (except perhaps Croatia) mean that they have little prospect of joining the Union before 2010, at the earliest. The conclusion, ratification, and implementation of association, partnership, and cooperation and trade agreements with south-eastern European states has been a slow process. Where implementation of agreements has begun, the substance of cooperation has been limited and slow to develop. Although the EU has sought to promote subregional cooperation between the former Yugoslav states through the Royaumont process, this initiative has had only limited success in actually facilitating substantive subregional cooperation between states.[7] Thus, the EU has probably made less progress than NATO in overcoming the bilateral character of its relations with south-eastern European states and encouraging multilateral, subregional forms of cooperation.

One way of promoting such cooperation would be to use the channels opened up by bilateral agreements and the PHARE aid program to promote multilateral and transfrontier cooperation in the areas of economic development, infrastructure, transport, environment, and crime prevention. At the politico-military level, more consideration should be given to ways in which the WEU (as the "defense arm" of the Union) can promote subregional cooperation in south-eastern Europe through, for example, defense education and training.[8]

The CoE, and particularly the OSCE, are also engaged in a wide range of activities in south-eastern Europe. In the context of the Dayton Peace Agreement, the OSCE is charged with election and human rights monitoring, promotion of democracy, and facilitation of the arms control and military confidence-building aspects of the peace process. Through the activities of the Chairman-in-Office (and his special representatives), the High Commissioner on National Minorities and its permanent mission in Macedonia, the OSCE has taken a leading role in efforts to prevent and contain conflict in Macedonia, Albania, and Kosovo. The OSCE has also facilitated various discussions on subregional cooperation within the framework of its Permanent Council in Vienna.[9] The CoE has also been involved in various election monitoring and democracy promotion activities in south-eastern Europe.[10] If the OSCE and the Council of Europe's roles in south-eastern Europe are to be strengthened, more attention must be paid to their operational roles, and they need to be given greater resources. Both organizations could consider more in-country democracy and human and minority rights promotion activities.[11] The OSCE might also provide an appropriate framework for initial discussion of how transnational problems might be addressed on a subregional basis.

One obstacle to greater external support for cooperation in south-eastern Europe has been the differing relationships of the states of the subregion with NATO and the EU. Slovenia, Romania, Bulgaria, Albania, and Macedonia are members of the PfP and the EAPC, while Croatia, Bosnia, and the Federal Republic of Yugoslavia are not. Slovenia, Romania, and Bulgaria have association agreements with the EU, while the other south-eastern European states have cooperation and trade agreements and, in the cases of Yugoslavia and Croatia, are subject to certain economic sanctions. As a consequence, south-eastern European states have differing degrees of access to institutionalized relations and political dialogue with NATO and EU and to the economic and military aid that both may provide. This makes it more difficult for the EU and NATO to engage all countries in subregional cooperation activities. Moreover, these differences will be exacerbated if and when some of the south-eastern European states become full members of NATO and the EU.

There are obvious and very good reasons for differentiated relations with NATO and the EU: Relations with NATO and the EU are dependent on states' progress in democratization, respect for human rights, economic reform, and the building of peaceful relations with ethnic minorities and neighboring states. This differentiation provides one of the main forms of western leverage over south-eastern European states and is likely to continue for the next few years. This will inevitably constrain the extent to which differing states can be drawn into western-supported subregional cooperation efforts. In the longer term, however, subregional cooperation in south-eastern Europe will have limited use if it excludes those countries that are, in fact, the greatest sources of instability and conflict in the subregion, i.e., Yugoslavia, Croatia, Bosnia, Macedonia, and Albania. The international community faces a delicate balancing act between finding ways of gradually drawing these countries into subregional cooperation and maintaining the conditionality of political and economic ties with them.

While the main European security organizations can and should do more to promote subregional cooperation in south-eastern Europe, the prospects for subregional cooperation cannot be divorced from wider political and security developments in the subregion. Subregional cooperation will not be able to develop or play a significant role if south-eastern Europe is characterized by continuing warfare and worsening interethnic and international relations. In this context, the west has arguably failed to develop an effective strategy for addressing the underlying cause of the subregion's problems, namely flawed democratization processes and virulent nationalism, above all in Serbia. In the long term, the resolution of the Bosnian and Kosovo crises and the creation of stability throughout south-eastern Europe will depend on the development of genuine democracies that respect human and minority rights as well as existing international borders. In order to achieve this goal, the key members of NATO, the EU, and the OSCE will have to remain deeply engaged in south-eastern Europe for many years to come. One element of that engagement should be intensified support for subregional cooperation.

**East-Central Europe**

As was noted already, Ukraine, Belarus, and Moldova's divergent domestic and foreign policy paths mean that there is neither an obvious rationale nor indigenous support for trilateral cooperation between the western NIS. Nor, given these realities, have international organizations treated these three states as a group. From a western perspective, the key issue has been how to promote the consolidation of statehood, democratization, and economic reform in Ukraine, Belarus, and Moldova. As a consequence, western actors have sought to develop separate individual relationships with each, and the international community has become engaged in each of the three states in different ways. Examples include western efforts to encourage Ukraine to surrender the former Soviet nuclear weapons on its territory in the early 1990s, the OSCE's efforts to help resolve Moldova's Transnistria conflict, and the OSCE's efforts to moderate Belarus's drift into authoritarianism. At the same time, the geostrategic situation of east-central Europe has made international organizations conscious of the need to avoid unnecessarily antagonizing Russia in this important subregion.

These dynamics have resulted in a strategy based on developing bilateral cooperation with and aid to Ukraine, Belarus, and Moldova (with particular support for Ukraine because of its size and geostrategic importance); excluding them from the prospect of

NATO or EU membership for the foreseeable future; and pursuing a parallel but separate bilateral relationship with Russia. This strategy has been reasonably successful in avoiding direct confrontation with Russia in east-central Europe and in providing various forms of support to Ukraine and Moldova. Russia, however, remains wary of western intentions in the subregion, while Ukraine and Moldova have been critical of the limited nature of western support for their sovereignty. In the case of Belarus, the increasing authoritarianism of President Alexander Lukashenka's regime has led to the freezing of NATO and EU relations with the country as well as to western diplomatic and economic sanctions. The Lukashenka regime has so far proved immune to western pressure for reform.

Given Russia's continuing wariness of NATO and its opposition to the alliance's eastward enlargement, the balancing act the Atlantic alliance faces in east-central Europe is particularly sensitive. In the context of NATO's initial enlargement into central Europe, the alliance adopted a strategy of pursuing parallel special relationships with Russia and Ukraine through the NATO-Russia Founding Act and the NATO-Ukraine Charter of 1997. NATO rejected a demand from Belarus for a similar special relationship, and as a result of Belarus's lack of interest, cooperation under the PfP agreement has been largely frozen.[12] Moldova has become one of NATO's more active PfP partners among the NIS. In the short-to-medium term, the main issue for NATO is how to give more substance to its support for Ukraine and Moldova without antagonizing Russia. NATO should encourage PfP activities relating to sovereignty support (civil-military relations, effective defense ministries, effective defense planning), rather than "harder" elements of military cooperation (joint exercises, provision of military equipment). Apart from providing useful support to Ukraine and Moldova in building effective state structures, such activities are also likely to be perceived as less threatening by Russia. There is probably relatively little NATO can do to engage Belarus as long as President Lukashenka retains tight control of the country. Nevertheless, the PfP relationship with Belarus should be retained as a channel for dialogue and could be reactivated if the political situation within the country changes.

One area that merits further exploration is the possibility of NATO/PfP/EAPC subregional cooperation between east-central Europe and its neighbors. NATO has already moved in this direction, with some military exercises involving Ukraine and its central European neighbors and some multilateral defense education/training activities. Further multilateral NATO/PfP/EAPC activities, involving flexible, ad hoc combinations of central and eastern European states should be considered. These could provide a means for expanding the western NIS-NATO relationship and for allowing Ukraine and Moldova to learn from the experiences of their central European neighbors' more advanced defense reforms. They could also help engage Belarus. In the context of NATO enlargement, progress in the Conventional Forces in Europe (CFE) treaty adaptation talks and new confidence-building measures could also help to promote long term confidence and cooperation. As far as possible, these initiatives should also include Russia.

Like NATO, the EU has concluded parallel bilateral partnership and cooperation agreements with the western NIS and Russia that provide frameworks for political and economic cooperation and gradual movement toward free trade. It has also provided significant aid to these countries under the TACIS (Technical Assistance to CIS) program. The issues facing the EU in its policy toward east-central Europe, however, differ somewhat from those facing NATO. Ukrainian leaders have explicitly stated that membership in the EU is their long-term goal and that the EU should conclude an association agreement with Ukraine. Officials in Kyiv have been quite critical of the EU for the slow progress in implementing the partnership and cooperation agreement and for the overall level of political and economic support provided by the Union. Ukraine has also expressed fears about the possible consequences of Poland and other central European states' membership in the EU. In particular, it is concerned about the likely tightening of controls on Ukraine's currently relatively open western border and the imposition of stricter visa regimes. These measures, Ukrainians argue, could undermine cooperation with central European states and push the country closer to Russia.[13] Russia, in contrast to its strong opposition to NATO enlargement, has expressed no similar general opposition to EU enlargement, although both Russia and Belarus share Ukraine's concerns with regard to the possible tightening of border controls and the introduction of visa regimes in central Europe.

Against this backdrop, the key challenge for the EU is how to intensify its support for Ukraine and Moldova and address potential "dividing lines" resulting from its own expansion into central Europe. Certainly, the EU needs to explore faster trade liberalization, the liberalization of visa regimes, and the provision of greater economic aid to Ukraine and Moldova. The EU should also explicitly acknowledge that Ukraine and Moldova have the long-term potential to become EU members and must commit itself to conclude association agreements with these countries when they have met the appropriate conditions. Although membership in the EU can only be a long-term prospect, such a policy would provide an important political signal that both countries are viewed as part of the European integration process and help to generate support for the domestic reforms necessary. In Belarus's case, the growing authoritarianism of the Lukashenka regime has resulted in the freezing of relations with the EU, but there is a clear case for maintaining channels of dialogue.[14]

The EU could also do more to promote flexible, ad hoc forms of subregional cooperation between the western NIS, their central European and Baltic neighbors, and Russia in functional areas such as economics, infrastructure, and the environment. Although the EU has made some progress in this area, the bilateral nature of its eastern agreements and of the PHARE and TACIS aid programs has limited this. The EU, therefore, needs to explore practical areas where it can facilitate such cooperation between these states.

The OSCE has been active in east-central Europe in a variety of dimensions: the efforts of the OSCE High Commissioner on National Minorities to prevent conflict in Crimea, the work of the OSCE mission in Moldova to help resolve the Transnistria conflict, and, since spring 1998, the OSCE mission mandated to monitor and promote democracy in Belarus. The OSCE and the CoE's ability to support state-building, democratization, and respect for human and minority rights in east-central Europe has, as elsewhere, been limited by the resources available to them. There may be a case for encouraging some democracy promotion activities on a subregional basis among east-central European states and their neighbors and for using the OSCE as a framework for bringing these states together to discuss common problems such as transnational crime and environmental degradation.

One could make the case for a more comprehensive reconsideration of international strategy toward Ukraine, Belarus, and Moldova as well as for the development of policies treating the three countries as a distinct group and east central Europe as a distinct subregion. In theory, such an approach could help build confidence between Ukraine, Belarus, and Moldova, help to draw Belarus out of its current isolation, and encourage reform in all three countries. The case for such an approach, however, is not convincing, nor would efforts to move in this direction be likely to succeed. Ukraine and Moldova would likely resist any international approach that treated them as a part of a group along with Belarus. Belarus would probably resist such an approach, perceiving it as a covert effort to weaken its ties with Russia. Russia would likely oppose such an approach, fearing a western-inspired effort to undermine its influence. Any such initiative would also risk intensifying Russian competition with the west for influence in the area.

While the case for treating Ukraine, Belarus, and Moldova as a distinct subregion is weak, there is a case for trying to engage the three with their central and eastern European neighbors and Russia in various looser forms of subregional cooperation.[15] Subregional cooperation that involves various ad hoc combinations of these states can help promote confidence and address specific functional problems to the extent that it is inclusive rather than exclusive. Such cooperation might be developed both within the context of existing subregional groupings (such as the CEI and the CBSS) and via NATO and the EU's own outreach programs. In this context, NATO, the EU, the OSCE, and the CoE could and should do more to overcome the bilateralism which has characterized their policies toward east-central Europe.

## The Southern NIS

As noted previously, the development of subregional cooperation in the southern NIS is inhibited by the many conflicts between the southern newly independent states themselves, the competing agendas of various external powers, and the absence of a strong sense of shared identity and interests, whether on a southern NIS-wide, Trans-Caucasian or central Asian basis. In this context, the involvement of international organizations in the southern NIS cannot be separated from the broader agendas and interests of their member states. The activities of international organizations in the southern NIS are thus highly sensitive issues, usually perceived in zero-sum terms by both the southern NIS and external states. To date, international organizations' support for subregional cooperation in the southern NIS has been limited. This raises two questions. Can international organizations do more to support subregional cooperation in the southern NIS? Which international efforts to promote subregional cooperation can best help to moderate the current zero-sum dynamics of the subregion?

NATO has become involved in the southern NIS primarily via PfP and the EAPC. All the southern NIS are EAPC members and, except for Tajikistan, have joined PfP. Those states seeking to counterbalance Russian influence, such as Georgia and Azerbaijan, have been among the more active in seeking PfP cooperation, while those dependent on close cooperation with Russia, such as Armenia, have been less actively engaged in PfP. Small-scale peacekeeping exercises have also been undertaken in central Asia within the framework of PfP, with the US playing the leading role. NATO has also played a low-key role in supporting Kazakhstan, Kyrgyzstan, and Uzbekistan in developing their joint central Asian peacekeeping battalion.

The underlying problem facing NATO in the southern NIS is the interaction of Russia's general wariness of the alliance with the wider competition for influence in the subregion. Russia, Iran, and China fear that NATO's activities in the southern NIS are part of a general US-European effort to achieve a dominant position in the subregion. There is a danger, therefore, that NATO's activities in the southern NIS could exacerbate the competition for influence in the subregion and give that competition a military dimension that has so far been relatively absent.[16] Such a development would undermine prospects for conflict resolution and stability within the southern NIS and increase the danger of future great power conflict over the subregion. NATO, therefore, faces a delicate balancing act in maintaining support for the independence of the southern NIS and sustaining cooperation with Russia, if not other powers.

Against this background, there is an obvious case for using inclusive, multilateral, subregionally-based PfP/EAPC activities to prevent NATO's engagement in the southern NIS from becoming dominated by the wider zero-sum dynamics of the subregion. In this context, it is a positive sign that subregional cooperation in the Trans-Caucasus is one of the leading subjects for discussion in the EAPC framework. One of the first fruits of this was an EAPC seminar on "Practical Approaches to Regional Security Cooperation in the Caucasus," held in Georgia in October 1998 and attended by NATO member states and PfP partners. The seminar was designed to increase awareness of the potential for security cooperation in the Trans-Caucasus, discuss experiences of subregional cooperation elsewhere, and explore areas for practical cooperation within the EAPC/PfP framework. The seminar covered defense-related economic issues, scientific and subregional cooperation, civil emergency and disaster preparedness, and technical military cooperation (e.g., mine clearance).[17] How far NATO can encourage more substantive Caucasian cooperation in the longer term within the EAPC/PfP framework remains to be seen.

There would appear to be a number of ways in which NATO could develop its engagement in the southern NIS and, in particular, encourage subregional cooperation. First, as in east-central Europe, PfP activities should center on the "softer" elements of sovereignty support rather than the "harder" elements of military cooperation. This would focus attention on those areas most likely to benefit the southern NIS and be less threatening for Russia. Second, NATO should maximize transparency with regard to its PfP activities in the southern NIS in order to reassure Russia, Iran, and China that such activities are not directed against them. In Russia's case, this should be relatively easy because of its own involvement with NATO. Transparency will be much more sensitive an issue with regard to Iran and China, although some informal provision of information on NATO's PfP activities in the southern NIS is conceivable. Third, NATO should continue to explore ways in which subregional cooperation in the southern NIS can be intensified via EAPC/PfP. A flexible approach is likely to be needed, with different groups of states involved in different activities. Appropriate activities might include subregionally organized defense education courses and more detailed discussion of practical issues such as environmental disaster management and multilateral peacekeeping activities. In general, the principles of transparency and openness to all interested PfP/EAPC members should be maintained. Iran, China, and other neighboring states might be involved as observers. As activities grow and confidence is built, more permanent arrangements might be considered, such as one or more regional peacekeeping centers or NATO/PfP/EAPC-sponsored hotlines and formal confidence-building measures.

The EU has engaged with Caucasian and some central Asian states through a series of partnership and cooperation agreements and the TACIS aid program. No partnership and cooperation agreement has been concluded with Tajikistan and that with Turkmenistan was only initialed in 1997 and has not yet been signed.[18] The partnership and cooperation agreements and TACIS have been relatively uncontroversial, certainly compared to NATO's engagement in the area. Like the EU's relations with the countries of south-eastern Europe and east-central Europe, these ties have been strongly bilateral.

A strong case could be made that the EU could do more, generally, to support the southern NIS in state-building, democratization, and economic reform, but particularly to promote subregional approaches to addressing shared problems. However, two specifically multilateral and subregional programs have been established by the EU: TRACECA (Transport Corridor Europe-Central Asia) and INOGATE (Interstate Oil and Gas to Europe). INOGATE involves technical assistance in the modernization of energy networks in the former Soviet Union. The larger and more politically significant TRACECA is aimed at the development of a transport corridor from central Asia and the Trans-Caucasus to Europe. Specific projects supported under TRACECA include the modernization of the Georgian port of Poti, the modernization of the Azeri port of Baku, the reconstruction of the Red Bridge on the Azerbaijan-Georgia border, and the redevelopment of ferry connections between Georgia and Ukraine. These projects are designed to promote the economic development of countries involved, reduce their economic dependence on Russia and former Soviet transport links, and encourage subregional cooperation between the southern NIS. The cumulative expenditure for TRACECA and INOGATE currently approaches 100 million ECU.

TRACECA, however, also illustrates why subregional cooperation, especially in relation to economics, transport links, and energy transit routes, cannot be separated from the wider international politics of the region. Russia is wary of TRACECA because the program will reduce the southern NIS's dependence on it and hence weaken its political influence in the subregion. Thus, while TRACECA provides an arguably positive example of subregional cooperation, it also illustrates that such cooperation has the potential to exacerbate existing competitive power dynamics in the subregion. The same dynamics exist with regard to the debate over possible pipeline routes for oil and gas from the southern NIS: Particular routes will encourage cooperation between certain groups of states, but they will also exclude or reduce the influence of other states.

The OSCE has been involved in the southern NIS as a result of its promotion of democracy and human rights and conflict prevention and resolution activities. The level of this activity, however, has been far lower than elsewhere in post-Communist Europe. Efforts in the last few years to encourage greater southern NIS (particularly central Asian) awareness of and engagement with the organization have implicitly acknowledged this fact. The OSCE has recognized the need to do more to promote cooperation in the Trans-Caucasus and central Asia, and has begun to develop some subregionally oriented activities, such as the seminar on central Asian "Regional Environmental Problems and Cooperative Approaches to Solving Them," in Uzbekistan in September 1998.[19] The OSCE's broad membership and its relative political neutrality (compared to NATO, the EU or the CIS) may make it particularly suited for the role of subregional promoter. The organization should continue to explore how it can do more to facilitate such cooperation, for example, through other seminars on common subregional problems and joint approaches to implementing OSCE norms and standards.

The poor democratization and human rights records of Trans-Caucasian and central Asian states have to date prevented them from joining the CoE as full members. The CoE has engaged with the three Trans-Caucasian states in assisting their promotion of democracy and respect for human rights. This has included an attempt by the parliamentary assembly of the CoE to organize hearings on the Nagorno-Karabakh conflict to be attended by the foreign ministers and parliamentary speakers of Armenia, Azerbaijan, and Georgia. As of October 1998, however, this meeting was delayed because of dispute between Armenia and Azerbaijan over whether representatives of Nagorno-Karabakh should attend, highlighting the difficulty of promoting subregional cooperation in the face of opposition from the subregion concerned.[20]

The UN and its specialized agencies have also been heavily involved in the Trans-Caucasus and central Asia, more so than in Europe's other "boundary zones." This involvement has included: UN humanitarian efforts in Georgia, Armenia, and Azerbaijan as a result of the conflicts in Abkhazia, Nagorno-Karabakh, and south Ossetia; UN Development Program efforts to address some of the subregion's environmental problems; and the UN Observer Mission in Georgia. These activities have been largely directed toward individual countries and conflicts, rather than the promotion of subregional cooperation. Two partial exceptions to this are the World

Food Program Trans-Caucasus Logistics Advisory Unit (which helped to restore the subregional transport infrastructure in 1994-96) and the UN Development Program's support for multilateral efforts to address the environmental problems of the Aral Sea area.

## Conclusion

This chapter has examined the potential role of the main international organizations in promoting subregional cooperation in Europe's new "boundary zones." Initially the post-Cold War policies of NATO, the EU, and the OSCE were based on bilateral ties with individual central and eastern European and former Soviet states, activities in or with individual states, or more general organization-wide commitments. There were and are good reasons for this approach. The pan-European commitments and standards of the OSCE provide the basic norms for international and domestic state behavior, and foster a sense of common European identity and security. The bilateral character of NATO and the EU's outreach policies and the country-specific character of much of the OSCE's operational work allow these organizations to tailor policies appropriate to each country and to make ties conditional on each country's progress in democratization and economic and foreign policy reforms.

This combination of policies, however, did little to encourage, and perhaps actively discouraged, multilateral, subregional cooperation in central and eastern Europe and the former Soviet Union. By the mid-1990s, there was a growing recognition of the need to adapt existing policies to provide greater support for subregional cooperation between the countries concerned. NATO, the EU, and the OSCE as well as other organizations such as the Council of Europe and the UN and its specialized agencies have begun this process of adaptation. As this chapter has shown, NATO has sought to encourage multilateral, subregional cooperation within the EAPC/PfP framework, while the EU has sought (perhaps less successfully than NATO) to break down the bilateralism of its association and partnership and cooperation agreements, and the OSCE has begun to facilitate discussion of subregional issues. Nevertheless, these organizations could and should do more to encourage subregional cooperation and to support existing subregional initiatives.

The differing political and geostrategic circumstances of the new "boundary zones" will require differing approaches to subregional cooperation. In south-eastern Europe, there appears to be a certain core of support for multilateral cooperation within the subregion which, combined with the leverage from NATO and the EU, may be sufficient to drive cooperation forward. The challenge will be to give more substance to existing frameworks and to find appropriate means of engaging the subregion's most troubled states (Croatia, Bosnia, and above all, FRY). Much may also depend on the success or failure of international efforts to contain and resolve the Bosnian and Kosovo conflicts. In east-central Europe, there is no real basis for trilateral cooperation between Ukraine, Moldova, and Belarus. There is, however, a case for greater subregional cooperation between the three, the central European states and Russia on an ad hoc, flexible basis. Support from NATO and the EU can help to provide both the political reassurance and the material resources necessary for such cooperation to develop. In the Trans-Caucasus and central Asia, subregional cooperation is likely to be inhibited by the conflicts between the southern NIS and the competing agendas of the external powers. Nevertheless, elements of subregional cooperation have begun to emerge. The task for the international community will be to encourage initiatives that promote cooperation on an inclusive basis within the Trans-Caucasus and central Asia.

While international organizations, particularly NATO, the EU, and the OSCE, can do more to promote subregional cooperation in Europe's "boundary zones," there will remain limits to what they can do, and expectations should be appropriately modest. Where serious internal and bilateral conflicts remain (as in Kosovo or between Armenia and Azerbaijan), more substantive subregional cooperation is likely to remain dependent on the resolution of these conflicts. Where there is little or no sense of common subregional identity or interests (as between the three western NIS), external powers or international organizations will not be able to create the basis for subregional cooperation. Where external powers are competing for influence (as in the southern NIS), subregional cooperation may be able to mitigate the character of that competition, but it is unlikely to be able to entirely overcome it. The challenge for the main international and European organizations will be to find the political spaces in which subregional cooperation can develop and to provide political and material support to maximize such cooperation.

## Notes

1. For useful recent reviews of the emerging situation in the southern NIS, see "Caspian oil: Not the great game revisited," in *The International Institute for Strategic Studies* (IISS), Strategic Survey 1997/98 (London: Oxford University Press, April 1998), pp. 22-29; and Zanny Minton Beddoes, "A Caspian gamble: A survey of Central Asia," *The Economist*, 7 February 1998.

2. Jane M. O. Sharp, "Dayton report card," *International Security* 22, no. 3, (Winter 1997-98): 101-37.

3. On PfP generally, see "The Enhanced Partnership for Peace," *NATO Fact Sheet* No. 9, July 1997 (http://www.nato.int/docu/facts/epfp.htm).

4. David Lightburn, "NATO Security Cooperation Activities with Bosnia and Herzegovina," *NATO Review* 46, no. 2 (Summer 1998): 31-34.

5. This has included a number of multilateral military exercises. See "Multinational Military Exercises in Albania," *OMRI Daily Digest* II, no. 136, 16 July 1996; "Navies of ten nations converge on Black Sea resort," *NATO AFSOUTH*, Release Number 96-17.2A, 19 July 1996; and Radu Busneag, "Romania: Peacekeeping exercise begins tomorrow," *Radio Free Europe/Radio Liberty*, 4 November 1997 (http://www.rferl.org/nca/news/1997/11/N.RU.971104152557.html).

6. "Balkan states discuss multinational peacekeeping force," *RFE/RL Newsline* 2, no. 54, Part II, 19 March 1998; and "Balkan Defense Ministers Agree to Form Joint Force," *RFE/RL Newsline* 2, no. 187, Part II, 28 September 1998.

7. The limitations of the Royaumont process are acknowledged by European Commission officials. See Renata Dwan and Andrew Cottey, "Frameworks for Security and Integration in Europe: Region-Building in South Eastern Europe – Summary of a workshop held in Sofia, 8-9 November 1997," Institute for EastWest Studies/Finnish Institute of International Affairs.

8. The WEU's associate partner status is limited to those states which have association agreements with the EU. Hence, the WEU's cooperation activities do not included Albania, Croatia, Macedonia, or FRY. This also limits the WEU's role in the western NIS and Southern NIS, since none of these states have association agreements with the EU. The WEU does, however, have more limited bilateral relationships with Ukraine and Russia. See Western European Union – Membership (http:www.weu.int/eng/info/info-0301.htm).

9. "OSCE Seminar within the framework of the Common and Comprehensive Security Model for Europe for the Twenty-First Century, 'Regional Security and Cooperation,' Vienna, 2-4 June 1997," Chairman's Summary, Organization for Security and Cooperation in Europe, Permanent Council, REF.PC/502/97, 4 June 1997.

10. On the Council of Europe generally, see Daniel Tarschys, "The Council of Europe: Strengthening European Security by Civilian Means," *NATO Review* 45, no. 1 (January 1997): 4-9.

11. As US President Bill Clinton has argued of the OSCE, "we should encourage even greater engagement in the areas where democracy's roots are still fragile – in the Balkans, in Central Asia, and the Trans-Caucasus – and we must develop practical new tools for the OSCE such as training police to support peacekeeping missions and dispatching democracy teams to build more open societies." Remarks by the President to the People of Germany, Schauspielhaus, Berlin, Germany, 13 May 1998, The White House, Office of the Press Secretary (Berlin Germany), (http://library.whitehouse.gov/.gifs/head-library.gif).

12. Jan de Weydenthal, "Belarus: Minsk demands NATO security guarantees," *Radio Free Europe/Radio Liberty*, 4 April 1997, (http://www.rferl.org/nac/features/

1997/04/F.RU.970404192931.html).

13. Bogdan Turek, "Ukraine: Diplomat appeals to Poland to keep border open," *Radio Free Europe/Radio Free Liberty*, 11 May 1998 (http://www.rferl.org/nca/features/1998/05/F.RU.980511124023.html).

14. Jan Maksymiuk, "EU punishes Belarusian leadership," *RFE/RL Newsline*, 2, no. 139, Part II, 22 July 1998.

15. As one potentially positive example of this sort of cooperation, it was reported in October 1998 that the foreign ministers of Russia, Ukraine, Moldova, and Poland would meet before the end of the year to discuss the Transnistria conflict. For more, see "Poland pledges to help Moldova resolve Transdniester," *RFE/RL Newsline* 2, no. 209, Part II, 29 October 1998. How useful this would be remains to be seen.

16. NATO's PfP involvement with Armenia and Azerbaijan, for example, has become linked to broader tensions between the two countries and between Russia and NATO. See "Aliev urges NATO to halt 'militarization of Armenia'," *RFE/RL Newsline* 2, no. 297, Part I, 26 October 1998.

17. EAPC, Seminar on Practical Approaches to Regional Security Cooperation in the Caucasus, Gudauri, Georgia, 15-16 October 1998, NATO, Press Release (98)113, 12 October 1998.

18. On the partnership and cooperation agreements, see *TACIS: Framework of the Program – PCA* (http://europa.eu.int/comm/dg1a/tacis/framework/frwrk_pca.htm).

19. "Seminar examines regional environmental problems and solutions in central Asia," *OSCE Newsletter* 5, no. 9, September 1998: 5-6.

20. "Armenia concerned by Council of Europe delay," *RFE/RL Newsline* 2, no. 207, Part I, 26 October 1998.

# Conclusion

## Renata Dwan

The three areas of the wider European space explored in this book share little in common. They differ in size, in the number of their constituent states, and in the extent to which they are perceived, or perceive themselves, as distinct subregions of the Eurasian continent. The chapters of the book, which focus on the particular physical, historical, political and economic factors that shape each area and interstate relations therein, amply demonstrate this fact. The distinctiveness of east-central Europe, south-eastern Europe and the southern tier of the Trans-Caucasus and central Asia has led each of the authors to emphasize the need for caution in delimiting these areas as subregions. As Charles King reminds us, "thinking a region does not make it so." It also underscores the impossibility of adapting a generic model of subregional cooperation to any particular area of the Eurasian continent.

Individual particularities have been also used to explain why there has been so little subregional cooperation to date among the countries of these three areas. At the same time, all of the contributors agree that processes of regularized, significant political and economic interaction among groups of states, such as that seen in parts of western, central, and north-western Europe, could significantly assist the subregions that are the subject of this volume. It could help create a more stable regional environment and enable states to concentrate on their socio-economic development. Such interaction could promote economic growth and the development of frameworks for trade and communication. It could contribute to the management of region-specific resource and environmental problems. It could facilitate the development of civil, democratic societies and stable ethnic relations within a subregion. It could offer a means for states to articulate their voice at the global level and bring international attention to their specific interests. These are all goals identified by Europe's "boundary zones." Yet it is the continued absence of these socioeconomic and political conditions that is said to constrain the emergence of cooperative subregional relations in each.

Can anything be done to break this seemingly vicious circle? Is it possible to identify the essential prerequisites for subregional cooperation in Europe's periphery spaces and thereby facilitate some subregional development that might, in time, lead to a "virtuous" circle of cooperation? Is a strategy for subregional cooperation even appropriate for east-central Europe, south-eastern Europe, the Trans-Caucasus, and central Asia? These are questions that the preceding chapters have addressed in the context of specific subregions and actors. This conclusion attempts to draw out some of the principal themes that have been identified and assess the prerequisites as well as the prospects for subregional cooperation in Europe's boundary zones. The influences dominating the emergence of subregional relations operate at the level of the nation-state, the immediate regional environment, and at the level of the wider international arena. The interplay between the forces at each level differs for east-central Europe, southeastern Europe, and the Trans-Caucasus and central Asia. It is this interplay that will determine the future for subregional cooperation in these "borderlands" of Europe.

## Subregional Cooperation and the Weak State

One of the most striking conclusions to emerge from the three cases is the significance of a functioning state for subregional cooperation. Many academics have claimed that the increase in regional cooperation is a global process reflecting the diminishing role of the nation-state in an interdependent world.[1] Regionalism, in this context, offers a way of managing the fragmentation of the state and the emergence of new transnational, non-state actors. Such a perspective tends to pay less attention to the state itself and concentrate, instead, on the interplay between different groups and issues. However, in central and eastern Europe subregional processes are usually viewed as strategies to strengthen the state. One of the most important motivating elements for subregional cooperation in the Baltic Sea area, for example, has been the desire of Nordic states to ensure the independence and stability of the three newly emergent Baltic states. Indeed, most existing subregional groupings implicitly include state-building as a common objective of their member states.[2] This approach to subregional cooperation reflects the increasing dominance of the independent nation-state in particular parts of the world. This reassertion of the nation-state is taking place, however, in an international environment of increasing interdependence. Central and eastern European states must thus negotiate the realization of self-determination, while adapting to the challenges of globalization. Subregionalism in this part of the world is a strategy for balancing national goals and international constraints, providing a framework of assistance to states seeking to consolidate independence, establish stable infrastructures, and manage transition to democratic, internationally integrated, market economies.

This strategy is, nonetheless, somewhat paradoxical. In order to initiate practical subregional cooperation processes in almost any area, whether promoting trade, environmental management, social development, or combating organized crime, a certain degree of state development is a prerequisite. A state must have already elaborated at least one state-building strategy to some degree of success before adopting a subregional approach to assist its further development. The implications for subregional cooperation of a dearth of mature or strong states in east-central Europe, south-eastern Europe, and the southern tier amply illustrate this paradox.

Given the common economic weakness of these states and the interest they share in increasing trade and investment in their immediate environment, practical economic cooperation is usually seen as the most promising area for subregional development between them. Such cooperation is an established goal between the states of central Asia, the south Caucasian states in the context of Black Sea Economic Cooperation (BSEC), various cooperative initiatives between south-eastern European countries, and between Ukraine, Moldova, and the neighboring state of Romania. Yet, practical results have been negligible in all cases. The weak rate of implementation of projects reflects the pace of economic transition and growth in many of these states. The structure of their economies is as significant an obstacle as their slow pace of economic develop-

ment. Nonmarket trading principles that governed economic interaction in the Soviet Union and the former Yugoslavia led to the
development of similarly structured peripheral economies linked to
each other only via the center. There is currently, therefore, only limited potential for trade and specialization between them on the basis
of comparative advantage, and there will not be until a substantial
degree of economic reform has been achieved.

Poor transport and communications infrastructures within and
between neighboring countries, for much of the same reason as
above, is another serious impediment to practical cooperation. As
a number of the authors in this book have noted, transport infrastructure development is an issue area in which common subregional interests have been recognized and articulated. Neighboring
states are potentially willing to initiate joint cooperation projects
in transport network development as early as possible. The high
financial cost of infrastructure projects, however, particularly
those with a large geographical scope, means that joint transport
and communications networks stand little chance of being implemented without massive funding and support from outside actors.
The EU's Trans-Europe-Central Asia Corridor project (TRACE-
CA) demonstrates this fact. TRACECA also illustrates that practical cooperation between states in central Asia and the Trans-
Caucasus is feasible in particular contexts. Indeed, common interest in transport development is arguably the most important factor
in the gradual amelioration of relations between Armenia and
Georgia as the December 1998 transport agreement between
Armenia, Georgia, and Bulgaria demonstrates.[3]

Lack of financial resources alone cannot explain the absence of
diverse forms of subregional cooperation. The lack of sub-state
frameworks within the states of Europe's boundary zones is,
arguably, a more substantial constraint on practical subregional
cooperation. Regional and local government structures in many of
these countries are either nonexistent or manifestations of rewards
among the political elite. Although countries such as Georgia have
given new priority to the development of regional and local authorities, there remain, in all three "borderlands," states that demonstrate little commitment to the democratic decentralization of
power. Yet, practical cooperation between regional authorities, initiated and supported by national governments, is seen as the core
of subregional cooperation in other parts of Europe. Sub-state

interaction is regarded as the distinctive element of subregionalism and the means by which groups of states can practically address local needs and problems. It is this multilateral cooperation that distinguishes subregionalism from traditional interstate relations and offers a democratizing contribution to the practice of international relations. Until the structures for sub-state cooperation are in place, therefore, the prospects for practical subregionalism remain poor.

The weakness of civil society in boundary zone states is a final constraint on the development of subregional cooperation. An active civil society can facilitate the implementation of government-initiated good-neighborly processes through social and commercial exchange and interaction. Nongovernmental organizations, private citizens' groups, and business communities can diversify and deepen processes begun by governments. They can serve as pressure groups on central authorities hesitant to assign scarce resources to cross-border cooperation. Civil society actors can even play a mitigating role in situations in which the government is hostile to subregional initiatives: The transborder links between nongovernmental actors in Slovakia under the recent regime of Vladimir Meciar are a case in point. These links helped contain the destabilizing effects of executive policies on relations in central Europe and prevented the state's further isolation in the region. The same could conceivably become the case in Belarus.

The emphasis of the South Eastern Cooperation Initiative (SECI) and the Royaumont Initiative on developing interaction between nonstate actors in south-eastern Europe suggests that western and, increasingly, south-eastern European policymakers are conscious of the significance of civil society for subregional cooperation. Substantial assistance to cross-border civil society programs is now underway in the region. The difficulty for much of east-central Europe, the Trans-Caucasus and central Asia, however, is that comparable frameworks of civil society are not yet even in place to begin such subregional processes.

It is hardly surprising, therefore, that most subregional cooperation in Europe's boundary zones to date has taken the form of high-level political initiatives between heads of state and government. In this environment the political will of political elites for subregional cooperation becomes paramount. As Charles King has observed in Belarus and Arif Yunusov in the three southern

Caucasian states, current patterns of interaction in east-central
Europe and the Trans-Caucasus indicate that individual leaders and
political elites are key actors in the development of subregional relations. Reliance on the perceptions and preferences of single individuals does not bode well for the development of sustainable subregional cooperation in the short term. It presents yet further challenges for the institutionalization of cooperative processes among
groups of states, and, where personal rivalries exist, may even be a
source of increased competition between neighboring states

In the medium term, however, a wider range of new political
elites is emerging in each of the three areas surveyed in this book.
The extent to which these elites can be exposed to and informed
about subregional processes may help encourage the evolution of
attitudes in east-central Europe, south-eastern Europe and the
southern tier. Elites from boundary zone countries engaged in
existing central and eastern European groupings are already
exposed to learning opportunities. The lessons they draw in one
context might well serve as the basis for subregional initiatives
elsewhere. Oleksandr Pavliuk gave an example of this in the case
of the Lower Danube and Upper Prut Euroregion initiatives
between Moldova, Romania, and Ukraine that have been directly
influenced by the experience of Ukrainian and Romanian participation in the Carpathian Euroregion. External actors, particularly
existing subregional groupings, could assist in this process by providing political elites with opportunities to learn about subregionalism and develop the technical skills necessary to initiate and
manage cooperative projects. Such training support focuses attention away from the structural and economic weaknesses of
Europe's boundary zones, while at the same time assisting the
political and societal development of their constituent states.

Emphasis on the weaknesses of the state may appear to yield
pessimistic prospects for subregional cooperation within Europe's
"borderlands" in the short to medium term. In one important way,
however, it represents a positive conclusion. As all of the writers
in this book demonstrate, there are no inherent factors that determine a subregion and the relations within it. Subregional cooperation cannot be viewed as an outcome  governed by ethnic, clan, or
religious identity. Given the traumatic experiences of Europe's
three "boundary zones" over the last ten years, this is a conclusion
that cannot be overemphasized.

## Subregional Cooperation and Conflict

The presence of ongoing or unresolved conflict in east-central Europe, south-eastern Europe, and the southern tier is identified by all the authors as a serious constraint on cooperation among states in the affected regions. It is not merely interstate dispute that ruptures relations between subregional actors: intrastate conflict, such as the Transnistria dispute in Moldova or the Georgian-Abkhaz war in the Trans-Caucasus, can severely destabilize the regional environment, and provoke fear and tension in neighboring states. That these cases are usually ethnic in nature, often involving a group with a kin state in the subregion, makes negative spillover all the more likely for the area. This is most often heralded by the arrival of large groups of refugees, which places further strains on the stability of all the states of the subregion.

At the same time, the relationship between subregional cooperation and conflict that emerges from this book is more nuanced than is often portrayed. Plamen Pantev's examination of evolving perceptions toward subregional cooperation among political elites in south-eastern Europe demonstrates that conflict may actually serve as a force for the initiation of cooperative relations among neighboring states. Balkan leaders have been motivated by a recognition of the high costs of conflicts for the development of all south-eastern Europe as well as by a desire to prevent the expansion of ongoing conflict. The threat of continued or increased violent conflict in an area may serve to encourage recognition of subregional interdependency and generate common interest in the containment of conflict among a group of states. Subregional cooperation in some parts of Europe's boundary zones may, therefore, develop around the explicit negotiation of security, unlike the central European experience which, as Anders Bjurner points out, has centered on a shared resolve not to address matters of "hard" security. The very centrality of conflict in some areas may make it impossible to shunt aside.

Low-level tensions and unresolved disputes in the three boundary zones may do more to impede cooperation between neighbors than actual conflict. Sophia Clèment, Oleksandr Pavliuk, and Arif Yunusov all show that a legacy of mistrust between two or more states can lead to a zero-sum perspective on subregional relations. Precisely because conflict is not overt, the possibility of mutual benefit for all parties is harder to accept. The entrenchment of attitudes that stems from protracted unresolved disputes further contributes to negative perceptions. In this context, any cooperative initiative is viewed as an inevitable strategy of unilateral gain for the state promoting it. Varying levels of grievances and frozen conflicts are a feature of all three of Europe's boundary zones and are one of the most significant factors in creating an environment that effectively precludes subregional development.

External actors could have a useful role to play in these contexts. As Andrew Cottey points out, international organizations, such as the UN, NATO's Partnership for Peace (PfP), the EU, or the World Bank can develop regional programs that encourage and reward subregional cooperation. Neighboring states could invite states of the subregion to participate in existing cooperative processes, and by placing the subregion concerned in a larger, more constructive environment, undercut the dominance of lingering rivalries. Third parties might, in some circumstances, even mediate between hostile neighbors. Larger non-neighboring western states could initiate, finance, and monitor subregional projects in specific areas. There should be no illusions that these processes produce anything but marriages of convenience in the short term. Over the longer term, however, cooperative frameworks initiated by actors external to the area may serve as an important first step toward the evolution of perceptions in a subregion with a record of unresolved disputes. The difficulty is that this requires sustained and active commitment by the international community in areas of Europe where the very absence of serious conflict is often seen to render a comprehensive presence unnecessary, if not untenable.

### Subregional Cooperation and External Actors

The involvement of external states in a subregion is a highly sensitive and often ambiguous issue. The geography of Europe's boundary zones means that for east-central Europe and the southern tier of the Trans-Caucasus and central Asia, at least, Russia is the dominant external actor. The presence of a large external state may serve to encourage subregional cooperation between smaller and/or recently established states that are keen to manifest and defend their sovereign independence. This was certainly viewed as an important element in central European subregional cooperative experiences. As the case of cooperation between Georgia, Ukraine, Azerbaijan, and Moldova

(GUAM) illustrates, this may take place even between noncontiguous states. However, the case of GUAM also reveals the limitation of cooperative processes that stem principally from a common attitude toward an outside neighbor. First, it can be perceived as a process directed against the external state, in this case Russia, and provoke a negative reaction from that state. Second, the participants in this form of subregional cooperation may find it difficult to generate wider support from an international community that seeks to adopt inclusive approaches to the management of Europe's boundary zones. Other neighboring states might view the process as an exclusionary gesture in a more immediate geographical context, notably Armenia in the south Caucasus. Finally, the extent to which non-proximate states can develop the practical interaction that is central to subregional cooperation remains an open question.

The presence of external states can, as Neil MacFarlane demonstrates, also serve to impede cooperative relations in a subregion. Larger, more powerful states often dominate political, economic, and security relations in a given area and establish an environment in which effective subregional cooperation is impossible. Central Asian dependency on the Russian communications infrastructure is a good example of this. Moreover, the external state may emphasize bilateral relations instead of multilateral approaches to the subregion, thereby effectively playing states off against each other. Where two or more external states have interests in the subregion, as is clearly the case in the Trans-Caucasus and central Asia, it is almost inevitable that subregional cooperation will be seriously constrained by power rivalries.

Yet interstate relations are not dictated solely by the larger state. The Russian-Belarusian Union offers a good example of a cooperative process that has been initiated and led by Belarusian President Alexander Lukashenka. Moreover, it is not always in the interest of external states to prevent subregional cooperation. While greater subregional interaction may lead to more assertive policies by smaller states, subregional cooperation can also contribute to political and economic stability. This would considerably reduce the costs incurred by larger states in maintaining order in troubled neighboring areas. States neighboring Europe's boundary zones such as Iran, Turkey, and Poland have sought to encourage subregional relations with certain states as a way of developing stability along their borders, a measure that may benefit all parties concerned.

Ultimately, practical subregional cooperation in Europe's boundary zones necessitates the involvement of large neighboring states. By virtue of their size, relations, and history these states have real interests in the subregions that border them. Such interests are legitimate. From the perspective of feasibility, it is impossible to engage in practical subregional cooperation in trade, investment, resource, and environmental management while excluding the strongest economic actor in the area. Without the acquiescence, if not active support, of large neighboring states, cooperative initiatives will stand little chance of generating the political and economic assistance necessary for implementation of projects. Finding strategies to engage large neighboring states in nonhierarchical cooperative processes will be one of the most important conditions for the development of sustainable subregional cooperation in Europe's boundary zones. This requires compromise and determined will from all sides.

**Subregional Cooperation and European Integration**

The nature of the states involved in subregional cooperation, the degree of conflict between them, and the role of larger states in their immediate environment significantly influence the emergence and nature of subregional cooperation in a given area. Perhaps the most significant influence on cooperation in Europe's boundary zones, however, is the integration processes currently taking place at the wider Euro-Atlantic level. Western institutional extension into central and eastern Europe is dominated by EU and NATO enlargement, and although these two parallel processes represent very distinct forms of integration, there is a tendency to view them collectively as a single process. This is certainly the case among the three boundary zones that are defined precisely by their peripheral status to the two most dominant institutions on the Eurasian continent.

In direct and indirect ways, European integration processes have served as the principal impetus for post-Cold War subregional cooperation. Western models of voluntary, noncoercive cooperation between states were perceived to emerge victorious over the more rigidified asymmetric relations defined by the Warsaw Pact and the Soviet Union. The comprehensive integration of western European states was perceived to have brought historical enmities between them to an end. It has certainly brought them economic well being. The visions of openness, free movement of people and goods, and cooperative relations between mutually sovereign states that dominated the international climate of the early 1990s were directly inspired by western integration experiences. It was hardly surprising that they should be articulated in central and eastern European contexts as the basis for the establishment of new relations between former Warsaw Pact states.

The desire to join western institutions is another strong motivation for the development of cooperative relations between groups of states in central and eastern Europe. The security protection and economic benefits that membership in NATO and the EU offer mean that a western orientation has never been in doubt for the overwhelming majority of these states. In some cases, support for integration into EU and NATO was the explicit basis for cooperative initiatives between central European states, as in the case of the Visegrad group, which was established in 1991-92 between then Czechoslovakia, Hungary, and Poland. Multilateral cooperation, in this instance, represented a way of articulating and securing international support for the claims of these states to belong to the institutions of the west. The EU and NATO stipulation of good neighborly relations as a fundamental condition for accession further encouraged this process and served to reinforce the interdependency between neighboring state relations and wider integration processes.

Subregional cooperation is also seen as a useful preparatory stage on the way to EU and NATO membership. Cooperation between a smaller group of neighboring states represents a way of socializing government, business, and civil society groups into the environment of dense networks of interaction that characterizes larger Euro-Atlantic processes. Subregional groups, in this context, may serve as arenas for states to exchange information and assistance on the common goal of EU and NATO membership, thereby strengthening the participation of all members in the European integration process. This, for example, is an implicit goal of subregional groupings such as the Central European Initiative (CEI), which counts south-eastern European states as well as the three east-central European countries among its members.

The subregional relations that have begun to emerge in Europe's boundary zones reflect the interrelationship between wider integration and subregional processes. The 1994 Central Asian Cooperative Initiative of Uzbek President Islom Karimov was launched as a model of European community processes adapted to a central Asian setting.

The recent name change of the grouping from the Central Asian Union to the Central Asian Economic Community reflects this influence. The states of south-eastern Europe, almost all of which have stated that EU and NATO membership are their primary goal, insist that nascent subregional cooperation between them must be seen in the context of their preparation for accession into these organizations. Subregional cooperation is understood in south-eastern Europe, Plamen Pantev suggests, as a way of speeding up the accession process itself and, according to Sophia Clément, is the lynchpin of the EU's conditional approach to relations in the area. Ukraine's (and, to some extent, Moldova's) desire for eventual EU and NATO membership is one of the strongest motivations for its engagement in multilateral and trilateral cooperative networks with a variety of partners to its west who are further advanced in the EU and NATO accession process. Subregional cooperation, for Ukraine, represents a useful backdoor in its relations with the EU.

Yet these very considerations demonstrate the potentially negative influence of wider integration processes on subregional cooperation in Europe's boundary zones. Subregional cooperation motivated primarily by the desire for EU and NATO membership is going to be viewed instrumentally by participating states. There is a risk, in such cases, that all subregional efforts will be regarded as contingent upon the success of EU and NATO goals, initiatives to be quietly left to wither if and when accession takes place or, worse, processes to be discarded if not seen to culminate in the immediate goal of EU and NATO membership. That disappointment in the latter might well have negative consequences for subregionalism was postulated in the case of  Romania's subregional enthusiasm after the NATO Madrid Summit of July 1997, as Oleksandr Pavliuk has noted. More significant, perhaps, is the direction in which the energies of resource-strapped states are focused. The goal of EU and NATO accession may, in south eastern European states, Ukraine, and, increasingly, Moldova and Georgia, direct attention and resources away from issues in the more immediate locale. As a result, these countries may fail to address some of the most serious challenges to their security and prosperity.

In some cases, wider integration goals may encourage states to take a hostile position toward subregional cooperation. The resistance of Slovenia, for example, toward south-eastern European cooperative initiatives stemmed in large part from its fear of having its EU accession chances diminished through association with a "troubled" geographical area. All central and eastern European states prior to 1997 feared that the EU might adopt an enlargement strategy of grouping states together and admitting them collectively rather than reviewing applications on an individual basis. The EU's explicit commitment to measure each state on its own merits thus constituted an important prerequisite for continuing subregional cooperation. Nevertheless, the fragility of being on the periphery of European integration continues to encourage many border zone states to view subregional cooperation only in westerly directed terms. Other south-eastern European states such as Bulgaria, Croatia, Romania, have, like Ukraine, embraced subregional cooperation with central European states much more enthusiastically than they have with their immediate border zone neighbors. Such patterns are unlikely to produce cooperation that addresses local, practical concerns. They may conceivably even generate tension with those neighbors that have chosen not to pursue EU and NATO integration. In this context, the relationship between subregional cooperation and wider integration in central Asia is quite distinct from east-central Europe, south-eastern Europe and even the southern Caucasian states. It may well be that genuine and effective subregional cooperation has more chance of emerging in those border zones where the prospect of EU and NATO membership is ruled out, either completely or for the long term, than in those areas closer to EU/NATO integration processes. This conclusion, it is worth noting, would appear to go against current subregional patterns in and around Europe's "boundary zones."

To a large extent, the dominance of the EU and NATO in subregional relations is not the "fault" of either institution. At the same time, it could be argued that NATO has been more successful than the EU in mitigating the potentially negative effects of its enlargement on subregional relations in central and eastern Europe. Admittedly, the expansion of the western collective security alliance to the Czech Republic, Hungary, and Poland is smaller in geographical scope and thus helps avoid a sense of an isolated periphery versus a large, strong center. More important, perhaps, is the framework of relations that NATO has developed with nonmembers. The PfP incorporates all the states of the boundary zones (with the exception of Bosnia, Croatia Former Republic of Yugoslavia and Serbia) in a structure that enables each state to negotiate its relationship with the alliance bilaterally (the

16+1 formula) without creating a hierarchy of closeness to the organization. Additionally, PfP programs have begun to develop a significant regional component that incorporates existing subregional initiatives in the security sphere, such as the central Asian battalion (CENTRABAT), as well as encouraging new ones through joint training exercises and cooperation. Most of the multilateral peacekeeping units that have recently been established in central and eastern Europe have taken place within the context of the PfP. Finally, as Andrew Cottey has outlined, NATO's EAPC forum for political dialogue has the potential to become a center for the discussion and development of cooperative subregional security approaches.

The EU, by contrast, has embarked on a complex series of differing relationships with its eastern neighbors. Ten central and eastern European states are accession partners. Of these, five have begun formal discussions for membership. Partnership and cooperation agreements exist with all of the Newly Independent States and Russia (except Tajikistan), although with differing rates of practical implementation. Relations with south-eastern European states take place along a range of individual trade and association agreements which, in some cases, are related to obligations set out in the Dayton Peace Agreement. This hierarchy of relations may reinforce the sense among nonassociated partner states' of peripherality as well as competition among them to enter the association fold. Practically, it means that there are a series of different institutional frameworks within which nonmember state-EU relations take place. This may well influence the relations between CEE states themselves. Associated partner states, in particular, might be more inclined to orient themselves toward other associated partners, rather than toward nonpartner states in their immediate geographical vicinity. Finally, the bilateral focus of the EU's assistance to the region, as Andrew Cottey has already pointed out, has not encouraged states to devise practical subregional projects for EU financing.

Fundamentally, however, there is tension between regional integration and subregional cooperation that no amount of regional fence building can easily overcome. Multilevel cooperation between central governments, sub-state authorities and nonstate actors is a necessary step toward integration. It is not a sufficient step, however. Integration, in the EU experience, is a process of comprehensive, structural cooperation between a group of states in which a significant degree of state sovereignty is voluntarily transferred to a supranational authority. A legal, political entity is created, the constituent units of which are bound together by a comprehensive body of norms, laws, and procedures, known in the EU as the *aquis communautaire*. This manifests itself in a wide range of ways, from a common commercial policy, to a common foreign and security policy, to a common system for regulating the movement of goods, labor, and persons. Within this integrated unit, intense forms of cooperation between a group of states or sub-states are perfectly feasible. Difficulties are raised, however, when individual member states seek to enter cooperative commitments with nonmembers in any of the economic, political, or security fields in which the EU *aquis* exists. Such sovereign freedom to act no longer exists.

The potential consequences of this for subregional cooperation in central and eastern Europe are serious. The case of visa requirements offers a trenchant example. States acceding into the EU must observe and enforce the obligations of the EU's Schengen arrangements, which provide for the removal of intra-EU borders on the basis of a secure external EU border. As a result, incoming EU members must impose strict conditions on the movement of goods and people along their eastern frontiers. This will not only significantly hamper practical cross-border and subregional cooperation between neighboring states, it marks a fundamentally new approach to relations in a multiethnic region where visa requirements have not previously been imposed. EU integration not only threatens states in Europe's border zones with greater political and economic isolation, it also precludes the strategy of subregional cooperation that many view as a way of preventing new dividing lines between Europe and its peripheries.

There is no easy way of resolving the tension between subregional cooperation and EU integration. Any attempt to mediate between the requirements of EU integration and the realities of relations between central and eastern European neighbors can only take place at the EU level and not by individual candidate states. The EU is adamant that no individual arrangements (so-called derogations) for particular states will be permitted. At the same time, the EU cannot afford to ignore efforts that certain groups of states have undertaken to establish cooperative relations and practical cooperation between them. Such initiatives reflect the very goals and policies by which EU has sought to define itself. Nor can it seek to shape these processes by encouraging, say, subregional relations only between nonaccession states or in certain, "noncontentious" issue areas, such as social exchanges. Ultimately, the extent to which strong EU eastern and southern borders will have to be established will depend on the stability, security, and prosperity of the states that lie outside them. The EU, therefore, has every interest in encouraging cooperative processes that contribute to development in and around its border zones and of finding ways that accommodate fruitful relations between member and nonmember neighbors.

The prospects for subregional cooperation in east-central Europe, south-eastern Europe and southern tier of the Trans-Caucasus and central Asia look set to be shaped by a combination of factors: the development of the states involved; the immediate environment in which they operate, particularly the level and character of regional conflict and the role played by larger neighboring states; and the future development of Euro-Atlantic integration processes. The way in which these forces play out will ultimately determine the extent to which these three areas will remain Europe's "border zones."

Subregional cooperation, therefore, does not represent an alternative to the processes taking place at national, regional and wider European levels. It is not a panacea to problems encountered in these contexts. It may, however, facilitate and forward the goals of security and stability in a particular subregion and thus contribute to the fulfillment of national and wider European goals. The way in which subregional cooperation may do this in Europe's boundary zones is unlikely to be through intense practical institutionalized economic, political or social interaction. Subregionalism's greatest contribution, in east-central Europe, south-eastern Europe, and the Trans-Caucasus and central Asia lies in the extent to which it may encourage the development of certain norms in Europe's boundary zones. These norms must, first, be based on recognition of a common interest in avoiding conflict and, second, recognition of the existing state system in the immediate neighborhood. The current task for subregional cooperation in Europe's border zones, therefore, is to establish a basic framework in which common objectives and interests may, over time, develop between the states involved. Ultimately, subregional cooperation may serve as a tool, enabling Europe's border zones to overcome their peripheral status, geographically, economically, and politically. The extent to which subregional cooperation can overcome such divisions in the wider Europe is its greatest challenge, paradox, and potential.

# Notes

1. Introduction in Jyrki Kakonen (ed.), *Dreaming of the Barents Region: Interpreting Cooperation in the Euro-Arctic Rim*, Tampere Research Institute Research Report, no. 73, 1996, p. 20.

2. See, for example, the CEI plan of action 1998-99 agreed at the meeting of CEI heads of government, Sarajevo, 28-29 November 1998.

3. RFE/RL Online Report, 24 December 1998.

# Appendices

Principal Subregional Groupings

# Appendix A

## Balkan Conference of Stability and Cooperation in Southeast Europe

Participating states: Albania, Bulgaria, the Former Yugoslav Republic of Macedonia, the Former Republic of Yugoslavia, Greece, Romania, Turkey

Established: 1996

### Origins

The Balkan Conference of Stability and Cooperation in Southeast Europe (BCSC) was launched in July 1996 as an attempt to revive multilateral subregional cooperation in south-eastern Europe (SEE) after the war in former Yugoslavia. The idea to organize a series of meetings for senior state officials from the region was initially presented by Bulgaria. Supported by Greece, Romania, and Turkey, the Bulgarian government organized a meeting of foreign ministers of the SEE countries in Sofia on July 6-7 1996. The Sophia Declaration on Good-Neighborly Relations, Stability, Security, and Cooperation in the Balkans, signed by foreign ministers and heads of delegation of Albania, Bosnia-Herzegovina, Bulgaria, the Former Republic of Yugoslavia, Greece, Romania, and Turkey, became a founding document of the Balkan Conference.

## Structure

The BCSC has no institutional structure. It operates through meetings of SEE government ministers and the heads of state. Foreign ministers and the heads of state meet once a year; other government ministers or their deputies meet on an ad hoc basis. Secretariat responsibilities for each year are borne by the country hosting the meeting of foreign ministers.

## Funding

The BCSC has no budget. Costs related to the meetings of government officials are borne by the host country and participating states.

## Cooperation to Date

The BCSC is not a subregional organization in any real sense. It is a plat-form that provides an opportunity for political leaders of the SEE states to meet on a regular basis and identify areas of common interest. Meetings of the Balkan Conference are not always attended by all participating states. To date, foreign ministers of SEE states have met three times – in Sophia, Bulgaria (1996), in Salonika, Greece (1997), and in Istanbul, Turkey (1998). The heads of state of the seven participating countries have met two times – in Heracleion, Crete (1997) and in Antalya, Turkey (1998). In addition, a meeting of deputy defense ministers of Albania, Bulgaria, the Former Yugoslav Republic of Macedonia, Greece, Romania, and Turkey took place in 1998. Each meeting has been concluded with an endorse-ment of a final document defining areas for potential cooperation, such as trade and investment promotion, protection of environment or the joint fight against drug and arms trafficking, organized crime, and terrorism. Specific projects within these areas have so far been initiated primarily through other subregional organizations and initiatives supported by actors from outside of the region (e.g., SECI, the Royaumont Initiative). The only significant example of an independent action taken by the Balkan Conference remains the 1998 agreement of the participating states (with the exception of the Former Republic of Yugoslavia) to form a joint rapid reaction force with Italian participation by September 1999.

## Web Page

The BCSC does not have a web page.

# Appendix B

## The Barents Euro-Arctic Council

Members: Denmark, European Commission, Finland, Iceland, Norway, Russia, Sweden

Established: 1993

### Origins

The Barents Euro-Arctic Council (BEAC) was formally established in January 1993 to encourage intergovernmental cooperation in the Barents region. The initiative reflected Norwegian efforts to normalize border relations with Russia in the Barents region after the end of the Cold War. The Barents region, covering an area twice the size of France, and forming a frontier between Russia and NATO, was during the Cold War one of the most militarized regions in the world. It also has a particularly high concentration of nuclear reactors. Although the political changes in Europe and the former Soviet Union in the early 1990s did not erase the NATO-Russia frontier, they did allow for a redefinition of policies addressing security and environmental challenges in the region. Mutual cooperation on a subregional level with the aim of increasing social, economic, and political stability in the Russian part of the Barents region, became the main pillar of this new policy.

The plan to initiate subregional cooperation in the Barents region was first raised by the Norwegian minister of foreign affairs in April 1992. As a first step, agreements on cooperation were signed between a number of Norwegian and Russian local administrative regions, later joined by Finnish and Swedish local authorities. In spring 1992, Finland, Russia, and Norway agreed to hold a meeting of their foreign ministers to discuss the framework for this subregional cooperation. This initiative was further extended in January 1993, when the foreign ministers of Russia and the five Nordic countries and a representative of the European Commission met in the Norwegian town of Kirkenes. As a result, a Declaration on Cooperation in the Barents Euro-Arctic Region, the founding document of the BEAC, was signed.

**Structure**

The BEAC is of strictly intergovernmental character. Foreign ministers of participating states meet once a year; meetings of other ministers are held as the need arises. To date, ministers of Environment, Transport, Economy, Culture and Education, and Health have convened on at least one occasion. The presidency of the BEAC rotates among the four core members having territories within the Barents region itself (Finland, Norway, Sweden, and Russia). Each presidency hosts a ministerial meeting at the end of its year in office. The BEAC has no permanent secretariat, and the administrative workload is borne by the state holding annual presidency.

Apart from cooperating on the national level, the four core countries of the BEAC have also instigated cooperation on the regional governmental level through the establishment of the Regional Council. This body consists of representatives of provincial authorities (two Russian oblasts, Murmansk and Arkhangelsk, and the Republic of Karelia; the counties of Finnmark, Troms, and Nordland in Norway; Lapland and Oulu in

Finland; and Norrbotten and Vasterbotten in Sweden) and the indigenous peoples (the Sami who live in all four countries of the region, the Nenets and the Komi of northwestern Russia). Chairmanship in the Regional Council alternates every two years among participating counties. The council convenes an annual extended meeting with the participation of three additional persons from each county and representatives of the indigenous peoples. This dual framework for cooperation in the Barents region reflects a desire of BEAC member states to ensure central political support and supervision while leaving day-to-day decision making over operations and practical initiatives to Barents local authorities.

## Funding

The BEAC has no permanent budget. All costs related to the BEAC meetings are borne by the presiding country. Most of the BEAC projects at the national and regional governmental level tend to be bilateral and are funded on a case-by-case basis by participating countries. In 1998, Norway spent a total amount of 194 million NOK (22.5 million Euro) on projects in the Barents region, Sweden more than 30 million SEK (3.3 million Euro), and Finland about 450.000 FIM (75,700 Euro). Russia has been allowed on a number of occasions to make contributions in the form of manpower, facilities or administrative resources. Some cross-border interaction in the region is funded through the EU assistance program to CIS states, TACIS (e.g., over 30 million Euro between 1992 and 1997 was spent on the improvement of safety conditions at the Kola Nuclear Power Plant) and the EU Barents Interreg-II Program set up especially for the Barents region in 1995 (e.g., 1.8 million Euro was spent on the improvement of border crossing facilities between Finland and Russia). Additional funding comes from the European Bank for Reconstruction and Development (EBRD) and the Nordic Investment Bank (as of 1997 the bank administers a lending facility that disposes over 100 million Euro for the financing of environmental investments in the region).

## Cooperation to Date

Since its inception, the BEAC has served as a platform for discussion on the extent and direction of intergovernmental cooperation in the Barents region. The meetings of the BEAC have enabled ministers from individual member states to define areas of common interest and launch a number of initiatives on the state and regional level. The BEAC has focused primarily on economic cooperation, transport, environment, energy, educational and research exchanges, and public health programs. Following the agreement of BEAC ministers, the Regional Council adopted a five-year program with 84 projects in 1994. These are currently at different stages of preparation, depending upon available funding. The most important projects include plans for the modernization of the Archangelsk and the Murmansk harbors, a plan for the construction of a ship-breaking and metals recycling plant in Murmansk, the introduction of the Environmental Management Program for the Murmansk region, and the introduction of the Cleaner Production Program in the region. Other projects include the establishment of bus, air, and ferry links in the region; improving telecommunications in the Russian part of the region; launching a monthly newspaper in Norwegian, Russian, and Finnish; erecting permanent and functional border-crossings; and the establishment of consulates and trade representations.

**Web Page**

The BEAC does not have a web page. For more information, go to "the Subregional Dimension" at http://www.iews.org/srd.nsf, maintained by the EastWest Institute.

# Appendix C

## The Black Sea Economic Cooperation

Members: Albania, Armenia, Azerbaijan, Bulgaria, Georgia, Greece, Moldova, Romania, Russia, Turkey, Ukraine

Established: 1992

**Origins**

The Black Sea Economic Cooperation (BSEC) was established in June 1992 to foster economic interaction among its members in order to promote peace and stability in the Black Sea region. The plan to initiate cooperation in the region was first officially put forward by the president of Turkey in 1990. The original initiative was followed in 1990 and 1991 by meetings between senior state officials from the four Black Sea coastal countries – Bulgaria, Romania, the Soviet Union, and Turkey. As a result, a draft document on the BSEC was prepared and reviewed. The scope of the draft agreement on the establishment of the BSEC was significantly modified by the collapse of the Soviet Union at the end of 1991. Newly independent, former Soviet republics of the Black Sea subregion quickly confirmed their interest in the project, as the BSEC became, for most of them, one of their first exposures to international politics on a multilateral level. In addition, two other countries – Albania and Greece – expressed their interest in taking part in the new organization. As a result, eleven heads of state and governments signed the Summit Declaration on the BSEC and the Bosphorus Statement in June 1992 in Istanbul. These two basic documents, outlining the aims and agenda of the BSEC, were further developed in the Bucharest Statement, signed in June 1995, and the Moscow Declaration, signed in October 1996. In June 1998, the eleven member states signed a charter converting the BSEC into a regional economic organization.

**Structure**

The BSEC is of strictly intergovernmental character. The highest executive body of the BSEC is the Meeting of the Ministers of Foreign Affairs (MMFA), which convenes at least twice a year. The MMFA makes decisions that relate to the functioning of the organization. Decisions over key issues such as admission of new members, creation of new BSEC bodies and approval of BSEC projects are made by consensus. Other decisions may be made by a two-thirds majority vote. The presidency rotates regularly among all BSEC members on a six-month basis. Agendas and draft documents of the MMFA are prepared in the meetings of BSEC senior foreign ministry officials. Administrative support is provided by the Permanent International Secretariat of the BSEC (PERMIS), which is based in Istanbul and run by more than ten employees.

The executive branch of the organization, the MMFA, is complemented by the Parliamentary Assembly of the BSEC (PABSEC). PABSEC consists of parliamentary representatives of all member states. The highest body of PABSEC is the General Assembly of representatives of national parliaments, which convenes twice a year. PABSEC's International Secretariat and its bureau are located in Istanbul, together with PABSEC's three standing committees (on Economic, Commercial, Technological, and Environmental Affairs; on Legal and Political Affairs; and on Cultural, Educational, and Social Affairs).

The structure of the BSEC further includes the Black Sea Trade and Development Bank established in Thessaloniki in March 1998 and the Istanbul based BSEC Business Council, acting as a platform for interaction of regional business representatives. Other permanent bodies of the BSEC include more than ten expert groups that focus their activity on different fields of cooperation in the region, the BSEC Coordination Center for Statistical Data and Economic Cooperation in Ankara, and the Black Sea Regional Energy Center in Sofia. In addition, the BSEC also has affiliated organizations, such as the Black Sea Economic Cooperation Council, the International Black Sea Club, and the Parliamentary Assembly of the Black Sea States.

## Funding

The BSEC has no permanent budget. The secretariat is funded from contributions by individual member states. According to the 1994 tentative agreement on the scale of contributions, Greece, Russia, Turkey, and Ukraine are expected to contribute sixteen percent each; Bulgaria and Romania eight percent each; and the other members four percent each. In reality, Turkey covers two-thirds of the secretariat's budget. Projects initiated within the BSCE framework are expected to receive funding primarily from the Black Sea Trade and Development Bank that is scheduled to become fully operational in 1999.

## Cooperation to Date

To date, most of the activities of the BSCE have been limited to discussions at different levels of the organization. Lack of funds and the highly diverse character of the organization have forced the BSCE to keep a fairly low profile with respect to the implementation of most discussed proposals for action. Yet, some steps toward the introduction of specific projects have been taken in the areas of transport, communication, and trade. The BSCE has launched a project for the development of a subregional transport infrastructure integrated into wider trans-European transport network. A comprehensive transportation map of the region has been prepared, and expert discussions are underway on practical steps to simplify passenger and cargo traffic in the region. BSEC members have also been interested in improving subregional telecommunications, and steps are being taken to develop fiber-optic and radio link systems connecting member states. Other projects pursued by the BSEC attempt to increase cooperation among the member states in attracting foreign investment and to create a BSEC free trade area. BSEC member states have also made some progress in the field of environmental cooperation. In 1992, BSEC members signed the Convention on the Protection of the Black Sea Against Pollution, and in 1996, they signed the Black Sea Strategic Action Plan. Furthermore, the Agreement on Collaboration in Emergency

Assistance and Emergency Response to Natural and Man-made Disasters was signed in 1998.

## Web Site

The BSCE does not have a web site. For more information, go to "the Subregional Dimension" at http://www.iews.org/srd.nsf, maintained by the EastWest Institute.

# Appendix D

## Central Asian Economic Community

Members: Kazakhstan, Kyrgyz Rep., Uzbekistan, Tajikistan

Established: 1994

### Origins

The Central Asian Economic Community (CAEC) was established in April 1994 to promote economic cooperation among its three founding members, Kazakhstan, Kyrgyz Republic, and Uzbekistan. Tajikistan joined the CAEC in March 1998.

### Structure

The CAEC serves as a platform for meetings of top senior officials from all member states. The highest executive body of the CAEC is the Council of the Heads of States, which convenes about once a year. Prime ministers, foreign ministers, and defense ministers meet as the need arises. The presidency rotates on a biennial basis among all member states. The CAEC has a secretariat based in Bishkek, the Kyrgyz Republic and a permanently operating executive committee that provides logistical support for the council. the other permanent body of the organization is the Central Asian Bank for Cooperation and Development with its headquarters in Almaty, Kazakhstan and branches in Bishkek, Kyrgyz Republic, and Tashkent, Uzbekistan.

## Funding

The CAEC has no budget. Costs related to the meetings of CAEC senior officials are borne by the host country. Programs and projects initiated within the CAEC framework are expected to receive funding primarily from the Central Asian Bank for Cooperation and Development.

## Cooperation to Date

To date, CAEC member states have signed more than 40 documents aimed at promoting interstate cooperation in the region. The Program for Economic Integration, adopted in 1995, defines steps that need to be taken before the year 2000 in order to create a single economic area in the region. The implementation of this plan has, in reality, been relatively slow so far, although CAEC members signed an agreement on the protection of mutual investments, adopted measures preventing double taxation, and endorsed a convention on a definition of common principles for capital markets. The CAEC has also demonstrated an ambition to pursue cooperation covering issues other than economic ones. In 1998, the four member states signed a treaty on mutual assistance in case of natural disasters, adopted a program for cooperation in the field of public health services, and outlined common principles against drug trafficking. In addition, CAEC member states formed a common peace-keeping battalion (CENTRABAT), which has already undertaken exercises under the NATO Partnership for Peace Program.

## Web Page

The CAEC does not have a web page.

# Appendix E

## The Central European Free Trade Agreement

Members: Bulgaria, Czech Republic, Hungary, Poland, Romania, Slovakia, Slovenia

Established: 1993

### Origins

The Central European Free Trade Agreement (CEFTA) was established in March 1993 in order to stimulate trade among the three Visegrad countries — the former Czechoslovakia, Hungary, and Poland — and to accelerate their integration into the EU. Trade liberalization in the region and the establishment of a relevant coordinating body for this purpose was discussed for the first time shortly after the collapse of the Council for Mutual Economic Assistance (COMECOM) at the October 1991 summit of the presidents of the three countries. A month later, trade ministers of the three countries signed a memorandum regarding the gradual elimination of all barriers to trade and began negotiating the scope of and timetable for trade liberalization. As a result, the CEFTA agreement was signed in December 1992 and came into force in March 1993. In January 1996, CEFTA accepted Slovenia as a new member. Romania joined the organization in July 1997, and Bulgaria gained membership in January 1999. Other countries that have expressed their interest in joining CEFTA include Croatia, Estonia, the Former Yugoslav Republic of Macedonia, Latvia, Lithuania, and Ukraine.

**Structure**

CEFTA has no formal institutional structure. Member states' prime ministers meet once a year; meetings of other ministers are held as the need arises. The presidency of CEFTA rotates among all members of the organization. Implementation of the trade agreement is supervised by individual member states. CEFTA has a Joint Committee in permanent session that deals with potential problems. The Joint Committee includes economy ministers and representatives from national ministries of Foreign Affairs, Agriculture, and Finance.

**Funding**

CEFTA has no budget. The costs related to the organization of annual meetings are borne by the presiding country.

**Cooperation to Date**

The principal aim of CEFTA member states is their accession into the EU. CEFTA was not created as a subregional integrative group per se but rather as a tool for accelerating integration of the member states into the EU. Cooperation within CEFTA has focused exclusively on gradual liberalization of trade in industrial and agricultural goods, with the aim of creating a free trade area in the region. Trade commodities were initially divided in three categories: (1) goods that became subject to zero tariffs once the CEFTA agreement came into force; (2) goods on which tariffs were to be phased out according to an agreed timetable; and (3) goods initially excluded from the liberalization process. Full liberalization of trade was to be completed by January 1, 2001.

The founding agreement that defined the goals of CEFTA was extended in 1994 with the endorsement of a special protocol increasing the number of goods subjected to the zero rating tariff. In August 1995, a further protocol was signed that applied zero tariff rates to goods of average sensitivity and reduced the duties on the most sensitive products by fifty percent. The protocol also called for the application of zero rates to all industrial trade as of January 1, 1997.

Gradual elimination of tariffs has helped to increase the level of trade within CEFTA, but the overall scope of inter-CEFTA trade remains small in relative terms as all CEFTA states trade primarily with the EU. For instance, trade with other CEFTA states constitutes only 6 percent of Polish foreign trade; the same figure for Hungary is less than 9 percent. Inter-CEFTA trade is more significant for the Czech Republic and Slovakia, but this is primarily due to their own strong mutual trade links established during their former coexistence in one federal state before 1993. Further increase in the scope of inter-CEFTA trade has been hindered by scant progress in the removal of non-tariff barriers and a lack of a clear agreement on many detailed questions, such as a mutual recognition of certificates and rules of customs procedure.

**Web Page**

CEFTA does not have a web page. For more information, go to "the Subregional Dimension" at http://www.iews.org/srd.nsf, maintained by the EastWest Institute.

# Appendix F

## The Central European Initiative

Members: Albania, Austria, Belarus, Bosnia-Herzegovina, Bulgaria, Croatia, Czech Republic, Hungary, Italy, Moldova, Poland, Romania, Slovakia, Slovenia, the Former Yugoslav Republic of Macedonia, Ukraine

Established: 1989

## Origins

The Central European Initiative (CEI) was originally established in November 1989 to stimulate political, technical, economic, scientific, and cultural cooperation among its founding members, Austria, Hungary, Italy, and Yugoslavia. The organization, initially called Quadrilaterale, grew out of the Alpe-Adria Working Group established in 1978 in order to encourage subregional cooperation between the border areas of Austria, Italy, Yugoslavia, and from early 1980s, Hungary. Each country agreed to take responsibility for one area of cooperation: Austria for the environment, Italy for roads and railways, Yugoslavia for communications and media, and Hungary for culture. Czechoslovakia joined the organization in May 1990, and Poland gained membership in July 1991. In 1992, the Yugoslav membership was suspended, and the organization took on the name CEI. The suspension of Yugoslav membership reflected the new political situation in Europe that resulted from the break-up of Yugoslavia. Three of the former Yugoslav republics – Croatia, Slovenia, and Bosnia-Herzegovina — subsequently joined the CEI in 1992. In January 1993, the organization accepted the two successor states of the former Czechoslovakia – the Czech Republic and Slovakia. Six months later, the CEI granted membership to the Former Yugoslav Republic of Macedonia. Further extension of CEI membership to other countries was discussed at the CEI 1994 and 1995 summits in Trieste and Warsaw, respectively. The principle of extending membership to other countries was eventually accepted, and in June 1996 Albania, Belarus, Bulgaria, Romania, and Ukraine joined the CEI. Moldova became a member of the CEI in November 1996.

## Structure

The CEI operates through a number of regular forums involving senior state officials of CEI members. Heads of governments and foreign ministers of CEI member states meet annually; other ministers meet as the need arises. Delegations representing national parliaments of CEI member states meet twice a year. The presidency of the CEI rotates among all member states. The state holding the annual presidency hosts meetings of the organization and provides all required administrative support. CEI meetings are planned and organized by national coordinators who represent all CEI members. The national coordinators, who meet on a monthly basis, work closely with CEI working groups, which are charged with identifying project ideas for cooperation in the region.

The lack of a clear permanent structure is, to some extent, compensated for by the work of the CEI Centre for Information and Documentation (CEI-CID) based in Trieste. The CEI-CID is primarily responsible for maintaining an archive of CEI documentation, but it also provides logistical support for the CEI itself. The CEI-CID is linked to the CEI permanent unit for Rehabilitation and Reconstruction of Bosnia-Herzegovina and the CEI unit for Central European Transport Reporting. In addition, CEI activities rest on the Secretariat for CEI Projects, which was originally based at the European Bank for Reconstruction and Development (EBRD) in London but which recently moved to Trieste. In the past, the Secretariat operated as a medium between both institutions, provided advice to the CEI committees on investment projects, translated CEI investment ideas into bankable projects, and provided technical support for EBRD investment projects in most of the CEI member states (e.g., studies, design, and implementation assistance).

**Funding**

The CEI has no permanent budget. The costs related to the organization of annual meetings are borne by the presiding country. The CEI-CID is funded by the Autonomous Region Friuli-Venezia Giulia in agreement with the Italian Foreign Ministry. Its director-general, an Austrian diplomat, is funded by the Austrian government. The Secretariat is funded by the Italian government and can also use Austrian funds for technical cooperation. Funding for individual projects initiated within the framework of the CEI comes primarily from EBRD (about two-thirds of the EBRD's investment goes to the CEI subregion, a total of 6.8 billion Euro), but also from other international and national financial institutions and from the EU.

**Cooperation to Date**

The CEI functions as a forum for identifying the needs of its member states, formulating joint decisions, and exchanging experiences. The organization does not put forward its own proposals for action, but rather encourages CEI members to initiate their own bilateral or multilateral projects and offers consulting on funding and implementation. Many of the initiatives encouraged by the CEI are designed to complement and reinforce strategic programs pursued in the region by the EU. CEI input usually includes assistance with preparation of a project proposal and monitoring of progress. To date, the CEI has focused primarily on the development of infrastructure in central and eastern Europe as well as on the reconstruction of Bosnia-Herzegovina and Croatia. Specific projects include a plan for the construction of a pan-European road corridor between Kiev and western Europe; a plan for the construction of a pan-European road corridor connecting Bulgaria, the Former Yugoslav Republic of Macedonia, Albania, and Italy; a plan for the reconstruction of roads in Albania; and a plan for the reconstruction of the airport in Skopje, the Former Yugoslav Republic of Macedonia. Smaller initiatives include various educational programs, such as a training course for young diplomats from CEI member states organized by the Diplomatic Academy in Vienna, full masters training for banking and finance candidates from CEI countries, organized by Fondazione Dell'Amore in Bologna, and a training course for election monitors offered by Italy at the University of Pisa.

**Web Page**

For more information, go to http://www.ceinet.org/.

# Appendix G

## The Council of Baltic Sea States

Members: Denmark, Estonia, European Commission, Finland, Germany, Iceland, Latvia, Lithuania, Norway, Poland, Russia, Sweden

Established: 1992

**Origins**

The Council of Baltic Sea States (CBSS) was established in March 1992 to encourage cooperation and coordination among the Baltic Sea states. The original impetus for its foundation came from a bilateral meeting between the Danish Foreign Minister Uffe

Ellemann-Jensen and his German counterpart Hans-Dietrich Genscher in autumn 1991. Some months later, the proposal to create a Baltic intergovernmental forum that would help to promote partnership and cooperation in the region was presented at a conference of foreign ministers of Denmark, Estonia, Finland, Germany, Latvia, Lithuania, Norway, Poland, Russia, and a representative of the European Commission in Copenhagen. The Copenhagen Declaration formed the founding document of the CBSS. Iceland became a member of the CBSS in 1996.

The Copenhagen Declaration outlines six main areas of cooperation. These include assistance to new democratic institutions; economic and technological assistance and cooperation; humanitarian matters and health; protection of the environment and energy; cooperation in the field of culture, education, tourism, and information; and transport and communication. These six areas reflect the ambition of the CBSS to ensure democratic development in the Baltic Sea region after the end of the Cold War and to achieve greater unity among the member countries.

**Structure**

The CBSS is designed as a forum for guidance and overall coordination among the governments of member states. Each CBSS member state is represented by its foreign minister. The presidency rotates on an annual basis among all CBSS members, and the CBSS convenes once a year in the country that currently holds the presidency. Two informal meetings of the heads of governments of the CBSS member states have taken place in 1996 and 1998. In autumn 1998, a small CBSS Secretariat was established in Sweden to assist the presiding country with the administrative workload related to the coordination of ongoing activities. The presiding state is further assisted by a Committee of Senior Officials (CSO), which consists of senior foreign ministry representatives of individual member states. The CSO supervises four working groups that are charged with drawing up proposals for action within individual areas of cooperation. The four groups are: the Working Group on Assistance to Democratic Institutions (WGDI), the Working Group on Economic Cooperation (WGEC), the Working Group on Nuclear and Radiation Safety (WGNS), and the Task Force on Organized Crime in the Baltic Sea Region.

## Funding

The CBSS has no permanent budget for cooperation. Each project is funded separately by participating member states. Some funding comes from the EU PHARE and TACIS programs. The CBSS secretariat operates on an annual budget of up to 2 million DM (1 million Euro). Four member states – Estonia, Iceland, Latvia, and Lithuania – contribute four percent each toward this budget, while the remaining seven members – Denmark, Finland, Germany, Norway, Poland, Russia, Sweden – each contribute 12 percent. The European Commission makes no direct contribution toward this budget.

## Cooperation to Date

The CBSS kept a rather low profile during the first few years of its existence, serving primarily as an annual meeting place for representatives of all the Baltic Sea states. Between 1993 and 1996, the CBSS, or its working committees, organized twelve seminars addressing various areas of cooperation in the region. In 1994, the CBSS appointed a special Commissioner on Democratic Institutions and Human Rights, Including the Rights of Persons Belonging to Minorities. The commissioner, whose mandate was extended in 1997 for another three years, conducts surveys on the state of democracy in the region and prepares annual yearly reports and recommendations for governments of the CBSS member states. In June 1996, the CBSS adopted three action programs outlining priorities for cooperation in the region: the Program on Participation and Stable Political Development aimed at supporting independent non-governmental organizations, encouraging student exchanges and education, and promoting cultural contacts in the region; the Program on Economic Integration and Prosperity aimed at supporting the integration of the Baltic states and Poland into the EU and encouraging trade liberalization in the region; and the Program on Sustainable Development and Environmental Protection aimed at instigating environmental cooperation between CBSS member states. Specific projects initiated by the CBSS include the establishment of the CBSS EuroFaculty, which helps key universities in the Baltic Sea states to meet common international standards for programs in law, economics, public administration, and political science; feasibility studies analyzing the idea of creating a common electricity market around the Black Sea; and research regarding the potential integration of the Baltic Sea gas transmission systems.

## Web Page

For more information, go to http://www.baltinfo.org/ or "the Subregional Dimension" at http://www.iews.org/srd.nsf, maintained by the EastWest Institute.

# Appendix H

## Economic Cooperation Organization

Members: Afghanistan, Azerbaijan, Iran, Kazakhstan, Kyrgyz Republic, Pakistan, Tajikistan, Turkey, Turkmenistan, Uzbekistan

Established: 1985

### Origins

The Economic Cooperation Organization (ECO) was established in 1985 to promote regional economic, technical, and cultural cooperation among its member states. The founding member states of the organization were Iran, Pakistan, and Turkey. The ECO is the successor organization of the Regional Cooperation for Development (RCD), which existed from 1964 to 1979. The basic charter of the RCD, the Treaty of Izmir of 1977, was amended in 1990 to provide a legal basis for a revival of the organization under its current name, the ECO. In 1992, the organization was expanded to include seven new member states – Afghanistan, Azerbaijan, Kazakhstan, Kyrgyz Republic, Tajikistan, Turkmenistan, and Uzbekistan.

The main objectives of the ECO are a progressive removal of trade barriers and promotion of interregional trade; development of a transport and communications infrastructure linking member states with each other and with the outside world; regional cooperation for drug abuse control as well as ecological and environmental protection; and strengthening of historical and cultural ties among the peoples of the ECO region.

**Structure**

The highest policy and decision-making body of the ECO is the Council of Ministers. The council is composed of the foreign ministers from individual member states or other high ranking officials designated by governments of ECO members. The council meets at least once a year. The presidency rotates among all member states. Meetings of foreign ministers are prepared by the Council of Permanent Representatives. This body, which is based permanently in Teheran and includes the ambassadors of the member states, is also responsible for implementation of decisions taken by the Council of Ministers. The ECO also has a Regional Planning Council composed of the heads of planning organizations of the member states. It meets once a year in one of the member states to review past programs, evaluate results achieved, and consider new projects for submission to the Council of Ministers. Apart from this formal structure, the ECO organizes a Summit of Heads of States in one of the ECO capitals every two years. The Summit meetings review overall performance and progress in implementation of ECO programs and projects. So far, five such meetings have been held.

**Funding**

The ECO has no permanent budget. Costs related to the meetings of foreign ministers and heads of state are borne by the host country. Feasibility studies for projects for regional cooperation are funded from a special fund established by the three original founding members of the ECO. To date, Iran, Pakistan, and Turkey have contributed $100,000 USD each to this fund. Projects initiated by the

ECO are expected to receive funding primarily from the ECO Trade and Development Bank to be based in Istanbul.

## Cooperation to Date

To date, ECO members have focused their attention primarily on cooperation in areas of trade, transport, education, and the fight against smuggling. In May 1991, the three founding members of the ECO signed the Protocol on Preferential Tariffs, which offered each of them a 10 percent tariff reduction on selected commodities. The impact of the protocol has been limited due to a low number of goods exposed to the agreed margin of preference. After the enlargement of the ECO in 1992, the organization received a new impetus. The first and second summits of the heads of states outlined a set of priorities for regional cooperation and adopted two documents calling for action, the 1992 Quetta Plan of Action and the 1993 Istanbul Declaration. In 1995, the leaders of ECO countries signed six documents regarding the establishment of six ECO institutions – ECO Trade and Development Bank, ECO Reinsurance Company, ECO Shipping Company, ECO Air, ECO Cultural Institute, and ECO Science Foundation. The institutions have yet to be established. In the same year, ECO members signed two documents aimed at increasing the scope of regional trade – ECO Transit Trade Agreement and ECO Agreement on Simplification of Visa Procedures for the Businessmen of ECO Countries. In 1998, steps were taken also toward cooperation in other fields. During the summit of heads of state held in Almaty, Kazakhstan, ECO member states signed the Transit Transport Framework Agreement and Memorandum of Understanding against Smuggling and Customs Fraud. Additionally, ECO members also agreed to establish an ECO Educational Institute in Ankara.

## Web Page

The ECO does not have a web page.

# Appendix I

## Royaumont Initiative

Participating states: Albania, Bosnia-Herzegovina, Bulgaria, Croatia, the Former Yugoslav Republic of Macedonia, European Commission, Hungary, Romania, Slovenia, Turkey, Yugoslavia

Established: 1995

## Origins

The Royaumont Initiative was launched by the EU Council of Ministers in December 1995 to promote stability and good neighborly relations among countries of south-eastern Europe. The aims of the initiative generally reflect the principles of peace and stability in the region outlined in the Stability Pact of Europe that was adopted by the EU in 1993 to help reinforce democratic processes and regional co-operation in central and eastern Europe. More directly, the Initiative is aimed at guiding the implementation of the 1995 Dayton Peace Accord and the following Paris Peace Agreement on the conflict in Bosnia. The Royaumont Initiative assigns crucial importance to the support and interaction of nongovernmental organizations, and the promotion of projects encouraging the development of a civil society in the region. The initiative supports regional cooperation primarily in the fields of education, culture, communication, institutions, and scientific research.

## Structure

The Royaumont Initiative does not have any permanent institutional structure. It functions as a loose forum for discussion among all participating states. The Action Plan of the Initiative was approved by the EU Council of Ministers. The council appointed a special Coordinator for the Initiative, Ambassador Panagiotis Roumeliotis at the end of 1997. The Royaumont Initiative has offices in Brussels and Athens.

## Funding

The Royaumont Initiative has no budget. Funding for projects initiated within the framework of the initiative comes from individual members of the European Union.

## Cooperation to Date

To date, the Royaumont Initiative has reviewed more than seventy project proposals, targeting almost all countries involved. Some 13 projects totaling 2.5 million Euro are already underway. Individual projects cover different domains of civil society such as media, interethnic dialogue, academic cooperation and education, cooperation between cities, and cooperation in culture, science, and the environment. Luxembourg has signed an agreement to fund the project "Promoting Positive Images through the Media," and it also financed a multilateral meeting on the "Legal Status of NGOs and their Role in a Pluralistic Society," which took place in October 1998. Greece is funding a project on the "Development of a Network of Young Southeast European Leaders," and the Netherlands is in charge of the "Workshop on Reporting Ethnic Minorities and Ethnic Conflict." The UK cosponsored the project "Regional Round Table on Free Media Perspectives" proposed by the Council of Europe. The UK has also decided to fund a summer camp for children from Turkey and the Former Yugoslav Republic of Macedonia. France has declared its interest in contributing financially to the project on "Television Across Borders." Other recent initiatives include a gathering of journalists from the region and a meeting in Greece of about 100 NGO representatives from south-eastern Europe.

## Web Page

For more information, go to http://royaumont.lrf.gr/.

# Appendix J

## Southeast European Cooperative Initiative

Participating states: Albania, Bosnia-Herzegovina, Bulgaria, Croatia, Greece, Hungary, Former Yugoslav Republic of Macedonia, Moldova, Romania, Slovenia, Turkey

Established: 1996

**Origins**

The Southeast European Cooperative Initiative (SECI) was established in December 1996 to encourage cooperation among its member states and to facilitate their integration into European structures. The initial plan for the creation of the SECI grew out of a US and EU interest in ensuring peace and stability in the region. The "Points of Common US-EU Understanding," which advocates the idea of regional economic and environmental cooperation among the countries of south-eastern Europe, became a driving force behind the implementation of this plan. Following review of the US-EU initiative, the participating states of the SECI held an inaugural meeting in Geneva on December 5-6, 1996 and adopted the SECI Statement of Purpose under the patronage of the Organization for Security and Cooperation in Europe (OSCE).

**Structure**

The SECI is not an organization in any real sense, but rather a loose platform, the purpose of which is to create new channels of communication between political leaders of south-eastern Europe. Its decision-making body and motivating force, the Agenda Committee, is comprised of high-ranking governmental officials representing each of the participating states. The Agenda Committee meets every other month. The body identifies areas of common interest in the fields of economy and environment and outlines priorities for potential cooperation. Project proposals are planned by six project groups established by the Agenda Committee at its first meeting in January 1997. The SECI cooperates closely with the United Nations Economic Commission for Europe (UNECE) and the OSCE. UNECE provides professional expertise and consultation to the SECI, including preparation of draft projects for the Agenda Committee and their further elaboration for individual working groups. The OSCE assists the SECI with technical support. It provides office space, computers, telephones and fax for the SECI secretariat administrated by the SECI Coordinator (currently former Austrian Vice-Chancellor Erhard Busek). The coordinator, appointed by the chairman of the OSCE, is responsible for the supervision of SECI activities. In addition, he also chairs the meetings of the Agenda Committee and works as a mediator between the SECI and other international institutions.

**Funding**

The SECI has no permanent budget. Costs related to the organization of SECI meetings are borne by the host country and participating states. The SECI Secretariat is funded on the principle of voluntary contributions from four nonmember states — the United States, Switzerland, Italy, and Austria. These contributions came to a total of $122,000 USD in 1997.

An additional $175,000 USD was provided by the US Government to fund travel costs of UNECE experts for the period from January 31, 1997 to September 30, 1998. During the same period, the US government also contributed $150,000 USD to UNECE for SECI-related technical assistance. In 1998 the SECI Secretariat received a total of $310,000 USD from the four contributing states. Projects initiated within the SECI framework receive funding either from individual member states, international financial institutions, or private investors. The World Bank, the European Bank for Reconstruction and Development (EBRD), and the European Investment Bank have expressed their willingness to cooperate with the SECI.

**Cooperation to Date**

The newly established SECI Agenda Committee currently oversees seven specific projects for cooperation in the region:
- The Border Crossing Facilitation Project aims to improve the physical infrastructure of border stations, to standardize trade procedures and simplify documentation among the SECI participating states, to create training programs and reform current border services, and to promote cooperation in combating cross-border crime and corruption.
- The Project on Energy Efficiency is focused on creating a network of energy efficiency demonstration zones in south-eastern Europe. The SECI is currently examining the concept of creating an SECI regional fund on energy efficiency under the umbrella of the EBRD and commercial banks.
- The Project on the Interconnection of Natural Gas Networks in the region attempts to attract investment for the extension of natural gas network systems and international pipeline interconnections. The first phase of the project was completed in January 1998 with the publication of a comprehensive report, which examined the present pipeline system in the region, analyzed the economics and security of new supply routes, and estimated future demand in the region.
- The Project on the Electric Power Systems in the SECI region examines the possibility of improving the reliability and economy of the electricity supply in the region through the interconnection of individual power systems.
- The Recovery Program for Rivers, Lakes, and Adjacent Seas aims to face the environmental challenges in the region. The project cur-

rently pursues two main points of action: designing a model for cooperation between international financial institutions and individual projects, and exploring models for financing waste water treatment and drinking water supply at the level of municipalities.

- The Project on Financial Policies, which would promote small and medium enterprises through microcredit and credit guarantee schemes, tries to explore ways for securing the capital needed by potential entrepreneurs from the region in order to obtain start-up credit for their operations.
- The Project on Investment Promotion aims to encourage cooperation among security markets in the region in order to increase capital inflow into the region.

## Web Page

SECI's web page is maintained by the UNECE. For more information, go to http://www.unece.org/seci.

# Index